Heritage Languages in the Digital Age

MULTILINGUAL MATTERS
Series Editors: Leigh Oakes, *Queen Mary, University of London, UK* and Jeroen Darquennes, *Université de Namur, Belgium*.

Multilingual Matters series publishes books on bilingualism, bilingual education, immersion education, second language learning, language policy, multiculturalism. The editor is particularly interested in 'macro' level studies of language policies, language maintenance, language shift, language revival and language planning. Books in the series discuss the relationship between language in a broad sense and larger cultural issues, particularly identity related ones.

All books in this series are externally peer-reviewed.

Full details of all the books in this series and of all our other publications can be found on http://www.multilingual-matters.com, or by writing to Multilingual Matters, BLOCK, The Fairfax, Pithay Court, Bristol, BS1 3BN, UK.

MULTILINGUAL MATTERS: 177

Heritage Languages in the Digital Age

The Case of Autochthonous Minority Languages in Western Europe

Edited by
Birte Arendt and Gertrud Reershemius

MULTILINGUAL MATTERS
Bristol • Jackson

DOI https://doi.org/10.21832/ARENDT4228
Library of Congress Cataloging in Publication Data
A catalog record for this book is available from the Library of Congress.
Names: Arendt, Birte, editor. | Reershemius, Gertrud, editor.
Title: Heritage Languages in the Digital Age: The Case of Autochthonous
   Minority Languages in Western Europe/Edited by Birte Arendt and Gertrud
   Reershemius.
Description: Bristol; Jackson: Multilingual Matters, 2024. | Series:
   Multilingual Matters: 177 | Includes bibliographical references and index. |
Summary: 'In light of changing digital communication, this book addresses
   issues including a shift from a focus on oral to written practices; the rise of
   new communities of practice and communicative domains; and the need for
   resulting shifts in language policy and teaching methods when applied to
   minority (or autochthonous) heritage languages' – Provided by publisher.
Identifiers: LCCN 2023048516 (print) | LCCN 2023048517 (ebook) | ISBN
   9781800414228 (hardback) | ISBN 9781800414242 (epub) | ISBN
   9781800414235 (pdf)
Subjects: LCSH: Heritage language speakers. | Linguistic minorities. |
   Digital media. | Language and languages – Study and
   teaching – Computer-assisted instruction. | LCGFT: Essays.
Classification: LCC P40.5.H47 H47 2024 (print) | LCC P40.5.H47 (ebook) |
   DDC 306.44/94 – dc23/eng/20231220
LC record available at https://lccn.loc.gov/2023048516
LC ebook record available at https://lccn.loc.gov/2023048517

British Library Cataloguing in Publication Data
A catalogue entry for this book is available from the British Library.

ISBN-13: 978-1-80041-422-8 (hbk)
ISBN-13: 978-1-80041-421-1 (pbk)

Multilingual Matters
UK: BLOCK, The Fairfax, Pithay Court, Bristol, BS1 3BN, UK.
USA: Ingram, Jackson, TN, USA.
Authorised Representative: Easy Access System Europe – Mustamäe tee 50, 10621
Tallinn, Estonia gpsr.requests@easproject.com.

Website: https://www.multilingual-matters.com
Twitter: Multi_Ling_Mat
Bluesky: https://bsky.app/profile/multi-ling-mat.bsky.social
Facebook: https://www.facebook.com/multilingualmatters
Blog: https://www.channelviewpublications.wordpress.com

Copyright © 2024 Birte Arendt and Gertrud Reershemius and the authors of individual chapters.

All rights reserved. No part of this work may be reproduced in any form or by any means without permission in writing from the publisher.

The policy of Multilingual Matters/Channel View Publications is to use papers that are natural, renewable and recyclable products, made from wood grown in sustainable forests. In the manufacturing process of our books, and to further support our policy, preference is given to printers that have FSC and PEFC Chain of Custody certification. The FSC and/or PEFC logos will appear on those books where full certification has been granted to the printer concerned.

Typeset by Riverside Publishing Solutions.

Contents

Contributors   vii

Acknowledgements   xi

Introduction: Can Digital Media Help to Prevent
Language Shift?   1
Gertrud Reershemius and Birte Arendt

Part 1: Shifting Ideologies

1 Language Ideologies, Digital Technology and Emerging
Hierarchies of Knowledge   15
Helen Kelly-Holmes

2 Myth Busters: Online Platforms and Emerging Ideological
Shift among Lombard Speakers   35
Marco Tamburelli

3 Focus on Faroese: Digital Insights into the Smallest
North Germanic Language Community   54
Laura Zieseler

4 Breton in the Online Context: A New Speaker Community?   77
Merryn Davies-Deacon

Part 2: Digital Tools and Practices

5 Language, Education and Community in a Digital Age:
A Welsh Digital Resources Case Study   103
Rhian Hodges and Cynog Prys

6 Teaching a Regional Language in Online Courses:
A Learner-Oriented Perspective on Agency, Practices
and Evaluation   128
Birte Arendt and Ulrike Stern

Part 3: Multilingual Practices on Social Media

7 North Frisian in Social Media: Looking for Computer-Mediated Communication in a Very Small Language 155
   Hauke Heyen

8 Unravelling Language Choice Online: Frisian Bilingual Teenagers on WhatsApp, Snapchat and Instagram 168
   Lysbeth Jongbloed-Faber

9 'Moin mitnanner': Digital Practices and Low German on Instagram 192
   Gertrud Reershemius

Epilogue: Agency, Ideologies and the Continuum of Language Practices – Towards an Integrated Theory 213
Yaron Matras

Index 220

Contributors

Birte Arendt is a Lecturer at the Institute for German Philology and director of the *Competence Centre for the Teaching of Low German* at the University of Greifswald. Her research interests include regional language teaching, digital language pedagogy, language acquisition in peer interactions and language attitudes. She is currently leading the project *Interuniversity Teaching Network: Low German teaching*. Relevant publications are the edited volume Arendt, B./Langhanke, R. *Niederdeutschdidaktik* (with R. Langhanke, Peter Lang, 2021) and a recent article published in the journal *Languages*, 'A Long-Lasting CofP of New and Native Speakers – Practices, Identities of Belonging and Motives for Participation'.

Merryn Davies-Deacon is Lecturer in French linguistics at Queen's University, Belfast, having completed a PhD on new speakers of Breton at the same institution in 2020 as part of the multi-institutional, cross-disciplinary *Multilingualism: Empowering Individuals, Transforming Societies* project. Merryn's research has mostly focused on the Cornish and Breton languages, and particular interests within the context of autochthonous heritage languages in new media include standardisation and the accommodation of non-standard varieties, orthographic variation, identity and group membership and the tensions inherent in the use of for-profit majority-centred social media by minority groups.

Hauke Heyen is a Graduate Student at the Europa-Universität Flensburg, Germany. At the Institute for Frisian and Minority Studies he is working on his PhD thesis on language use and language choices in messenger chats of speakers of North Frisian. In 2018, he graduated from Kiel University in Frisian and Scandinavian studies with a focus on linguistics. His main research interests are sociolinguistics and language contact, language use in social media communication and the North Frisian varieties of the islands Amrum and Föhr. He worked as a research assistant for the past five years before becoming programme coordinator in spring 2023.

Rhian Hodges is a Senior Lecturer in Sociology and Social Policy at the School of History, Law and Social Sciences, Bangor University. She lectures on many Welsh-medium undergraduate and postgraduate modules at Bangor and specialises in the field of language policy and planning. Rhian leads the MA Language Policy and Planning and her research interests include new speakers of minoritised languages, minority language education and the community language use of minoritised languages.

Lysbeth Jongbloed-Faber is part of the Frisian-speaking community in the province of Fryslân, the Netherlands, where Frisian is an official language besides Dutch. Lysbeth has a Bachelor degree in Business and Languages and a Master's in Communication and Information Sciences. After a career in business, she made a switch to science and defended her PhD dissertation 'Frisian on Social Media: The Vitality of Minority Languages in a Multilingual Online World' in 2021 (Maastricht University/Fryske Akademy). Lysbeth currently works as a language policy advisor for the province of Fryslân – the ideal place to employ her knowledge to strengthen the position of Frisian.

Helen Kelly-Holmes is Professor of Applied Languages at Ollscoil Luimnigh/University of Limerick. Helen's work focuses on the interrelationship between media, markets, technologies and languages and the management of these relationships. She is particularly interested in the economic aspects of multilingualism in relation to minority languages and the global political economy of English, and she has published widely on these topics. Recent books include: *Language, Global Mobilities, Blue-Collar Workers and Blue-Collar Workplaces* (edited with K. Gonçalves, Routledge, 2020); *Sociolinguistics from the Periphery: Small Languages in New Circumstances* (with S. Pietikainen, A. Jaffe & N. Coupland, Cambridge University Press, 2016).

Yaron Matras is former Professor of Linguistics at the University of Manchester, where he founded and led the Multilingual Manchester project; he was also British Academy Wolfson Professorial Fellow and Fellow of the Hanse Wissenschaftskolleg Institute for Advanced Study. He holds honorary affiliations with the Aston Institute for Forensic Linguistics in Birmingham and the Department of Hebrew Language at the University of Haifa. His books include *Language Contact* (CUP, 2009/2020) and *Romani: A Linguistic Introduction* (CUP, 2002).

Cynog Prys is a Lecturer in Sociology and Social Policy at Bangor University in Wales. His area of expertise is the sociology of language and language policy and planning. His current research focuses on language use in civil society, particularly the use of Welsh in the community and on digital platforms. He has published several research projects in this field. In addition to his research, Cynog is also passionate about teaching sociology in Welsh and making Welsh-medium higher education accessible to people of all ages and backgrounds.

Gertrud Reershemius is Professor of Linguistics and Language Contact at Aston University (Birmingham). She was awarded a PhD from Hamburg University for her work on spoken Yiddish in Israel. Gertrud's work focuses on pragmatics, language contact and multilingualism with a focus on speakers of smaller or lesser used languages such as Yiddish and Low German. She is particularly interested in mediatisation processes and the study of semiotic landscapes, and she has published widely on these topics.

Ulrike Stern is a Research Associate at the *Competence Centre for the Teaching of Low German* at the University of Greifswald. After her degree in Cultural Studies at the University of Hildesheim she worked as a literary adviser for the Low German theatre of the Mecklenburg State Theatre in Schwerin. Her research focus is on Low German literature and on teaching Low German on digital platforms. Recent publications include articles in Arendt, Birte/Langhanke, Robert (eds) Niederdeutschdidaktik. Ansätze, Problemfelder, Perspektiven. Frankfurt/M., and Altenhofen, Cleo Vilson: "Uff mein Mottersproch": Wissen durch Sprachen / "Em minha língua materna": conhecimento por meio de línguas (ebook + Video).

Marco Tamburelli is Professor of Linguistics at Bangor University. His research focuses on bi- and multilingualism. He has worked on bilingual language acquisition, particularly in relation to transfer effects in simultaneous bilinguals, and on lexical and phonological development in typically developing children and in children with SLI. He also works on social and comparative aspects of bilingualism, particularly regional/minority and contested languages, the measurement and assessment of linguistic attitudes, the measurement of linguistic distance in language continua, and the application of intelligibility as a criterion of demarcation between 'languages' and 'dialects'. He is currently director of the International Research Network on Contested Languages.

Laura Zieseler is a Research Assistant at the Chair of Scandinavian Linguistics at the University of Greifswald. She graduated with a BA in Scandinavian, English and American Studies, and an MA in Intercultural Linguistics in Greifswald. From 2009 until 2012, she received a scholarship from the German Academic Scholarship Foundation. In 2020, she won an award for her PhD thesis 'On the Integration of Non-Native Nouns in Faroese'. Her main research interests include language contact and language change, sociolinguistics, computer-mediated communication and language ideology. Although she has so far mainly been focused on Faroese and Norwegian, her research scope ultimately covers all Scandinavian languages, also in comparison to German.

Acknowledgements

The selection of case studies in this book originates in the responses to a call for papers for the conference 'Minority Languages in the Digital Age', which took place as an online event in Greifswald in December 2020 and was funded by the German Research Foundation (DFG), the Alfried Krupp Wissenschaftskolleg and the Competence Centre for Low German Teaching at the University of Greifswald.

Introduction: Can Digital Media Help to Prevent Language Shift?

Gertrud Reershemius and Birte Arendt

> As people use technologies, these become media, and they do so because the new possibilities and functions are helpful for them.
> Friedrich Krotz (2014: 155)

Over the last three decades, new digital technologies have been and still are emerging, many of them turning into new media and some of them fundamentally changing the way people communicate. These processes – generally conceptualised as mediatisation (see, for example, Androutsopoulos, 2014; Krotz, 2014) – have the potential to instigate wide-reaching changes to culture and society. A medium can be defined as a technology that is turned into a tool for communication by people using and adapting it to their needs and then has the potential to change communication and social interaction itself (Krotz, 2014: 156). Mediatisation has been described as a meta-process alongside other complex and wide-reaching current developments, such as globalisation, individualisation and commercialisation, which drive the societies of modernity.

Mediatisation in its various aspects forms the theoretical framework for this book, although, as the title indicates, the focus will be on digital media and the opportunities they offer to speakers of autochthonous minority languages in Europe.[1] There is uncertainty among linguists, language planners and activists as to what term to use to describe the entities we refer to here as autochthonous minority languages. The European Charter for Regional or Minority Languages, for example, uses the term *regional or minority languages*. However, many years of participant observation have convinced us that speakers of these languages do not see themselves as part of a minority, but rather as people who share a common heritage as well as cultural and linguistic practices. Autochthonous minority languages such as Breton, Faroese, Lombard, Gaelic, Frisian, Low German and Welsh fall under the category of smaller or lesser-used languages (see, for example, Pietikäinen *et al.*, 2016).[2]

Such languages tend to be in competition for communicative domains with their dominant contact languages and the global language English, and are all facing language shift to varying degrees: Faroese, Low German, Welsh and West Frisian are categorised as 'vulnerable' by the UNESCO Atlas of the World's Languages in Danger, Lombard and Irish as 'definitely endangered', Breton and North Frisian as 'severely endangered'. In the bigger picture of smaller and minoritised languages worldwide, the languages presented in this book can be seen as privileged: compared with many other smaller languages, they are still spoken by a considerable number of people and enjoy varying and varied forms of institutional, legal, financial and ideological support.[3] They also tend to be spoken in areas and countries with high levels of access to digital technology. At the current stage, they also have in common that while their overall numbers of speakers are declining, their importance as linguistic resources for identity construction and commodification processes tends to be increasing, as many of the case studies in this volume show.

The media have long been seen as a vital component of language policy and maintenance efforts for minority languages: they can potentially increase the status of a language, aid corpus planning through the dissemination of new terminology, support language acquisition by increasing language visibility and use in both public and private domains, and create fashionable domains of language use (for example Cormack & Hourigan, 2007; Honeycutt & Cunliffe, 2010; Lenihan, 2011; Pietikäinen, 2010). It appears that media studies in the field of smaller or endangered languages always differ rather fundamentally from media studies in general due to their specific focus: here, the dominant question raised by researchers and language planners tends to be how the media or a particular medium can be used to support a language (Cormack, 2013). Researchers have stressed both the opportunities and the pitfalls of digital technologies for smaller languages (for example Cunliffe & Herring, 2005). The view was expressed that effective use of computer-mediated communication could be the mainstay of successful maintenance efforts in the future: 'An endangered language will progress if its speakers can make use of electronic technology' (Crystal, 2001: 141).

Of particular importance here is the contextually appropriate mastery of digital tools and typical communicative practices, expressed in the concept of *digital literacies*. Current studies (for example Ceberio *et al*., 2018; Jones & Hafner, 2021; Knobel & Lankhear, 2015) outline a complex set of skills required to achieve digital competences. Jones and Hafner (2021) define digital literacies as

> ways in which people use the mediational means available to them to take actions and make meaning in particular social, cultural and economic contexts. Consequently, they are inevitably tied up with values,

ideologies, power, relationships, and cultural understanding that are part of these contexts. They involve not just being able to 'operate' tools like computers and smartphones, but also the ability to adapt the affordances and constraints of these tools to particular circumstances. (Jones & Hafner, 2021: 18)

While users need to be able to apply digital tools appropriate to their communicative needs, they should also critically reflect on and, if necessary, edit linguistic ideologies established and shared online by using critical literacy, a conscious stance to interrogate and question language ideologies. Language ideologies (for example Irvine & Gal, 2000) as meta-linguistic belief systems construct discourses about languages which establish hierarchies of knowledge both, online and offline (Androutsopoulos, 2013).

New speakers of autochthonous minority languages need to acquire these competences while at the same time adapt them for their communicative needs in a smaller or lesser used language. Only by going through this process can merely passive recipients of digital change become 'active shapers of this technology, ... able to create their own tools, adapt existing tools to local needs and to create culturally authentic, indigenous Internet media' (Cunliffe, 2007: 146).

Earlier studies in the field of minority language media generally expressed the hope that the internet could provide spaces for virtual communities which would function as immersion settings for speakers of smaller languages to meet, interact and communicate (Buszard-Welcher, 2000; Hinton & Hale, 2001). Other studies examined whether and how the internet could be used in various ways to support status and corpus planning initiatives for smaller languages (Mensching, 2000; Ouakrime, 2001; Sperlich, 2005; Warschauer, 2002). These studies all emphasise the opportunities the internet offers, for example by making smaller languages visible to global audiences, developing literacy in thus far predominantly oral languages and providing language teaching materials and concepts. The internet is also seen as a potential archive for threatened languages, although the point is made that access to computer-mediated communication technology is far from equal in different parts of the world (Ouakrime, 2001). Some of the earlier case studies also report interesting failures: Sperlich (2005), for example, analyses the impact of online discussion forums on the endangered Polynesian language Niue, spoken on islands in the South Pacific as well as by a growing number of diaspora speakers in Australia. He shows that speakers of Niue do actually come together in these forums but mainly communicate in English, with only 5% of contributions being in Niue.

Jumping forward in time, a recent study on Mapudungun (or Mapuzugun), a minority language spoken by roughly 100,000 people in Chile and Argentina, shows how the predictions of earlier research have taken shape: Alvarado Pavez (2022) describes how social media, in particular Facebook, have enabled language activists to establish a media presence for the language, which had hitherto been mainly ignored by monolingual Spanish-focused state media. Recent governmental maintenance initiatives focusing on standardisation were of limited success since 'language planning has paid too much attention to spelling, ignoring other urgent aspects of language revival, particularly the dwindling number of actual speakers and spaces where the language can be actively used' (Alvarado Pavez, 2022: 156). Debates on the most popular Mapudungun Facebook groups are lively and in themselves an interesting discussion forum for different language ideologies. However, these discussions hardly ever take place in Mapudungun: 'The situation can be summarised in a somewhat alarming statement made by the interviewees: "there is plenty of talk on Mapuzugun, but little in Mapuzugun"' (Alvarado Pavez, 2022: 154).

While earlier studies on the impact of digital media on smaller and lesser-used languages sometimes saw them as yet another addition to the catalogue of established mass media, such as newspapers, radio or television, to use and navigate for language maintenance purposes, researchers have now become aware of the dimensions of digital mediatisation and the all-encompassing ways digital media change social interaction – to the extent that people experience communication increasingly in relation to media, whether at work, at home or in the context of various leisure activities (Krotz, 2014: 138). Jenkins (2004) introduced a theory of media convergence to conceptualise these processes:

> Media convergence is more than simply a technological shift. Convergence alters the relationship between existing technologies, industries, markets, genres and audiences. Convergence refers to a process, but not an endpoint. Thanks to the proliferation of channels and the portability of new computing and telecommunications technologies, we are entering an era where media will be everywhere and we will use all kinds of media in relation to each other. (Jenkins, 2004: 34)

Jenkins points out that previous ideas of audience, media content and its regulation, the role of media in a globalised economy and the relationship between media producers and consumers will need to be re-evaluated and defined as part of the convergence process.

The impact of media on endangered languages has sometimes been a contentious issue among sociolinguists and language planners in the past. Fishman (2001) for example, referring to the traditional mass media of the pre-convergence age, thought that the role the media could potentially play in maintaining smaller languages was probably overrated. With the advent of technologies leading to what has been described as Web 2.0, however, there is little doubt that the new converged media landscape will also change the ways speakers of endangered languages communicate with each other (see e.g. Gruffydd Jones, 2013).

A theoretical framework to conceptualise the changing impact of media and media policies on smaller and lesser-used languages has been proposed by Pietikäinen and Kelly-Holmes (2011). They suggest framing media policies for smaller languages by distinguishing between three eras they call gifting, service and performance. Gifting describes a phase when limited media spaces in the mass media were dedicated to programmes in the smaller languages, normally by the state: 'The state is the key agent and actor with the ultimate power. The speech community is perceived as demarcated, monolingual, internally unified; and language is conceived as an objective, isolated system with material properties which can be fixed, kept pure, maintained etc.' (Kelly-Holmes, 2014: 539). The second phase, the service era, saw media professionals engaged to secure and shape media spaces for smaller and lesser-used languages. Performance, the final phase thus far, focuses on the individual user as the main agent, empowered by the opportunities of content development systems and social media. These individual users might have access to smaller or lesser-used language as part of their linguistic repertoire and may or may not apply it as a resource in some of the many media contexts they are engaged in. As a result, 'languages become "detached" from their established geographical "habitat", becoming "mobile" resources' (Kelly-Holmes, 2014: 541). It is important to emphasise that all three processes – gifting by governmental and official institutions, services of media professionals hired and performance of individual users – are currently happening to various extents at the same time.

The focus of the contributions to this volume tends to be on the performance era and individual users, be it as creators or recipients of social media content, teaching professionals applying or developing digital learning tools or language activists endeavouring to shape discourses about a language. Some of the studies, however, show the overlap between gifting, service and performance, for example when Arendt and Stern (in this volume) report on their innovative digital approaches to teaching Low German that are paid for by local government and inspired by gaming technologies.

In this fast-changing environment, researchers interested in autochthonous minority languages see the need to frequently take stock and critically evaluate opportunities and challenges that may arise, but also to share good practices. Thus, case studies based on a variety of autochthonous minority languages are a research requirement in the current environment. The case of Mapuzugun described earlier underlines the opportunities and challenges speakers of smaller languages face when taking maintenance efforts to social media. Researchers analysing the impact of digital media on endangered languages need to get to a better understanding in order to establish whether they are looking at general patterns or at individual cases.

At this stage, it is probably time to return to the speakers of autochthonous minority languages: the smaller language is normally only one part of their overall linguistic repertoire, whether they have been raised with the language since childhood or are *new speakers* who have acquired it at some stage later in life (for example Hornsby, 2015; O'Rourke, 2018). Different to previous eras, when the use of autochthonous minority languages was normally only possible in certain fixed geographical entities, it has now become part of an individual's mobile linguistic resources (Deumert, 2014; Pietikäinen, 2010). The advent of the interactive possibilities of social media present speakers with the opportunity to create their own mediatised *affinity spaces* and communities of practice so that they can apply their extended multilingual repertoires should they wish to do so (for example Cunliffe, 2018; Gee, 2013; Kelly-Holmes, 2014; Moriarty, 2014; Reershemius, 2017). Taking the point of view of speakers who include autochthonous minority languages in their bi- or multilingual repertoires, this volume aims to address the following questions:

- Can social media provide new communicative domains for speakers of autochthonous minority languages in a time of increasing and accelerating mediatisation?
- Are communicative domains online an opportunity for new speakers to integrate into emerging communities of practice?
- How do digital technologies and communication online impact on standardisation processes?
- How is digital communication taken into account by policymakers?
- Are new forms of digital literacies emerging online?
- Which innovative digital teaching tools and methods are emerging in various autochthonous minority language contexts?
- Which (new) ideologies and discourses are conveyed in the use of autochthonous minority languages online, for example on social media?

The chapters in this book are written by experts in the fields of specific autochthonous minority languages, including socio-, applied or historical linguists. They describe and analyse the impact digital mediatisation is having on the linguistic communities they are observing. At the same time, many of them are involved in designing and evaluating digital tools in order to create communicative spaces online or to support the learning and teaching of autochthonous heritage languages. In their case studies, they show how digital media impact on various aspects of the status, corpus, acquisition and prestige (Cooper, 1989) of autochthonous minority languages.

The book approaches its complex topic in three parts: 1. Shifting Ideologies 2. Digital Tools and Practices, 3. Multilingual Practices on Social Media.

Part 1 Shifting Ideologies

The participatory Web has become a rich archive of discourses on language and languages. Examining how social media technologies as such drive ideological debates on language issues, Kelly-Holmes analyses a Twitter debate on a question of Irish English where the autochthonous minority language Irish Gaelic is applied as an authenticity scale. She shows how Twitter's commercial blueprint is driving discursive action by creating occasions for specific stances rather than others via its algorithms. Kelly-Holmes also introduces innovative methodological approaches for the in-depth analysis of the interplay between political economies and the technological functions of social network sites.

Tamburelli's case study analyses online discourses around Lombard, a contested language spoken in Northern Italy and Southern Switzerland, and in particular the role of social media in perpetuating ideological statements about smaller languages, in this instance the 'unintelligibility myth', the perception that dialects of Lombard are not intelligible across the overall community of speakers. Although social media play a major role in disseminating these detrimental discourses, Tamburelli also makes the point that speakers and language planners turn to the same social media platforms to counteract these discourses.

Zieseler's contribution to this volume shows how speakers of Faroese modernise their language by using it online in what she calls 'bottom-up Faroeisation': against a backdrop of purist language policies which tend to prevent borrowing, speakers use Faroese in computer-mediated communication, in particular on social media sites, adapting lexemes and structures from the dominant contact language Danish, and thus making Faroese easier to apply to more genres and writing styles online.

Davies-Deacon shows in her contribution on Breton in an online context that the perceived dichotomy between traditional and new speakers of autochthonous heritage languages may need to be re-evaluated when it comes to computer-mediated communication: new speakers of Breton, often described as young, well educated, mobile and computer savvy, tend to be seen as adhering to standard Breton and neologisms derived from Celtic languages. Traditional speakers tend to be seen as older, less well educated, less computer literate and citizens of rural areas of Brittany whose language often features borrowings from French or favours dialectal words and structures. However, Davies-Deacon's analysis of the most popular Facebook group dedicated to Breton shows users applying neologisms, borrowings and various orthographic conventions as well as language play and creative innovation, thus engaging in heteroglossic practices which may in time contribute to the corpus development of Breton.

Part 2 Digital Tools and Practices

The two chapters in this section present digital tools and practices which have been tried and tested in their respective environments, focusing on language learning and maintenance. These have the potential to be adapted for other minority language contexts. Hodges and Prys present two tangible digital products which they have designed and created in cooperation with the Welsh government and speaker organisations in order to support the use of Welsh in the community as well as in a specific educational setting. The first product is a toolkit to encourage the use of Welsh in private settings which contains, for example, a YouTube channel offering video games in Welsh, a Welsh dictionary app (including a spellchecker) and a 'Welsh Hour' initiative on Twitter where Welsh speakers are encouraged, for a specific time and day, to use their language as the main medium of communication. The second product is a resource pack for teachers and lecturers of sociology consisting of teaching materials for the A-Level Sociology examination in Welsh. This initiative also led to the standardisation of sociological terminology in Welsh, thus also adding to language corpus development.

Arendt and Stern present an innovative online course teaching Low German to new speakers at beginner and advanced levels. They have designed and created an extracurricular learning space based on gamification approaches that allows participants to create their own digital 'worlds' in which they act using an avatar role. This approach makes it worthwhile for participants to attend the courses repeatedly, thus increasing their opportunities to practise their Low German in ever-changing environments. In their analysis of the learning and teaching experiences of course participants, Arendt and Stern can show that the courses attract learners from a large geographical catchment area and a wide variety of age groups and professional backgrounds who often see the courses as a stepping stone to learning and using Low German.

Part 3 Multilingual Practices on Social Media

Heyen raises the question of how speakers of a small language such as North Frisian (5000 to 10,000 speakers approximately) engage in the performance era. Reporting on three research initiatives based on a survey, the analysis of Facebook groups dedicated to North Frisian and the use of hashtags on Instagram, he shows that, while speakers rarely apply North Frisian on Twitter, they do engage – albeit in small numbers – in dedicated North Frisian Facebook groups, described as *breathing spaces* (Fishman, 1991). Heyen also shows that speakers (and probably non-speakers) of North Frisian use hashtags on Instagram, often in a playful way, to flag their identities or to tag locations from geographical areas normally associated with North Frisian.

Jongbloed-Faber presents the results of a follow-up study on social media and language use among 1982 teenagers in the Frisian-speaking province of Fryslân in the Netherlands, based on an extensive survey with a new focus on audience design (Bell, 1984, 2001). She shows that teenagers now prefer to communicate via WhatsApp, Snapchat and Instagram, with each platform serving slightly different communicative purposes. Frisian is used to a higher degree on those platforms which are normally preferred for more intimate communication with friends and family, in this case WhatsApp and Snapchat. Jongbloed-Faber also shows that speaking practices and language use offline is the most important factor for online behaviour: teenagers who frequently speak Frisian offline also use it most online. The main reasons for not using Frisian online are a lack of writing skills and questions of audience design: not all 'friends' on social media can understand Frisian.

Reershemius combines quantitative and qualitative methods to examine how Low German is used and applied on Instagram. Her analysis of *#Plattdeutsch* 'Low German' reveals that only a minority of users post in the actual language, while the majority apply a repository of indexicalised words and phrases for commercial purposes or as geographical and biographical contextualisation cues.

Which directions could research into lesser used languages such as the autochthonous minority languages discussed in this volume take in the future? In his epilogue, Yaron Matras observes that many of the cases discussed in this volume examine bottom-up processes which present ongoing discussions about ideologies and practices in the digital age. Accelerated mediatisation changes patterns of social interactions and shapes ideologies and practices for everyone with access to it; for speakers of lesser-used languages it adds further components to individual repertoires and increases linguistic choice. For future research into autochthonous minority languages, Matras recommends a theoretical approach involving a shift of focus from languages to the agency of 'heritage speakers' from both immigrant and autochthonous language backgrounds.

Notes

(1) The editors would like to thank two anonymous reviewers for their thorough and diligent reading and their constructive criticism.
(2) Terms such as *Welsh, Frisian* or *Low German* are used here as umbrella terms for all varieties that form the totality of what would be referred to as a language. German, for example, would include standard varieties, regional varieties ('dialects'), sociolects, etc. (see, for example, Blommaert, 2005: 10).

(3) The selection of case studies in this book originates in the responses to a call for papers for the conference 'Minority Languages in the Digital Age', which took place in December 2020 as an online event in Greifswald, Germany.

References

Alvarado Pavez, G. (2022) Language ideologies of emerging institutional frameworks of Mapudungun revitalization in contemporary Chile: Nation, Facebook, and the moon of Pandora. *Multilingua* 41 (2), 153–179.
Androutsopoulos, J. (2013) Participatory culture and metalinguistic discourse. Performing and negotiating German dialects on YouTube. *Discourse* 2, 47–71.
Androutsopoulos, J. (2014) (ed.) *Mediatization and Sociolinguistic Change*. De Gruyter.
Bell, A. (1984) Language style as audience design. *Language in Society* 13 (2), 145–204.
Bell, A. (2001) Back in style: Reworking audience design. In P. Eckert and R. Rickford (eds) *Style and Sociolinguistic Variation* (pp. 139–169). Cambridge University Press.
Blommaert, J. (2005) *Discourse: A Critical Introduction*. Cambridge University Press.
Buszard-Welcher, L. (2000) Can the web help save my language? In L. Hinton and K. Hale (eds) *The Green Book of Language Revitalization in Practic: Towards a Sustainable World* (pp. 331–345). Academic Press.
Ceberio, K., Gurrutxaga, A., Soria, C., Russo, I. and Quochi, V. (2018) *The Digital Language Diversity Project: How to Use the Digital Language Vitality Scale*. See http://www.dldp.eu/sites/default/files/documents/DLDP_Digital-Language-Vitality-Scale.pdf (accessed July 2022).
Cooper, R.L. (1989) *Language Planning and Social Change*. Cambridge University Press.
Cormack, M. (2013) Concluding remarks: Towards an understanding of media impact on minority language use. In E.H. Gruffydd Jones and E. Uribe-Jongbloed (eds) *Social Media and Minority Languages: Convergence and the Creative Industries* (pp. 255–265). Multilingual Matters.
Cormack, M. and Hourigan, N. (2007) (eds) *Minority Language Media: Concepts, Critiques and Case Studies*. Multilingual Matters.
Crystal, D. (2001) *Language and the Internet*. Cambridge University Press.
Cunliffe, D. (2007) Minority languages and the internet: New threats, new opportunities. In M. Cormack and N. Hourigan (eds) *Minority Language Media: Concepts, Critiques, and Case Studies* (pp. 133–150). Multilingual Matters.
Cunliffe, D. (2018) Minority languages and social media. In G. Hogan-Brun and B. O'Rourke (eds) *The Palgrave Handbook of Minority Languages and Communities* (pp. 451–480). Springer.
Cunliffe, D. and Herring, S. (2005) Introduction to minority languages, multimedia and the web. *New Review in Hypermedia and Multimedia* 11 (2), 131–137.
Deumert, A. (2014) *Sociolinguistics and Mobile Communication*. Edinburgh University Press.
Fishman, J.A. (1991) *Reversing Language Shift. Theoretical and Empirical Foundations of Assistance to Threatened Languages*. Multilingual Matters.
Fishman, J.A. (2001) From theory to practice (and vice versa): Review, reconsideration, and reiteration. In J.A. Fishman *Can Threatened Languages be Saved? Reversing Language Shift Revisited: A 21st Century Perspective* (pp. 451–482). Multilingual Matters.
Gee, J. (2013) *Good Video Games + Good Learning* (2nd edn). Peter Lang.
Gruffydd Jones, E.H. (2013) Minority language media, convergence culture and the indices of linguistic vitality. In E.H. Gruffydd Jones and E. Uribe-Jongbloed (eds) *Social Media and Minority Languages: Convergence and the Creative Industries* (pp. 58–72). Multilingual Matters.
Hinton, L and Hale, K. (eds) (2001) *The Green Book of Language Revitalization in Practice: Towards a Sustainable World*. Academic Press.

Honeycutt, C. and Cunliffe, D. (2010) The use of the Welsh language on Facebook: An initial investigation. *Information, Community & Society* 13 (2), 226–248.

Hornsby, M. (2015) The 'new' and 'traditional' speaker dichotomy: Bridging the gap. *International Journal for the Sociology of Language* 231, 107–125.

Irvine, J.K. and Gal, S. (2000) Language ideology and linguistic differentiation. In P. Kroskrity (ed.) *Regimes of Language* (pp. 35–84). School of American Research Press.

Jenkins, H. (2004) The cultural logic of media convergence. *International Journal of Cultural Studies* 7 (1), 33–43.

Jones, R.H. and Hafner, C.A. (2021) *Understanding Digital Literacies: A Practical Introduction* (2nd edn). Routledge.

Kelly-Holmes, H. (2014) Mediatized spaces for minoritized languages. In J. Androutsopoulos (ed.) *Mediatization and Sociolinguistic Change* (pp. 539–543). De Gruyter.

Knobel, M. and Lankshear, C. (2015) Digital media and literacy development. In A. Georgakopoulou and T. Spilioti (eds) *The Routledge Handbook of Language and Digital Communication* (pp. 151–165). Routledge.

Krotz, F. (2014) Mediatization as a mover in modernity: Social and cultural change in the context of media change. In K. Lundby (ed.) *Mediatization of Communication* (pp. 131–161). De Gruyter.

Lenihan, A. (2011) 'Join our community of translators': Language ideologies and/in Facebook. In C. Thurlow and C. Mrotzek (eds) *Digital Discourse: Language in the New Media* (pp. 48–64). Oxford University Press.

Mensching, G. (2000) The internet as a rescue tool of endangered languages: Sardinian. Paper presented at the conference 'Multimedia and Minority Languages' (San Sebastian 8–9 November 2000). See https://www.yumpu.com/en/document/view/3642791/the-internet-as-a-rescue-tool-of-endangered-languages-gaia (accessed June 2022).

Moriarty, M. (2014) Súil Eile: Sociolinguistic change and the Irish language. In J. Androutsopoulos (ed.) *Mediatization and Sociolinguistic Change* (pp. 463–486). De Gruyter.

Ouakrime, M. (2001) Promoting the maintenance of endangered languages through the internet: The case of Tamazight. In C. Moseley, N. Ostler and H. Ouzzate (eds) *Endangered Languages and the Media: Proceedings of the Fifth FEL Conference* (Agadir, Morocco, 20–23 September, 2001) (pp. 61–67). FEL.

O'Rourke, B. (2018) New speakers of minority languages. In L. Hinton, L. Huss and G. Roche (eds) *The Routledge Handbook of Language Revitalization* (pp. 265–274). Routledge.

Pietikäinen, S. (2010) Sámi language mobility: Scales and discourses of multilingualism in a polycentric environment. *International Journal of the Sociology of Language* 20 (2), 79–101.

Pietikäinen, S. and Kelly-Holmes, H. (2011) Gifting, service, and performance: Three eras in minority-language media policy and practice. *International Journal of Applied Linguistics* 21 (1), 51–70.

Pietikäinen, S., Jaffe, A., Kelly-Holmes, H. and Coupland, N. (2016) *Sociolinguistics from the Periphery: Small Languages in New Circumstances*. Cambridge University Press.

Reershemius, G. (2017) Autochthonous heritage languages and social media: Writing and bilingual practices in Low German on Facebook. *Journal of Multilingual and Multicultural Development* 38 (1), 35–49.

Sperlich, W. (2005) Will cyberforums save endangered languages? A Niuean case. *International Journal of the Sociology of Language* 172, 51–77.

UNESCO (2021) World Atlas of Languages. http://www.unesco.org/languages-atlas/index.php?hl=en&page=atlasmap (accessed June 2022).

Warschauer, M. (2002) Languages.com. The internet and linguistic pluralism. In I. Snyder (ed.) *Silicon Literacies: Communication, Innovation and Education in the Electronic Age* (pp. 62–74). Routledge.

Part 1
Shifting Ideologies

1 Language Ideologies, Digital Technology and Emerging Hierarchies of Knowledge

Helen Kelly-Holmes

The emergence and evolution of the participatory web, i.e. Web 2.0, has not only created more spaces for observing 'naturally occurring', 'spontaneous' language data, but also for language ideological data. As Pearce (2015: 16) points out, 'the conditions of late modernity not only increase sociolinguistic awareness, they also offer more contexts for expressing it in'. Online spaces have thus proven to be ideal sites for studying language ideologies and for understanding how they become mediatised and what the implications of this might be (see for example Androutsopoulos, 2013, 2014, 2016; Barton & Lee, 2013; de Bres, 2015; Hachimi, 2013; Lee, 2017; Lenihan, 2013; Leppänen *et al.*, 2018; Pearce, 2015; Squires, 2010; Thurlow & Mroczek, 2011; Vessey, 2016). Language ideologies are understood here as shared beliefs about language in the broadest possible sense: so, for example, ideologies around differences between languages, dialects, accents, around texts and genres, ways of speaking and writing as well as '…who is authorised to speak or write or to be listened to or read, and in what sorts of social and institutional spaces' (Bauman & Briggs, 2003: 142). Such ideologies exist and are shared within all cultures – again understood in the broadest possible sense. Language ideologies are totalising, incorporating much more than just language; they simplify complex linguistic situations (Irvine & Gal, 2009). They are political and moral, pervasive and powerful with very real consequences, often when they seem at their most banal.

The approach has been to use the web as a resource for the study of language ideologies, given that it offers a full archive of 'discussions' with details of who said what, when, where etc. Thus, it largely involves the transfer of the offline study of language ideologies to online spaces. While the integration of computer-mediated discourse analysis

(CMDA), virtual ethnography, discourse-centred online ethnography (Androutsopoulos, 2008) and multi-modal discourse analysis (Deumert, 2014) have all enriched our understanding, our approaches would further benefit from paying greater attention to the political and technological economy of the data that we are studying. The current chapter attempts to respond to Androutsopoulos's (2016: 282) call for new ways for sociolinguists to address the methodological and paradigmatical challenge posed by 'the rise of digitally mediated language as a new type of everyday language-in-use, and the circuit of mediatized representation, uptake, and recontextualization of linguistic fragments'.

When we look into the political economy and technical functions of social networking sites, it becomes very clear that we do not come across things by chance – even when we search for them. In fact, in cyberspace, it is more often the case that data find us than the other way around. Thus, based on previous search histories and online behaviours, as well as our networks and connections, we are guided to content that aligns with our cyber profile or 'algorithmic identity' (Blommaert, 2017). Technology has always impacted on language and on our ideologies around language (see, for example Androutsopolous, 2016; Kelly-Holmes, 2022; Kristiansen, 2014). It seems clear that the digital technological revolution too is shaping our ideas about language and how we discuss these and how they get distributed. There is a need to understand fully how that technology might in fact shape and change language ideologies and knowledge about language that is in circulation, 'even if there is presently hardly a way in which we can profoundly and directly examine this' given that 'these algorithms are among the best-kept industrial secrets' (Blommaert, 2017: 39–40).

Two of the founding principles of the internet and the web are parity and universality, and they both concern equality of content. Digital media are not intended to function like traditional, monologic media, whereby authoritative information is transmitted from a recognised, respected and resourced centre. Instead, everyone should have the ability to create and contribute content and all of that content should be equal. Likewise, in relation to universality, the internet and later the web were intended to be experienced in the same way everywhere and by everyone. This rather naïve aspiration of course belies a monolingual mindset – the programming languages and organisation of the internet and the web are all products of this mindset, as well as the fact that the technology was developed for a narrow group of users in a focused domain, a very particular speech and communication community (see Kelly-Holmes, 2019, for an overview). It was only as the internet and later the web developed that this monolingualism was exposed and challenged and online linguistic diversity also evolved. Likewise, despite the aspiration towards parity, there are, as we know, knowledge hierarchies online – authoritative centres of knowledge do emerge or are manipulated to emerge. So, in investigating knowledge about language online, we need to ask: which knowledge and ideologies come to the fore and how and what other knowledge and ideologies are suppressed? Is new knowledge created through 'collective intelligence' (Bonabeau, 2009) and does this process simply maintain or instead challenge and subvert existing ideologies about language, and what might the consequences be?

With these questions in mind, I set about trying to understand a thread on Twitter which involved a discussion about what the correct word for 'mother' in Irish English is, not just using my usual methods which involve CMDA, virtual ethnography and language-ideological analysis, but also by trying to adapt my methods to incorporate the technology and political economy of Twitter (now known as X) as well as learnings from the burgeoning field of cyber-criminology and computational criminology (Jakubowicz, 2012; Jakubowicz *et al.*, 2017; Williams & Burnap, 2016). In these fields, language is a number one focus and tool, but with little input, as far as I can see, from sociolinguists. My aim is to try to explain the complex intersections of technology, economics and discourse that result in the development and distribution of language ideologies and ultimately new knowledge about language in digital spaces. These issues are, I argue, of particular relevance to small or minoritised languages in relation to questions of maintenance and revitalisation. Since the thread in question involves a discussion about the Irish language and Irish English, I begin with a very brief overview of these.

The Irish Language and Irish English

As highlighted in the Introduction to the volume, describing Irish, like many of the languages in the chapters of this book, is a fraught and complex process. With these caveats in mind, Irish can perhaps best be described as a privileged, minoritised language. It is privileged in that it is the first official language of Ireland, and has official status in Northern Ireland and within the European Union. It is also privileged by being a compulsory subject (along with English and Maths) for the duration of primary and secondary education for the majority of mainstream pupils (for overviews of language policy and planning see Moriarty, 2015; Ó Laoire, 2008; Ó Riagáin, 1997; Walsh, 2012). However, it is minoritised in relation to English in everyday life and domains such as business, entertainment and media. Anyone who has ever travelled to Ireland will have struggled to encounter the language outside of official signage (see Moriarty, 2015) or the bilingual Gaeltacht areas, where the language survives as a community language, albeit in a challenging context (see Ó Giollagáin *et al.*, 2007). As with all situations of minoritisation, language ideologies have played and continue to play a major role in the association of the language, for example, with economic failure and 'uselessness', and a raft of language policy and planning measures in corpus, acquisition, status and maintenance have been used since the founding of the state to counter these associations (see Walsh, 2010). For example, Irish has instrumental value in the education system and also has strong symbolic value as an identity and authenticating resource (see Walsh, 2020). It can be argued as a result of all of this that, leaving aside fluent and first language speakers, the Irish language plays a varying role in many people's linguistic and communicative repertoire. Thinking about Twitter in terms of the three eras model discussed in the Introduction to the volume, we can see how it allows a space for all three facets: gifting by government in the form of official sites and language agencies providing linguistic resources and content; service by the Irish language media established in previous eras as well as community broadcasters and print media; and, performance of Irish by individuals – generally, but not always by fluent or first-language speakers and frequently in combination with other modes and linguistic resources.

Irish English, the variety of English spoken in Ireland, is also seen as both a competing and a complementary resource for identity and expression of authenticity (see Hickey & Amador-Moreno, 2020, for a comprehensive overview of these issues). Within this context, the relationship between Irish English and the Irish language and knowledge about this can be a point of contention – and the Twitter discussion that provides the data for the study is a good example of this. The variety of English spoken in Ireland is seen to have two main sources: the – fossilised – English brought as a result of colonisation; and the influence of Irish words and grammatical structures on this English (see, e.g. Hickey, 2007). In the thread that follows, the 'authentic' discourse is strongly arguing for the latter as being the source of the term for mother in Irish English.

The Thread

As stated above, the thread in question thematises a perceived change in how Irish people collectively name and refer to their mother. The spark for the thread is the claim that there has been a change from 'mum' to 'mom'. The topic of the thread is not particularly controversial compared to many language ideological debates and the tone in general is not aggressive or overly confrontational, compared for example to a discussion about the same topic in the North of England which was analysed by Pearce (2015), in which some of the comments contained language that would be tagged as cyber-hate. Nonetheless, the thread can be seen as an example of language policing, namely 'the production of "order" [in language behaviours and ideologies]—normatively organised and policed conduct—which is infinitely detailed and regulated by a variety of actors' (Blommaert *et al.*, 2009: 203) or 'verbal hygiene' (Cameron, 2005), in other words talking about and caring about language change and what language other people use or do not use. I purposively selected a Twitter thread which had appeared in my feed about terms of address for 'mother' in Irish English. I collected all of the tweets manually and so did not use any web crawling or scraping tools. I am using 'Originator' as the pseudonym for the person who posted the original tweet and then 'Poster A', 'Poster B', 'Poster C' etc. to refer to the people who tweet comments in the thread. The numbering of the extracts is in relation to the order in which these comments are presented here, not in relation to how they are presented in the thread.

The original tweet that started the thread read as follows:

```
Extract 1, Originator: When did Irish people who
said 'mum' replace it with 'mom'? Nobody said mom in
the 90s. I'm asking because I find it fascinating.
```

The tweet was posted by an Irish writer who then followed it up by replying with an explanatory tweet:

```
Extract 2, Originator: When I did a Tefl course in
Dublin years ago, we looked at hoe U.K. lexicon
was replaced by US, mirroring the rise of American
influence and the fall of British. Is the mum/mom
mystery as simple as that?
```

And, yet another one:

```
Extract 3, Originator: Mam is still going strong,
but as I said as far as I can see people who said
MUM now say MOM.
Mam is still going strong.
```

In their study of cyber-hate, Jakubowicz *et al.* (2017: 45) explain how 'the clustering of Internet users around points of attraction', what they term 'sticky spots', creates a 'swarm', which in turn creates value:

Any process that enables such clustering into online communities ... becomes effectively sealed into the underpinnings of the Internet. Any actor or motivator who can create a sticky spot that enables a swarm to form and to stay attached over time becomes a value creator of significant importance in the vast universe of value nodes. (Jakubowicz *et al.*, 2017: 45)

We can understand this original tweet (just as with any tweet) as having the potential (or even the aim) to create such a 'swarm', i.e. a 'clustering of users around a point of attraction' (Jakubowicz *et al.*, 2017: 45). The tweet in question about 'Mum' versus 'Mom' generates

240 likes, 179 comments and 23 retweets. This 'swarm' is sustained over three days (from 1 December, when the original tweet was posted, to the last reply on 4 December 2018), with a peak on the first day which accounts for the vast majority of replies and likes. In terms of our concern with language ideologies, we can see that the way in which the sticky spot is created, and how and whether or not it attracts a swarm and whether or not that swarm is sustained, involves the creation of a hierarchy of content, i.e. of 'information' or knowledge. The commercialisation of the web is necessarily based on undermining the principles of parity and equality of knowledge that were outlined above. If all information really was equal, then there would be no way to sell advertising. The by-product of this commercialisation is the creation of hierarchies of knowledge, which are determined by whether or not a tweet can attract and sustain interest. The fact that something comes to our attention at all, e.g. this thread coming to my feed, is an example of a hierarchisation – some content is promoted in favour of some other type of content based on our 'algorithmic identity' and it comes to our attention. So 'how did I find this?' or, perhaps more accurately, 'how did it find me' are critical questions to pose when investigating language ideological data.

My next question was around how it is possible to create and sustain a 'sticky spot' around language ideological content. By understanding this, we can understand how new knowledge is created. This involves exploring how and why certain ideologies come to the fore while others do not, and how existing ideologies might be challenged or reinforced. My original research question when I first 'found' the thread was: What does this Twitter thread tell us about language ideologies? Having read more widely about the economic and technological basis of Twitter and approaches from cyber-criminology, this changed to: How does language ideological content like this thread create value on Twitter?

Trying to understand this in the context of the Twitter thread that I studied involved for me a reworking, rethinking and adapting of how and why I study mediatised language ideologies in these online spaces. Value is, not surprisingly, created through the emergence of linguistic authority, 'explicit discursive representations of language, and linguistic practices' (Woolard, 2016: 16). However, what is of concern here is the role of technology in how that linguistic authority emerges and what form it takes, and from my analysis the following concepts emerged as crucial for understanding this: anonymity/de-factoism, authenticity, alignment, influence, validation and expertise.

A preliminary model of how language knowledge emerges

The first two elements of this model, namely anonymity and authenticity, are familiar ones to scholars of language ideologies and

Kathryn Woolard's work in particular. As she points out, 'linguistic authority in modern Western societies is underpinned by one of two different ideological complexes' (Woolard, 2016: 21), namely anonymity and authenticity. These ideological 'complexes' dominate the current thread and the dialogue/dialectic between them would seem to be needed in order to create the 'sticky spot' and initially attract as well as sustain a swarm of posts. Almost all responses can be seen to fall into these two ideologies.

Anonymity/de factoism

As Woolard (2006) puts it, anonymity refers to how 'the tenets of dominant ideologies in the modern public sphere appear not to belong to any identifiable individuals but rather seem to be socially neutral, universally available, natural and objective truths. In a sense then, they are anonymous' (Woolard, 2006: 306). Thus, 'the citizen participating in public discourse as a speaker of disinterested truths speaks in what we could call a 'voice from nowhere' (Woolard, 2006: 306).

Anonymity is the basis for arguments such as English being a logical and useful global lingua franca, agreed standards for a language being efficient or monolingualism being easier and fairer in a country or region. The ideology of anonymity most prevalent in this thread was a discourse of de factoism, an ideology of 'that's just the way people speak (in this place or that place)'.

Significantly, while the ideological basis of the anonymity discourse in the thread is universalism, these citizen-speakers may in fact be endorsing vernacular prescriptivism, i.e. the idea that people in this place speak this way, sound like this and perhaps more importantly *should* sound like this. It is therefore a type of 'super-localism' (Milroy & Milroy, 2014), yet they are still endorsing an ideology of 'this is just the way the world is'. This is illustrated in Extracts 4 (people in Ireland), 5 (Working Class Dublin speech) and 6 (Cork – city in south of Ireland) below, all of which reference place. Anonymity is therefore not 'alocational' and not about breaking the language-territory link, quite the opposite. It is the ideology of 'this is how it is – and always has been – in this place' and this needs no further discussion/challenge.

> Extract 4, Poster A: People who say 'mum' or 'mom' are mental. 'mam' is the only true title of an Irish mammy! ☺ (3 comments, 47 likes, 1 retweet).

> Extract 5, Poster B: Working class Dublin it was always Ma and Da. When did Nan, Nanny or Granny became Grandma? (1 comment, 2 likes).

> Extract 6, Poster C: Mam, ma or mom in Cork. Mum is how the English say it. I go back to the 70s! How interesting. I was out of Ireland in the 90s. (1 like).

We can see many examples throughout the thread and it is arguably the most powerful discourse running through it, precisely because, as Woolard points out, it does not seem ideological. These are the words of the 'ordinary person' who 'tells it like it is':

As Woolard (2006; 2016), Schiffman (1996) and Shohamy (2006) and others have shown, de factoism is highly powerful: it represents the mainstream and hegemonic, and this kind of mainstream ideology and culture is favoured by the political economy of the web. For example, research has shown that mainstream content is promoted by YouTube's algorithms making it harder for alternative content to gain prominence (May, 2010). Anonymity or de factoism appears to be a powerful way of creating and sustaining value on Twitter and of contributing to a sticky spot and the ensuing swarm. However, it needs the dialogue with and challenge from authenticity in order for this to be sustained.

Authenticity

In Kathryn Woolard's words, 'that which is authentic is viewed as the genuine expression of a community, or of a person's essential "self". This ideology of authenticity locates the value of a language in its relationship to a particular community' (Woolard, 2016: 22). This goes beyond the commonsense approach of de factoism or anonymity and involves making a singular and particular case about a language and the people who speak it. In the current thread, this becomes about connecting the English spoken in Ireland today to the Irish language, which as mentioned above is a key authenticating and identity resource. In Extract 7, a link is made to the Irish (language) word for mother and its pronunciation as well as the territorial linkage to the West of Ireland, which is iconic for the Irish language; while in Extract 8, reference is made to the different dialects of Irish and their pronunciation, which is closer to 'Mom':

> Extract 7, Poster D: Mom has been big in the West of Ireland since forever – it's close to the Irish pronunciation of Mam...

> Extract 8, Poster E: Some of the moms in Dublin can be explained by American TV for sure ... but listen to how 'mam' is pronounced here on focloir. ie (press the C, M or U for Connacht, Ulster or Munster.

Extract 9, Poster F: Very common in Gaeltacht areas, stemming from a Mhamaí, but usage seems to have extended beyond that lately. (1 comment, 29 likes).

In Extract 7, the assertion in the original tweet that 'mom' is a new and possibly foreign/American influenced language change is challenged and the poster claims that this pronunciation is in fact much closer to the pronunciation of 'mam' in the Irish language. The juxtaposing of the West of Ireland in Extract 7 with the capital city of Dublin on the East Coast in Extract 8 draws attention to the iconic home of Irish and the 'real' Ireland. Extract 9 mentions the Gaeltacht areas, officially bilingual areas which have been the focus of language maintenance policies, largely but not exclusively located in the West of the country. The reference to the online Irish dictionary and the three dialects of Irish and their different pronunciation all strengthen the claim being made in Extract 8. In Woolard's words, 'the primary significance of the authentic voice is what it signals about *who* one is, rather than what one has to say. In fact, speech is often taken as not just an indexical sign associated with a particular group or type of person, but even as an iconic representation, a natural image of the essence of that person' (Woolard, 2016: 22). Extracts 10 and 11 reference a kind of essential Irish motherhood, one linked to the Irish language and crucially linking to locations outside of the urbane Dublin:

Extract 10, Poster G (in reply to Extract 9): Yup we grew up saying 'a mhama' and it just translted to Mom (2 likes).

Extract 11, Poster H: My Mam grew up in an Irish speaking household in Dublin with parents from West Cork – they always called her mother Mom but would spell it Mam/Maim, which is also what I do.

As Kathryn Woolard (2006) has pointed out, anonymity and authenticity are interrelated rather than separate, and in these extracts we can see that they are both about language in a particular place and as spoken by particular people. But while the former is constructed as commonsensical and not thinking too much about these things because this is just the way 'we' are (rational, universal), the latter is about going into depth, tracing profound connections and emphasising the distinctiveness of a particular language which makes 'us' the way 'we' are (Romantic, particular). An extreme form of anonymity is represented in the thread by non-engagement with particular comments, 'so-what' type comments, and attempts to invalidate the originator's and other posters' stances (see, for example, Extract 17 below), especially the authentic stance.

So, to create and maintain a language ideological sticky spot and a swarm around it, it would appear that anonymity and authenticity need to be present, and come into dialogue with each other. However, as became clear to me, they can only work in connection with a number of other enablers, which are particular to the economy and technology of Twitter, which I will now explore.

Alignment

Alignment refers to the ideological congruence of a particular tweet or tweeting behaviour with the poster's Twitter identity. I would argue that apart from 'famous' people (and that could even be challenged), the actual offline identity is of less relevance in relation to alignment than the online identity that has been created. So, this is not about who the person is in real life, what expertise they have, what language(s) they speak or what kinds of attitudes and ideologies they have, but is instead about the extent to which the language and linguistic ideologies expressed in their tweet – or in their liking, commenting and retweeting of a particular tweet – align with their other content, their profile page (visuals and text) and their Twitter biography. All of these of course contribute to a person's 'algorithmic identity'. As mentioned previously, Twitter is a public forum and for many people on Twitter, identifiability and verifiability are crucial to their value and 'brand', thus the coherence of the content they post, like or retweet needs to create, cohere with and reinforce their Twitter identity and narrative. If there is misalignment between some content or behaviours and the established narrative/identity, then this could undermine either their anonymity–authenticity position in the current language ideological debate, i.e. it would undermine their linguistic authority, and/or it could undermine their existing narrative, identity or brand. As Douglas *et al.* (2005: 70) point out in relation to Twitter, 'people communicate strategically depending on their identifiability and their audience'.

Two examples from the thread under discussion illustrate the importance of alignment in establishing/maintaining linguistic authority online. In response to the discussion of a switch from 'mum' (considered a British English pronunciation) to 'mom', the following comment is posted:

```
Extract 12, Poster I: Obviously their colonial
guilt is kicking in.
```

A look at Poster I's Twitter history shows a strong alignment between this post and their Twitter identity, which reinforces their 'authentic' position in relation to the debate. For example, their most recent activity before this post consisted of: a retweet of a message about the Centenary commemoration of the Soloheadbeg Ambush, an event carried out by the Irish volunteers against the Royal Irish Constabulary and often seen as the opening incident of the Irish War of Independence in 1919; a retweet of a post by a Sinn Féin Member of the European Parliament commemorating IRA Hunger Striker Bobby Sands, who died in 1981; and a retweet of content mocking the stance of the Democratic Unionist Party in Northern Ireland in relation to Brexit. All of this recent activity can be seen as constructing a pro-nationalist identity on Twitter, which chimes perfectly with the tweet in the current thread about the 'colonial guilt' of people who use what are deemed to be British English words and pronunciations ('Mum') instead of those deemed to be Irish English.

Alignment – as with authenticity/anonymity – is not always as straightforward as in the previous case, as we discover when we analyse the online narrative or identity of Poster J , who posted as follows in relation to Mum/Mom on the thread:

Extract 13, Poster J: I'm Mom because I didn't like Mammy, Mam or Ma, kept looking over my shoulder for my own Irish mammy. Mum was never an option. So, I'm Mom or Mommy and it's a title I happily hold.

As we can see, Poster J chooses not to go for an explicit anonymity/authenticity ideology, but instead takes an individualist stance on the topic. In addition to the sentiment of the post, we can note the prevalence of the first person in their contribution compared to other posts and that there is no reference to where they are from. In fact, there appears to be a strong desire to disassociate from these stances and instead adopt a type of 'live and let live' stance, which is in perfect alignment with this individual's Twitter profile and recent tweet activity at the time of the thread. Her pinned tweet (a tweet that is selected to stay in first place on people's profiles and does not get moved down over time by newer tweets) uses the motto 'Love is all you need, Find your tribe by joining us at BUSINESS'. Recent retweets include one about being understanding to the royal couple, Meghan Markle and Prince Harry, about the fact that their birth plan for their first child did not work out, and another about encouraging empathy for people in difficult and abusive situations. The 'Find your own tribe' exhortation represents an interesting ideological stance: on the one hand it is used by groups and individuals wanting to espouse and pursue new types of relationships and ties not based on family, heredity, duty or legal ties, and as such can be seen as refreshing and empowering; on the other, it is also a major trope of contemporary advertising, in which the consumer tribe offers an alternative to traditional units and relationships, and as such is further evidence of marketisation of society. It is important to note that these two interpretations are not necessarily exclusive. Either way, the alignment with a 'live and let live' philosophy and an individualist ideological stance in relation to language choices reinforces Poster J's contribution rather than undermining it and overall it can be seen to add to their Twitter identity and cohere with their narrative.

Influence

Twitter is at its core about 'the ability to drive action' (klear.com), which as discussed above creates sticky spots and swarms that attach to them, and certain tweeters have more potential to do this than others. In their study of cyber-hate, Williams and Burnap (2016: 217) found that 'tweets emanating from particular agents will be significantly predicative of information flow, size and survival'. Influence refers to the power of an individual tweeter to 'drive action' (i.e. attract views, likes, retweets, comments), in the form of distributing and mainstreaming content across the platform and possibly beyond. Based on my analysis of the thread and on reading about Twitter and how it functions, I used the following dimensions to estimate influence in relation to language ideologies and linguistic authority:

- Total number of followers (given that the average number of followers on Twitter is 700, as mentioned above, a number above this should indicate influence and the ability to drive action).
- Ratio of followers to following (i.e. does the person have more people following them than they are following; the logic here would be that a greater number of followers would indicate greater influence).
- Total activity in terms of tweets and likes (implying that more active tweeters are more likely to have more influence).
- Ratio of tweets to likes (this ratio would indicate whether the individual's tweets to date have attracted a significant number of likes, indicating an ability to drive action).
- Twitter age (the assumption here would be that the longer a person has been on the platform, the more likely they are to have influence).
- Ratio of original tweets to retweets for the last 20 tweets (original content is generally seen as more personal and authentic and likely to attract more activity than retweets of other people's content (Guo & Harlow, 2014) – see also discussion of 'media richness' below)
- Maximum and minimum numbers of likes and replies received by the person's last 20 tweets (again a crude indication of the tweeter's ability to drive action).
- Statistics for their tweet in the thread under investigation (number of likes, comments, retweets – how much action did this particular tweet drive).

Using this I attempted to estimate the potential influence of the original tweet and a comment by Poster L, which I picked at random

Table 1.1 Influence of originator versus Poster L

	Originator (posted original tweet)	Poster L (posted a reply)
Number of followers (<700>)	16,000	983
Followers to following ratio	9 (i.e. nine times as many people are following the originator than they are following)	0.79
Total tweets to likes ratio	19,200:18,200 = 1.05	3100:2800 = 1.107
Twitter age (years since joining as per profile)	7	1
This thread	240 likes 23 retweets 178 replies	1 like 1 reply
Last 20 tweets	1 pinned tweet – original content advertising new book 1.2 k likes 255 retweets 90 replies 1 original tweet (visual and comment) 13 likes 1 retweet 17 retweets 51 likes 22 retweets 1 retweet with comment 3 replies	1 pinned tweet – original content 23 likes 2 retweets 4 replies 5 original tweets 6 retweets with comments 8 retweets 42 likes 7 retweets 12 replies

(see Table 1.1). We can conclude from the basic analysis, that the Originator, who wrote the original tweet, has significantly more influence and ability to 'drive action' on Twitter than Poster L, meaning in this case that they can 'start' and maintain a language ideological debate that in turn creates a sticky spot, which may not be the case for L.

Validation

An additional feature that seems crucial in establishing and maintaining linguistic authority in the thread is what I am terming 'validation'. This refers to the way in which certain tweets are validated, either by the person who started the thread (which can be particularly powerful) and/or by other contributors to the thread, while some tweets can be ignored and some can even be invalidated. In their study of cyber-hate, Bliuc *et al.* (2018) identify 'media richness' as enhancing the capacity of a message to persuade or change a point of view. As they put it, 'this richness is increased when the medium can provide immediate feedback, when there is a high number of cues and channels used and when it is personalised' (Bliuc *et al.*, 2018: 81). Twitter provides this immediate feedback in the form of likes, retweets, replies etc. Validation in the form of a like from the originator of the thread (ideally) or from another poster can make the tweet more physically prominent by moving it up the thread and can also affect how other people view the content of the tweet. Validation from like-minded people together with other types of personalised interaction, e.g. by mentioning the tweeter's name in a reply using the @ icon, through use of emojis and other visual cues, can all be seen to contribute to media richness, which in turn enhances the validity of the tweet and its ability to persuade or change a point of view. The following extract illustrates how validation works:

> Extract 14, Poster M: Never said mum or mam in our lives – Belfast it's ma and da pronounced maw and daw (6 likes).
>
> Extract 15, Originator: I'm talking about people who said mum.
>
> Extract 16, Poster M: Just letting' ya know okey dokey (2 likes).

In their reply to Extract 14, the Originator invalidates M's contribution (stating that nobody has ever said 'mum' in Belfast, Northern Ireland) to the thread by restating the parameters of the discussion ('I'm talking about people who said mum') and effectively ruling them out of the thread. It is signficant that M's post, despite attracting likes, is not liked by the originator or any of the mainstream and/or more active contributors to the thread, who are validated by the originator and often by each other.

Extract 17 is another example of a tweet that does not get validated:

> Extract 17, Poster N: Mam, mum, mom.

This tweet is effectively ignored – even though Poster N mentions the originator in their reply, and no-one likes or interacts with this contribution and so it falls to the end of the thread. This tweet could be seen to be espousing the 'live and let live' ideology that we discussed earlier, however it may be ignored and not validated because it is undermining the whole point of the thread which is that language change is significant and interesting. This poster simply refuses to engage in the debate by refusing to acknowledge that these differences are interesting or significant. It was actually hard and took quite a lot of work to find extracts like 14 and 17 and that is important to understand in our analysis of Twitter threads – the chronology or 'script' that is presented to us is ever-changing and does not reflect how the thread develops in 'real time'.

In Extract 18, Poster O comes to the defence of the originator of the thread, by challenging Poster P who has in turn challenged the originator's assertion about the use of 'Mum' when they were growing up:

> Extract 18, Poster O: Can't agree with @Poster P. Born in 1975 'mum' is what I and most of my friends used, still do. TV & especially Netflix have influenced the growth of 'Mom' (6 likes, including a like from thread originator).
>
> Extract 19, Originator: Exactly. This mirrors my experience too. (liked by commenter 4).
>
> Extract 20, Poster P: Born in 62. Mom the norm in N Dublin middle class, otherwise Mam.

Extract 18, in which O agrees with and validates the originator's assertion in their original tweet and defends them against P, is liked by the originator and mainstream contributors to the thread. The originator then replies, reaffirming this assertion and further validating this contribution which aligns with their way of thinking. P attempts to come back in by reasserting their authority in relation to language change by giving their age credentials (they are older than O or the originator and so should know more about how people have called their mothers in Ireland for longer) and their origin (North Dublin) and class status (middle class). Age, origin/location and class are all fundamental, essential categorisers in relation to language and so these claims should enhance the authority of the post. However, neither the originator nor any of the mainstream contributors engage with the tweet (Extract 20), it attracts no likes or replies and is thus invalidated.

Some tweets in the thread are also blanked out with the message 'This tweet is unavailable', which can mean a variety of things. This is of course the ultimate invalidation, having the content erased. Twitter stated in 2019 that their policy at the time was not to mediate content or intervene in disputes between users. They emphasised, however, that targeted abuse or harassment may have constituted a violation of the Twitter Rules and Terms of Service. There is official (in)validation possible in the form of blocking of certain users, reporting and deleting of tweets and of accounts, and users can now moderate replies to their tweets. However, there is also indirect regulation of the thread by the originator, which in turn validates or invalidates certain types of contribution and signals this to other potential and actual contributors. This is illustrated in Extract 21:

> Extract 21, Originator: To point out the parameters of my question again I'm very specifically talking about the demographic that said 'mum' that now

says 'mom' EMOJI (crying laughing) (7 replies, 10 likes).

Extract 22, Poster Q: Sorry i only just saw your parameters! ignore all my comments! (1 like from originator).

Extract 23, Originator: Hahaha no problem. The parameters have been clearly disregarded my most EMOJI (laughing crying) x (1 like from Q).

After a number of what the originator deems to be irrelevant contributions, they effectively reset the discussion, which invalidates these contributions and also discourages further contributions of this sort – a type of advance or pre-emptive invalidation. This 'resetting' is explicitly remarked on in Extract 22 by Q, who apologizes for their non-relevant contribution and allows their contributions to date to be invalidated ('ignore all my comments!'). The reply is liked by the originator, who responds with a light-hearted tweet, which is in turn liked by Q, thus revalidating this contributor.

Expertise

Expertise has to do with the extent to which the tweeter displays specialist knowledge about language in general or about the particular language which they are discussing. This could be explicit, e.g. posting content relating to relevant educational qualifications or professional activity or the identification with a particular primary categorisation that gives authority in relation to the particular language (e.g. age, gender, social class or place of origin); or it could be implicit, e.g. the display of multilingual competence or of specialist linguistic vocabulary. Expertise may be discussed or referenced explicitly in the particular tweet or might also be explicitly stated in the tweeter's biography or profile. So, for example, the originator states that they did a TEFL (Teaching English as a Foreign Language) course (Extract 24), while Poster R states in their Twitter biography that they are a historian of language education and a university lecturer. This kind of 'professional' expertise may or may not add to the authority of the individual: in some ways, in the current context, where professionals and experts are often undermined, this can be framed as a kind of elitism in language ideological debates online and may in fact serve to reduce their 'professional' authority in favour of 'popular' or 'everyman' authority. However, even the latter can be enhanced by a reference to a primary categorisation by the tweeter such as place of origin or age, as we saw in some of the extracts.

One type of 'expertise' that certainly adds to the authentic stance in the thread (in relation to asserting the connection between 'Mom' and the Irish language and disputing that its use is the result of a foreign influence) is if the tweeter has an Irish language name, as in the case of Posters D and G for example (see Extracts 7 and 10 above).

Expertise can also be implied by a type of language display, not just multilingual display, but one in which specialist vocabulary ('Tefl' and 'lexicon' in Extract 24 and 'shibboleth' in Extract 25) in relation to language is deployed by the posters:

Extract 24, Originator: when I did a Tefl course in Dublin years ago, we looked at how U.K. lexicon was replaced by US, mirroring the rise of American influence and the fall of British. Is the mum/mom mystery as simple as that? (29 likes, 10 replies).

Extract 25, Poster R: It's like a kind of shibboleth. How you say it says everything about your background, class education etc. Personally I say mum, and my other half says ma. (1 like and reply from originator).

Discussion

As we have seen, Twitter's commercial model relies on the creation of knowledge hierarchies: not all spaces or pieces of content on the web can be equal because if they were there would not be the possibility to attract advertising. Certain knowledge and content rise to the top or need to rise to the top, leaving other content behind and this applies to language ideological content also. On Twitter, this happens through the creation of content which has the potential to be a language ideological 'sticky spot', which can attract 'swarms' of attention and crucially also sustain attention. In this way, linguistic authority is established, maintained or challenged, and knowledge about language is also either reinforced or undermined with new knowledge hierarchies about language emerging through this process. In a context of a founding principle of equality of content on the web, and the ability of anyone, anywhere to post language ideological content and assert linguistic authority (with certain caveats of course), understanding how new hierarchies of knowledge about language are created, in this performance era for minoritised languages, matters just as which ones we choose to study (and why and how) also matter.

Authentic and anonymous discourses frame language-ideological content on Twitter, but alignment, influence, expertise and validation are facilitated by its techno-economy and they are all necessary in order to ensure that a language ideological post becomes a 'sticky spot' and ultimately is authoritative or not. We can of course see parallels with how language ideological debates such as these previously took place 'offline' and it is clear that issues of influence, alignment, expertise and validation have always played a role. For example, the letter penned to the newspaper editor from the professor of linguistics would inevitably hold more weight in such debates (see, for example, Johnson, 2005). So, the supporting concepts in this model of linguistic authority online are not new. However, there are significant differences, I would argue, which have an impact on and ultimately change the nature of language ideological debates, the constitution of new knowledge about language or consolidation of existing knowledge and the dissemination of language ideologies. Spaces such as Twitter make these processes explicit – everyone contributing to these debates has a biography on Twitter, as well as an 'algorithmic identity' based on their online lives which means that we have a lot more information about someone who is posting (at least in relation to their digital existence) than we would previously have had. It is therefore easier to categorise contributors to posts. Where previously more space would have been given to the expert voice, the – albeit imperfect – constitution of the web as a space of equality of knowledge and access means that it is as easy or difficult for an expert to post an opinion about language as it is for an ordinary 'citizen-speaker' in line with the affordances of the performance era. The gate-keeping carried out in the gifting and service eras is not generally possible, although as we have seen, validation processes mean that localised, ad hoc gatekeeping does still happen, and expertise is self-declared.

At first glance, it might seem that the new possibilities offered by Twitter would favour the authentic ideological stance by affording the opportunity to point to and mark expertise (e.g. location, language, name) and display alignment (e.g. online linguistic behaviour). However it became clear to me as I went deeper into the study that platforms like Twitter in fact favour the mainstream and 'everyman' stance, far more than previous media or spaces within which language ideologies were debated and mediatised and linguistic authority asserted. At first, I was seduced by how those representing the authentic voice differentiated and distinguished themselves, dismissing the blander profiles of the anonymous voices. But of course, as Critical Discourse Analysis teaches us, what is there is not nearly as important as what is not there, and I soon realised the effort involved in creating that blandness and of tethering oneself to the mainstream. This led me to recognise the ensuing – albeit hidden and implicit but nonetheless powerful – expertise and influence that this bestows, which in fact seems to favour the anonymous, de facto stance.

References

Androutsopoulos, J. (2008) Potentials and limitations of discourse-centred online ethnography. *Language@ internet* 5 (8), N.P.

Androutsopoulos, J. (2013) Participatory culture and metalinguistic discourse: Performing and negotiating German dialects on YouTube. *Discourse* 2, 47–71.

Androutsopoulos, J. (2014) Moments of sharing: Entextualization and linguistic repertoires in social networking. *Journal of Pragmatics* 73, 4–18.

Androutsopoulos, J. (2016) Theorizing media, mediation and mediatization. In N. Coupland (ed.) *Sociolinguistics. Theoretical Debates* (pp. 282–303). Cambridge University Press.

Barton, D. and Lee, C. (2013) *Language Online: Investigating Digital Texts and Practices*. Routledge.

Bauman, R., and Briggs, C.L. (2003) *Voices of Modernity: Language Ideologies and the Politics of Inequality*. Cambridge University Press.

Bliuc, A-M., Faulkner, N., Jakubowicz, A. and McGarty, C. (2018) Online networks of racial hate: A systematic review of 10 years of research on cyber-racism. *Computers in Human Behavior* 87, 75–86.

Blommaert, J. (2017) Durkheim and the internet: On sociolinguistics and the sociological imagination. *Tilburg Papers in Culture Studies* 173, N.P.

Blommaert, J., Kelly-Holmes, H., Lane, P., Leppänen, S., Moriarty, M., Pietikäinen, S. and Piirainen-Marsh, A. (2009) Media, multilingualism and language policing: An introduction. *Language Policy* 8 (3), 203–207.

Bonabeau, E. (2009) Decisions 2.0: The power of collective intelligence. *MIT Sloan Management Review* 50 (2), 45–52.

Cameron, D. (2005) *Verbal Hygiene*. Routledge.

De Bres, J. (2015) Introduction: Language policies on social network sites. *Language Policy* 14 (4), 309–314.

Deumert, A (2014) *Sociolinguistics and Mobile Communication*. Edinburgh: Edinburgh University Press.

Douglas, K.M., McGarty, C., Bliuc, A-M. and Lala, G. (2005) Understanding cyberhate: Social competition and social creativity in online white supremacist groups. *Social Science Computer Review* 23 (1), 68–76.

Guo, L., and Harlow, S. (2014) User-generated racism: An analysis of stereotypes of African Americans, Latinos, and Asians in YouTube videos. *Howard Journal of Communications* 25 (3), 281–302.

Hachimi, A. (2013) The Maghreb-Mashreq language ideology and the politics of identity in a globalized Arab world. *Journal of Sociolinguistics* 17 (3), 269–296.

Hickey, R. (2007) *Irish English. History and Present-day Forms*. Cambridge University Press.

Hickey, R. and Amador-Moreno, C. (eds) (2020) *Irish Identities. Socioloinguistic Perspectives*. De Gruyter.

Irvine, J.T. and Gal, S. (2009) Language ideology and linguistic differentiation. In A. Duranti (ed.) *Linguistic Anthropology – A Reader* (pp. 402–434). Blackwell.

Jakubowicz, A. (2012) Cyber racism. *More or Less: Democracy and New Media*. Future Leaders (futureleaders.com.au). See http://www.futureleaders.com.au/book_chapters/pdf/More-or-Less/Andrew_Jakubowicz.pdf (accessed October 2023).

Jakubowicz, A., Dunn, K., Mason, G., Paradies, Y., Bliuc, A-M., Bahfen, N., Oboler, A., Atie, R. and Connelly, K. (2017) *Cyber Racism and Community Resilience*. Palgrave Macmillan. https://doi. org/10.1007/978-3-319-64388-5.

Johnson, S. (2005) *Spelling Trouble? Language, Ideology and the Reform of German Orthography*. Multilingual Matters.

Kelly-Holmes, H. (2019) Multilingualism and technology: A review of developments in digital communication from monolingualism to idiolingualism. *Annual Review of Applied Linguistics* 39, 24–39.

Kelly-Holmes, H. (2022) Sociolinguistics in an increasingly technologized reality. *Sociolinguistica* 36 (1-2), 99–110. https://doi.org/10.1515/soci-2022-0005.

Kristiansen, T. (2014) Does mediated language influence immediate language? In J. Androutsopoulos (ed.) *Mediatization and Sociolinguistic Change* (pp. 99–126). Mouton de Gruyter.

Lee, C. (2017) *Multilingualism Online*. Routledge.
Lenihan, A. (2013) The interaction of language policy, minority languages and new media: A study of the Facebook translations application. Unpublished PhD Thesis, University of Limerick.
Leppänen, S., Peuronen, S. and Westinen, E. (2018) Superdiversity perspective and the sociolinguistics of social media. In A. Creese and A. Blackledge (eds) *The Routledge Handbook of Language and Superdiversity* (pp. 30–42). Routledge.
May, A.L. (2010) Who tube? How YouTube's news and politics space is going mainstream. *The International Journal of Press/Politics* 15 (4), 499–511.
Milroy, J. and Milroy, L. (2014) *Real English: The Grammar of English Dialects in the British Isles*. Routledge.
Moriarty, M. (2015) *Globalizing Language Policy and Planning: An Irish Language Perspective*. Springer.
Ó Giollagáin, C., Mac Donnacha, S., Ní Chualáin, F., Ní Shéaghdha, A. and O'Brien, M. (2007) *Comprehensive Linguistic Study of the use of Irish in the Gaeltacht. Principal Findings and Recommendations: A Research Report*. Stationery Office.
Ó Laoire, M. (2008) The language situation in Ireland: An update. In R.B. Kaplan and R.B. Baldauf (eds) *Language Planning and Policy in Europe, Vol. 3: The Baltic States, Ireland and Italy* (pp. 193–255). Multilingual Matters.
Ó Riagáin, P. (1997) *Language Policy and Social Reproduction: Ireland 1893-1993*. Clarendon Press.
Pearce, M. (2015) *Mam* or *mum*? Sociolinguistic awareness and language-ideological debates online. *Sociolinguistic Studies* 9 (1), 115–135.
Schiffman, H.F. (1996) *Linguistic Culture and Language Policy*. Routledge.
Shohamy, E.G. (2006) *Language Policy: Hidden Agendas and New Approaches*. Routledge.
Squires, L. (2010) Enregistering internet language. *Language in Society* 39 (4), 457–492.
Thurlow, C. and Mroczek, K. (eds) (2011) *Digital Discourse: Language in the New Media*. Oxford University Press.
Vessey, R. (2016) Language ideologies in social media: the case of Pastagate. *Journal of Language and Politics* 15 (1), 1–24.
Walsh, J. (2010) *Contests and Contexts: The Irish Language and Ireland's Socio-economic Development*. Peter Lang.
Walsh, J. (2012) Language policy and language governance: A case-study of Irish language legislation. *Language Policy* 11 (4), 323–341.
Walsh, J. (2020) The Irish language and contemporary Irish identity. In R. Hickey and C. Amador-Moreno (eds) *Irish Identities. Sociolonguistic Perspective*s (pp. 21–44). De Gruyter.
Williams, M.L. and Burnap, P. (2016) Cyberhate on social media in the aftermath of Woolwich: A case study in computational criminology and big data. *British Journal of Criminology* 56 (2), 211–238.
Woolard, K. (2006) Language and identity choice in Catalonia: The interplay of contrasting ideologies of linguistic authority. In U. Muhlschlegel, K. Suselbeck and P. Masson (eds) *Regulations of Societal Multilingualism in Linguistic Policies* (pp. 303–323). Ibero-Amerikanisches Institut.
Woolard, K.A. (2016) *Singular and Plural: Ideologies of Linguistic Authority in 21st Century Catalonia*. Oxford University Press.

2 Myth Busters: Online Platforms and Emerging Ideological Shift among Lombard Speakers

Marco Tamburelli

Online platforms offer a wealth of sociolinguistic data that are not only highly relevant to the study of language use (e.g. Belmar & Glass, 2019) but also to the investigation of new and emerging linguistic ideologies (e.g. Androutsopoulos, 2013; Lee & Barton, 2013; Vessey, 2016; see also Kelly-Holmes in this volume). With this in mind, the aim of this chapter is twofold. First, it introduces a long-standing but hitherto undiscussed language myth, the 'unintelligibility myth', which I argue plays a strong part in hindering the linguistic emancipation of regional, minoritised, contested or heritage languages. Second, the chapter reports data from online exchanges showing that the unintelligibility myth is being questioned and to some extent eroded via new media. As we shall see, the unintelligibility myth is rooted in Ausbau-centrism (Tamburelli, 2014, 2021), a wider ideology that promotes language shift in favour of highly sociopolitically developed languages and away from lesser used languages. Itself rooted in the wider concept of language attitudes, Ausbau-centrism is an ideology in the sense of Rumsey (1990: 346), as it is part of 'shared bodies of commonsense notions about the nature of language in the world'. Thus, the potential erosion of the unintelligibility myth discussed in this chapter is of great importance to the overall question of whether and how digital media can contribute to counteracting language shift.

The degree of decline of a regional, minoritised, contested or heritage language[1] is closely linked to and frequently driven by the attitudes associated with that language (e.g. Gibbons & Ramirez, 2004). Negative attitudes, which tend to underlie language abandonment (e.g. Price & Tamburelli, 2016), may include the belief that a regional/minority language is somewhat inferior to the dominant language, or that it is not 'useful' or even 'not a real language' (e.g. Lawson, 2014). While these beliefs have often been reported for and are particularly strong in cases of creole languages (e.g. Flórez, 2006), they are by no means limited to creoles. For example, an investigation into the perceptions and attitudes towards Scots revealed that 64% of respondents agreed with the statement 'I don't really think of Scots as a language – it's more just a way of speaking' (TNS-BRMB, 2010: 2), suggesting that Scots is viewed as somewhat 'less' than a language. Comparable attitudes have also been reported in relation to Yiddish (Kahn, 2014), Mayan (Langan, 1996) and the so-called Arabic 'dialects' (see for example Marley, 2004); they have played a central part in the continuous refusal to recognise AAVE as a language (Sealey-Ruiz, 2006), and have plagued the history of sign languages (see Lucas, 2001, for an overview).

These attitudes are rooted in a tradition that insists on giving precedence to sociopolitical considerations when distinguishing between what counts as a 'language' and what does not. Alas, Weinreich's (1954: 13) infamous adage about the role of armies and navies[2] has been taken to heart to the point that the absurd has now become commonplace, with statements such as 'X is not a language because it is not written/official/standardised' routinely used as a defence for refusing to uphold a community's right to introduce their regional/minority language in official settings. In Tamburelli (2014, 2021), I dubbed this phenomenon 'Ausbau-centrism', namely the widespread and mainstream practice of viewing languages as sociopolitical constructs that cannot be identified through linguistic means. As shown in Tamburelli (2021), Ausbau-centrism is rife in the academic literature, besides being common among laypeople and warmly welcomed by governmental institutions. In fact, the Ausbau-centric approach serves the interests of governmental institutions quite well, as it legitimises their tendency to be rather penurious when it comes to extending linguistic support beyond the language of the central state, especially in cases of regional/minority languages that cover a relatively large area of the state and count a relatively high number of speakers (see Tosco, 2021, on a similar point). It should therefore come as no surprise that the results of the Scots language survey were welcomed by several Members of the Scottish Parliament, including Ted Brocklebank (cited in Young, 2023), who stated that Scots 'is not a separate language, but a collection of regional dialects of the English language'. This statement offers a clear example of how the Ausbau-centric doctrine equates 'language' with '*Ausbau* language' (in the sense of Kloss, 1967), favouring varieties that have undergone high degrees of social construction (Blommaert, 2005) or *Ausbau*-isation (Fishman, 2008; Tosco, 2008) and have thus been socially elevated through systematic status, corpus, and acquisition planning, subsequently becoming a 'standardised tool of literary expression'

(Kloss, 1967: 69) within a polity (more often than not a nation-state), to the detriment of all other languages. To the Ausbau-centric mind, Scots *must* be a dialect of English and cannot be anything else because: (1) Scots is related to English, the *de facto* official language of the nation-state and (2) English has undergone high degrees of Ausbau-isation while Scots has not. Note how this stance entirely disregards issues of linguistic distance and/or (un)intelligibility between the two languages, leading to the treatment of Scots speakers as simply ignorant of what is their supposed mother tongue – i.e. English – rather than being treated as bilingual in two related languages as, for example, Spanish–Portuguese bilinguals usually are. Many would probably be appalled, and rightly so, if Spanish-speaking children were sent to Portuguese language schools to be told that Portuguese is their mother tongue and then called 'ignorant' for not being fluent in it. This does not tend to happen, and provisions are usually duly made for Spanish speakers who wish to learn Portuguese (e.g. Carvalho *et al.*, 2010). Yet, Scots-speaking children have been routinely treated as somewhat 'defective' English speakers (e.g. Matheson, 2014), regardless of how linguistically distant the two languages might be, and thus regardless of how much ground a Scots-speaking child might have to cover when being schooled in English. Of course, it may be the case that Scots and English are in fact linguistically closer than Spanish and Portuguese, and that therefore it is linguistically appropriate to treat as bilinguals those who speak Spanish and Portuguese but not those who speak Scots and English. However, the point here is that the Ausbau-centric doctrine prevents such a question from ever being asked; Scots is simply treated as a dialect of English on sociopolitical grounds, and its speakers treated as defective English speakers.

The deleterious effects of Ausbau-centrism are by no means limited to Scots, which is only used here as a working example. Similar situations have been reported for many languages whose only sin is to not be as sociopolitically powerful as their close relative (see for example Adler, 2021, on Low German; Berthele, 2016, on Alemannic; Dołowy-Rybińska & Soria, 2021, on Kashubian and Piedmontese; Leonardi & Tamburelli, 2021, on Bavarian; and Tamburelli, 2014, 2021, on Lombard).

While the development and perpetuation of Ausbau-centrism have been discussed in detail elsewhere (Tamburelli, 2014; Tamburelli & Tosco, 2021), in this chapter, I present an additional characteristic that contributes to sustaining Ausbau-centrism, namely the 'unintelligibility myth'. While part of the broader Ausbau-centric ideology, the unintelligibility myth has surfaced particularly strongly in online fora, predominantly on social media (and specifically Facebook) and in discussions among Wikipedia contributors, where issues of language classification and labelling have for the first time involved the wider public. Looking at data from the Lombard-speaking community, I show how the unintelligibility myth is a direct product of Ausbau-centric linguistics and how it plays a role in hindering linguistic emancipation within a language community. However, as we will see, a novel discourse in opposition to the myth has also been developing through the same online platforms, with a new 'myth-busting' perspective being conveyed in favour of developing regional/minority languages. The message of this chapter is therefore twofold: on the one hand, it shows that the potentially pernicious effects of the unintelligibility myth should be of interest to academics and policymakers alike, and should be taken into consideration when evaluating regional/minority language situations around the world. On the other, the chapter contributes evidence of how the use of electronic technologies can challenge established ideologies, such as Ausbau-centrism, that are detrimental to regional/minority languages, ushering in an important shift in how these languages are viewed.

The Unintelligibility Myth: The Case of Lombard

As a working example of how the unintelligibility myth operates, I will discuss the case of Lombard, a language spoken in Northern Italy and Southern Switzerland. Lombard is a contested language (in the sense of Tamburelli & Tosco, 2021), as it lacks official recognition by the states within which it is spoken, despite being linguistically quite distant from the official language with which it is associated (i.e. Italian, which belongs to a separate genealogical branch of Romance, see Tamburelli & Brasca, 2018) as well as only marginally intelligible with Italian (Tamburelli, 2014) while being relatively highly intelligible with its other Gallo-Romance neighbours, e.g. Occitan (Brasca, 2021b). Lombard is also an endangered language (Moseley, 2010), where endangerment is directly linked to its being contested. By treating it as a 'dialect of Italy' (a conveniently ambiguous label, seeing as it is widely agreed that Lombard is not a dialect <u>of Italian</u>, e.g. Maiden & Parry, 2006), the state denies Lombard any official recognition on the basis that it is *languages*, not dialects, that are owed protection (for a detailed overview of how this stance applies across Italy, see Coluzzi, 2008). The contestation of Lombard comes primarily from the Ausbau-centric stance developed in the Italian dialectological tradition (see Brasca, 2021a) whose bias is to portray any Romance variety spoken in Italy as 'a dialect', regardless of structural linguistic or genealogical considerations, a position which has unsurprisingly been embraced by Italian institutions (for a detailed discussion of how and why modern nation-states seek to recognise as few languages as possible, see Romaine, 2002 and Tosco, 2021. For a discussion of how this position affects the languages of Northern Italy in particular, among them Lombard, see Brasca, 2021a).

Lombard has often been portrayed as 'not a language' by institutions and by its speakers alike, a situation that is rather common in cases of language contestation, where negative attitudes are known to play a fundamental part (Tamburelli, 2021), besides being a recurrent issue in the maintenance of regional/minority languages in general (e.g. Bell, 2013; Loureiro-Rodríguez et al., 2013). However, what I would like to propose here is that the unintelligibility myth plays a central role in the justification and thus the perpetuation of negative attitudes, and that its study should therefore be included in any research endeavour keen to understand how language attitudes are developed and maintained. As we will see, the unintelligibility myth is regularly relied upon to justify continued efforts to prevent Lombard from extending its domains of use and, ultimately, to oppose any attempt at its official recognition, thus playing a central role in maintaining, if not worsening, the situation of endangerment. Reliance on the unintelligibility myth can be observed every time Lombard is deemed 'not a language' on the basis that its varieties are purportedly unintelligible with each other. In 2016, as part of a proposal for the reorganisation of regional policies, the regional government of Lombardy proposed the addition of a comma for the 'promotion of the Lombard language'.[3] This triggered a backlash in the media and among a number of national institutions, all of which opposed the proposal by appealing to some form of the unintelligibility myth.

For example, the academy for the Italian language (*Accademia della Crusca*) published an article in response to the proposal, stating that 'one should talk of "Lombard languages", because in Lombardy there is no single "Lombard dialect"'.[4] Besides its apparent linguistic naivety (one is hard pressed to find any natural language that is formed by a single dialect, so why would dialectal variation be an issue for Lombard alone?), this attack against the regional proposal appeals to a form of the unintelligibility myth, albeit without openly introducing the concept of intelligibility itself. Instead, the article appeals to some purportedly unsurmountable differences which are tacitly presumed to be sufficiently large to prevent successful communication between speakers of different Lombard dialects, as we can see from the following passage cited in the same article: 'Lombard dialects are well differentiated between those to the west and those to the east of the Adda river'.[5] Note that the term 'well differentiated' is never defined, least of all in this instance, with the author simply claiming that such differentiation is so great as to give rise to more than one language. This runs counter to established research, which has provided ample evidence of the linguistic unity of Lombard varieties, and of the fact that dialectal differences are largely due to 'later, more superficial developments' (Sanga, 1997: 253). Nevertheless, the author repeats the same claim in a response to a comment on his article, where he states that 'rather different dialects are spoken in Lombardy' and that therefore 'they can't be considered varieties of a Lombard language'.[6] Other representatives of the Italian establishment came out in support of this view. Giovanni Gobber, Professor of Linguistics at the University of Milan, was asked by the national newspaper *La Repubblica* whether it makes sense to talk about a Lombard language, to which he replied, 'no, in Lombardy there are many dialects, all different from one another'.[7] Similarly, Gian Luigi Beccaria, a philologist and member of the *Accademia della Crusca*, stated that 'Lombard does not exist ... there are very many dialects'.[8] This position was embraced and further propagated by the national media. More than a year after the Lombard proposal, the national newspaper *La Repubblica* continued to contest the language status of Lombard, claiming that it is wrong to use the term 'Lombard language', because 'between Bergamasque and Milanese and the Varese dialect we do not find fewer differences than between Italian and Portuguese'.[9] Besides being another example of appeal to the unintelligibility myth, this statement is also blatantly false. In fact, the degree of genealogical distance between Italian and Portuguese is demonstrably larger, with each language belonging to a different branch of Romance languages (Eastern and Western Romance respectively, e.g. Posner, 1996), while all Lombard varieties belong to the same branch as well as to the same sub-branch of Western Romance, namely Cisalpine (e.g. Hull, 1982; Pellegrini, 1995). Note how Lombard, like Portuguese but unlike Italian, also belongs to the Western Romance branch, being genealogically closer to Portuguese than to Italian, a fact that unsurprisingly remains unmentioned in any discussion on the presumed linguistic distance of Lombard dialects.

As to individual speakers' opinions, many examples can be found in online forums and on social media. Using Google's built-in search tools, several searches were run for the string 'lingua lombarda' (i.e. 'Lombard language') and its variations, which returned a number of cases where the very label 'language' was being contested. For example, in a series of long and tortuous exchanges on Italian Wikipedia for the article 'Lingua lombarda' (Lombard language) we find the following statements from a user and a Wikipedia administrator:[10]

> User 1: Non esiste nessuna lingua lombarda, e lo dico da lombardo. ... e direi che i dialetti orientali (bergamasco, bresciano ecc.) e i dialetti occidentali (milanese, pavese ecc.) non si somigliano proprio per niente.
>
> (There is no Lombard language, and I say this as a Lombard. ... and I would say that the Eastern dialects (of Bergamo, Brescia, etc.) and the Western dialects (Milanese, Pavia, etc.) are not similar at all.)
>
> User 2: Questo lo so' perche conosco persone da queste parti che parlano una lingua similissima al milanese, cosi' simile di fatto

che loro dicono che, pur facendo parte della provincia di Pavia, non capiscono bene il pavese.

(I know this because I know people in these parts who speak a language very similar to Milanese, so similar in fact that they say that, despite being part of the province of Pavia, they do not understand the variety of Pavia well.)

User 3: non si tratta di una lingua ma semplicemente di uno dei tanti dialetti italiani

(it is not a language but simply one of the many Italian dialects)

Wikipedia administrator:

Non esiste una 'lingua lombarda'. Esistono numerosi dialetti lombardi.

(A Lombard language does not exist. There are numerous Lombard dialects.)

chi parla bergamasco fa proprio riferimento a un sistema linguistico ben diverso da quello di chi parla milanese o legnanese ecc. Insomma, una 'lingua lombarda' non esiste.

(Those who speak Bergamasque refer to a linguistic system that is very different from that of those who speak Milanese, Legnanese, etc. In short, a Lombard language does not exist.)

Comparable statements can be found in various online media outlets. In a reply to a newspaper article, a user states that his dialect 'does not resemble the one spoken in Bergamo at all, yet I am from the Bergamo province',[11] suggesting that major differences – and presumably issues of intelligibility – arise every few kilometres. Similarly, in a letter to the online newspaper *varesenews.it*, a reader reiterates that Lombard does not exist because each Lombard dialect is 'a different language' which is 'absolutely incomprehensible'[12] to speakers of other dialects.

A search for the same string (i.e. 'lingua lombarda') with Facebook's search engine reveals more examples across several discussions on the Lombard language. One user, for instance, states that his variety includes words that are 'almost incomprehensible even for people who speak the same dialect just 30 kms away',[13] while another intimates that for 'a Milanese and a Bergamasque to have a discussion, I imagine a third party is needed to translate'.[14] In a separate discussion, one user reports a conversation with a friend who insisted that 'there is no Lombard language. Besides the differences in sounds and terms, Milanese and Bergamasque have different conjugations'.[15] Another user states that Lombard does not exist because 'we find enormous differentiations' and 'profound differences'.[16] The same user reiterates the unintelligibility myth by stating: 'I challenge you to talk to someone from Bagolino or from Cimbergo in Valcamonica and (see if you) understand something'.[17]

Examples like those listed above are widespread and not limited to Lombard (a point to which I will return later). The logical conclusion forced upon us by the purported unintelligibility and its interaction with Ausbau-centrism is typically this: *there is no Lombard language because the varieties attributed to such entity are unintelligible with each other. Therefore, one should speak of Lombard languages, in which case let us speak of 'Lombard dialects' because these varieties do not have the sociopolitical characteristics of a language.* Note how this stance sets an almost unattainable standard for languagehood: a variety is not a language unless it has the degree of Ausbau-isation typical of major European languages. Besides the blatantly Ausbau-centric assumptions it makes, this whole idea relies on the belief that Lombard varieties are indeed unintelligible, something for which there is absolutely no empirical evidence. On the contrary, there is in fact evidence of relatively low degrees of linguistic distance between Lombard varieties (Tamburelli & Brasca, 2018) and of relatively high degrees of intelligibility (Brasca, 2021b), which raises the question: How did the unintelligibility myth come about?

I would like to suggest that the construction and subsequent spread of this unintelligibility myth (similar to other 'language myths', e.g. Bauer & Trudgill, 1998) have been accelerated by the rampant loss of communicative domains that Lombard has undergone in the last century. In terms of the Expanded Graded Intergenerational Disruption Scale (EGIDS, Lewis & Simons, 2010), Lombard gradually shifted from being a language of trade (EGIDS level 3) to becoming threatened (EGIDS level 6b) and in some cases moribund (EGIDS 8a) between the early and late 20th century, as its domains of use became increasingly reduced and localised. This loss of communicative domains has fuelled the unintelligibility myth through a vicious circle, as represented in Figure 2.1 below. With the use of Lombard becoming limited, speakers have inevitably had less exposure to varieties spoken outside their immediate dialectal area, thus losing familiarity with the peculiarities of other Lombard dialects; which consequently strengthens their belief that those dialects are 'unintelligible' with their own, which in turn leads speakers to avoid using Lombard with speakers from outside their own dialectal area, hence keeping the domains of use to a minimum and perpetuating the myth.

Importantly, the unintelligibility myth, and the vicious circle it feeds, is in no way limited to Lombard. In an online discussion on Andalusian, language activists lament that one recurrent claim presented to them against the recognition of Andalusian is that 'Andalusian is not a language because it is not spoken the same throughout Andalusia',[18] where this presumed lack of 'sameness' points towards supposed issues

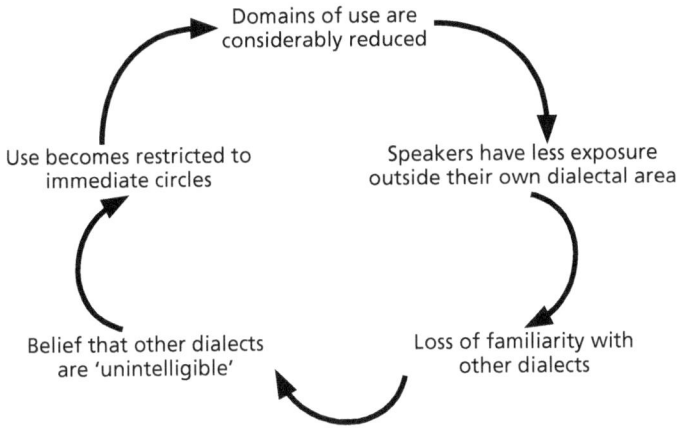

Figure 2.1 Fuelling the myth: The vicious circle of the unintelligibility myth

of unintelligibility. Echoing positions that are remarkably similar to those we have seen presented against Lombard, Nuñez (2001: 27) reports the widespread belief that Andalusian is 'not a language' since it 'has a great linguistic diversity, because a Granada-born person does not speak the same as a Sevillian, a Cadiz, a Cordovan, etc.'.[19] Similarly, in a discussion on the article entitled 'Kurdish Language' on Wikipedia, a user states: 'Kurdish is not a language ... One dialect is so different from the other dialect even they cannot understand each other!'. Similar positions were relayed in interviews with speakers of Jamaican Creole (Sanchez-Alcolea, 2017) who, among the purported reasons why Jamaican is not a language, included this: 'Creole in Kingston is different from Creole in Manchester, and Creole in Mandeville may be different from Creole in Malvern' (Sanchez-Alcolea, 2017: 156).

As is clear from these examples, some form of the unintelligibility myth is active in many language communities. I believe this suggests that it should be included as a useful evaluative tool when measuring language attitudes. In fact, one shortcoming in current approaches to language attitudes is that they are framed as and aim to gather information on attitudes towards *a language*. However, as we have seen, the very notion of 'a language' is itself intertwined with attitudes, with the very same phenomenon, i.e. diatopic variation, being taken as a knock-down argument against languagehood only in cases where the attitudes towards the language in question are negative. While both Lombard and Italian display dialectal variation, only the former is regularly attacked as a 'non-language' on the basis of its variation (on the concept of 'attack' in sociolinguistics, see Trudgill, 1992). As we have seen from the examples above, a similar case can be made for Kurdish vs Turkish or Andalusian vs Spanish; the difference between the two members of these pairs is not that one has the property of dialectal

Table 2.1 Evaluative factor including community members' attitudes towards an endangered language

Grade	Community members' attitudes toward language
5	*All* members value their language and wish to see it promoted.
4	*Most* members support language maintenance.
3	*Many* members support language maintenance; others are indifferent or may even support language loss.
2	*Some* members support language maintenance; others are indifferent or may even support language loss.
1	Only a *few* members support language maintenance; others are indifferent or may even support language loss.
0	*No one* cares if the language is lost; all prefer to use a dominant language.

Source: UNESCO (2003).

variation while the other does not, but that only for one member is the existence of dialectal variation viewed as evidence that it therefore is 'not a language'. This suggests that we are dealing with a matter of attitudes, since it is the attitude towards a property (i.e. variation) and the value associated with it that changes across languages, not the property itself. Consequently, studies on language attitudes, and particularly studies concerned with measuring attitudes towards a regional/minority language, ought to involve considerations about the unintelligibility myth as part of, or a prerequisite to, attitude measurement. In the case of scales such as UNESCO (2003), eliciting information about the unintelligibility myth should run as a prerequisite to more generic considerations such as those in Table 2.1.

As shown in Table 2.1, evaluative factors with regard to attitudes towards a regional/minority language tend to presume that the speaker community and/or the members of the majority community perceive the language at issue as being a language. Nonetheless, as we saw earlier, this is often not the case and cannot therefore be assumed *a priori*, especially in cases where the language status is contested through the perpetuation of the unintelligibility myth. I would therefore like to propose that evaluative factors include attitudes towards the notion that the language at issue is indeed a language, and specifically in relation to whether its dialects are perceived as intelligible. The notion of *perceived* intelligibility as opposed to actual intelligibility is rather crucial here. We would not be dealing with a matter of attitudes if what is perceived as low intelligibility stems from actual low intelligibility. The issue here is that low intelligibility is perceived to be the case despite the demonstrable presence of relatively high intelligibility.

The inclusion of perceived languagehood as an evaluative factor could be extended to research that is interested in understanding the traits associated with a language. For example, some researchers (e.g. Baker, 1992; Zahn & Hopper, 1985) have investigated attitudes as preconceptions about the 'beauty' of a language (e.g. whether the language is perceived as beautiful or ugly), its 'complexity' (e.g. whether the language is perceived as easy or difficult) and its 'importance' (e.g. whether the language is perceived as important or unimportant). Again, this type of research would benefit from also investigating whether the language at issue is perceived as 'a language' at all and, specifically, whether its dialectal variation is seen as some sort of insurmountable obstacle to achieving languagehood.

In the next section I will return to the case of Lombard as our working example, looking at some recent developments that give us an insight into how the unintelligibility myth can be dispelled in order to strengthen speakers' perception, align it with linguistic reality and, ultimately, improve a language's chances of survival.

Recent Maintenance Activities for Lombard

As outlined in Coluzzi *et al.* (2021), recent years have seen the beginning of a shift whereby some individuals as well as several small non-profit organisations have begun to actively promote the use of Lombard. While this is not part of an overarching planning strategy, arising instead from independent and usually uncoordinated efforts, it has nevertheless ushered in a positive, albeit small, change in the history of Lombard, whereby the presence of Lombard is seen and felt outside of the narrow home domains to which it had been relegated since the middle of the 20th century. New activities involve some radio and TV programmes, the dubbing of a few famous films,[20] as well as several social media groups, particularly on Facebook, where members use Lombard as the main language of communication, employing different dialects and several orthographies (see for example Coluzzi *et al.*, 2019). One particular set of initiatives which are highly relevant to the current discussion have been pioneered by the cultural association *Far Lombard* ('to do Lombard'), whose members have specifically focused on trying to dispel the unintelligibility myth.

Tackling the unintelligibility myth

The initiatives organised by Far Lombard include public lectures, a YouTube channel for video interviews, and an online forum for video chats in Lombard (*ciiciarade in lombard*) using the Zoom platform. I will present them in turn.

The public lectures followed a simple but effective format: a speaker with expertise in a specific subject would be invited to give a talk outside of his or her dialectal area, and they would be asked to give the talk entirely in their own Lombard variety. A wide range of subjects has been covered so far, including biology, archaeology, gastronomy, linguistics, statistics, urban planning and history. The public lecture series was specifically devised with two goals in mind: (1) to raise the profile of Lombard by showing that it can be used to discuss academic topics, something which modern speakers have never been exposed to, and (2) to directly show, rather than 'tell', that there is a high degree of intelligibility between Lombard dialects. It is this second point that makes the lecture series rather unique, not just within the Lombard context but among language planning efforts more generally. While the importance of raising the profile of a language (i.e. goal 1) is well known and often at the core of any status planning (e.g. Johnson & Ricento, 2013; Olko & Sallabank, 2021), the second goal is rather innovative, and one which – as far as I know – has received hardly any attention in the literature nor has it been tackled so overtly in other regional/minority language contexts.

The video interviews were also specifically devised to tackle the unintelligibility myth and have a crucial characteristic in common with the public lecture series: they involve inter-dialectal communication. In each interview, the interviewer and interviewee come from different parts of Lombardy, sometimes hundreds of miles apart, and speak different dialects of the language. Again, this initiative was specifically devised to show, rather than tell, the high degree of intelligibility between different Lombard varieties.

Lastly, the online video chats feature a regular forum (usually on Sunday evenings) where Lombard speakers from all over the world can meet and chat in Lombard via Zoom. Every chat evening begins with a short (usually 5 to 10 minutes) introduction by one of the guests, who presents a few ideas about a topic they are interested in, an experience they would like to share or a story they wish to tell. This acts as an icebreaker, after which the host opens the floor to all participants, who are invited to contribute their views. These turn into full discussions with different participants taking part to different degrees depending on their language ability and level of interest in the topic. Crucially, however, all participants get a chance to hear dialects different from their own as well as to converse with speakers of other dialects. Given that some of these dialects may be from areas over 200 miles away, the online forum gives participants the opportunity to hear and converse with speakers of dialects who they would probably never have had the opportunity to meet otherwise, and whose dialect they would be unlikely to be exposed to, certainly not with any regularity.

Overall, the activities organised by the association Far Lombard have brought about an increase in exposure to various Lombard dialects, thus providing very much needed opportunities to dispel the unintelligibility myth and to break the circle that fuels it (see Figure 2.1). Providing speakers with regular exposure achieves two goals: (1) speakers realise how highly intelligible Lombard dialects actually are, thus becoming less susceptible to the unintelligibility myth; and (2) regular exposure to dialects other than one's own allows speakers to learn the lexical peculiarities of other dialects, thus further enhancing their ability to engage in cross-dialectal communication and reduce the chances of actual intelligibility issues arising.

While these activities are reaching hundreds and possibly thousands of Lombard speakers, this is only a tiny percentage of their overall number. With an estimated 3.8 million speakers (Lewis *et al.*, 2015) embedded within a large population size of over 10 million (comparable to the population of Sweden or Greece) and scattered across approximately 10,000 sq mi, reaching large parts of the Lombard-speaking community presents serious challenges. Even relatively successful grass-roots campaigns that may reach as many as five or six thousand speakers are reaching less than 0.2% of the total number of speakers. Hence, increasing speakers' exposure to dialects other than their own remains a challenge, as does the possibility of reaching a potential critical mass of speakers. Nevertheless, we can already see signs that a number of rather vocal speakers no longer buy into the unintelligibility myth.

A series of telling examples stem from a post on the very popular Facebook page 'Steve the vagabond and silly linguist', which at the time of writing has over 500,000 subscribers. The main point of the post was to list the ten Romance languages with the highest number of speakers, with Lombard featuring at number nine (below Catalan and above Galician). Predictably, one user attacked the post with the unintelligibility myth: '"Lombard" is not a language. It might be considered a dialect, EXCEPT there is no "Lombard" dialect, every city has its own!'.

However, what makes this particular case unusual in recent history is that a number of users have replied to this comment by disputing the unintelligibility myth. Some examples are reported below:

(1) The intelligibility between Maghrebi Arabic and Levantine Arabic is much lower than the one between, let's say, Milanese Lombard and Bergamo Lombard, however the former are often considered variants of the same language.
(2) There is more difference between me and my Calabrian neighbour speaking Italian than between me and a person from Bergamo speaking Lombard.

Other users point out the fallacy of bringing up the unintelligibility myth only with regard to Lombard:

(3) Yes, there are many variants between one Lombard area and another, but this could be said about every language (Italian spoken in Lombardy is way different from Italian spoken in Sicily …).

(4) tutte le lingue funzionano così, lombardo è semplicemente un raggruppamento basato su determinati principi, così come tutti i vernacoli inglesi sono classificati come 'inglese' anche se tre (sic) Londra e Newcastle ne passa di acqua.

(all languages work like this, Lombard is simply a grouping based on certain principles, just as all English vernaculars are classified as 'English' even if differences are obvious between London and Newcastle.)

Another user makes the point that actual unintelligibility runs between Lombard and Italian rather than between Lombard dialects: 'By the way good luck watching "L'albero degli zoccoli" (a film entirely shot in Lombard) without subtitles, those things you need to understand *another* language'.

Similar exchanges can be found in other social media posts where Lombard is mentioned, with one or two users questioning its legitimacy on the basis of the unintelligibility myth and a larger number of users (usually 10 or more) countering their position. In a page dedicated to the languages of Italy, users rebuked attempts at perpetuating the unintelligibility myth, as follows:

(5) Praticamente stai dicendo che, per un milanese, tedesco e cremonese pari sono. È chiaro che non è così. (i dialetti Lombardi) condividono tanti di quegli aspetti (sotto il profilo dell'evoluzione dal latino, grammatica, formazione della frase, lessico) da rimanere stupiti

(Basically you are saying that, for a Milanese, German and Cremonese are equal. It is clear that this is not the case. (Lombard dialects) share so many aspects (in terms of evolution from Latin, grammar, sentence formation, vocabulary) to leave you amazed)

(6) il buon senso mi dice che fino a che ci capiamo senza bisogno di dizionari e interpreti parliamo la stessa lingua. Con qualche variante locale magari, come tutte le lingue.

(common sense tells me that as long as we understand each other without the need for dictionaries and interpreters, we speak the same language. With some local variation maybe, like in all languages.)

(7) Da bergamasco delle valli il mio dialetto è diverso da quello del Vava e anche naturalmente da quello milanese, ma è ovvio che ci capiamo

(As a Bergamasque from the valleys my dialect is different from Vava's and also of course from that of Milan, but it is obvious that we understand each other)

While these make up a relatively low number of cases in a relatively limited social media context, it is important to remember that only a few years ago the reverse was the norm: dozens of users would recite the unintelligibility myth, with one or possibly two users trying to question it and usually ending up being ridiculed or told that they have never tried to communicate with a speaker of this or that dialect (by implication a supposedly unintelligible one). The examples above are therefore symbolic of what appears to be a slow but important shift in how speakers of Lombard varieties see themselves in relation to other speakers: no longer as using different linguistic systems that 'happen' to have traits in common, but as speakers of the same language.

Conclusions

In this chapter I have outlined what I called the 'unintelligibility myth'. Using examples form the Lombard situation, I argued that the unintelligibility myth is both a product of Ausbau-centrism (Tamburelli, 2014) and a characteristic that contributes to sustaining it, thus playing an active part in threatening linguistic diversity (for details of why Ausbau-centrism is a threat to linguistic diversity, see Tamburelli & Tosco, 2021). I have discussed some examples from the Lombard-speaking community to show how the unintelligibility myth is perpetuated and regularly presented as a supposed reason to defend the hindering of linguistic emancipation. Some examples taken from other language communities (Andalusian, Jamaican Creole and Kurdish) suggest that the unintelligibility myth is potentially a widespread phenomenon, and that it should therefore be taken into consideration when evaluating regional/minority language situations around the world, and eventually it should be built into current models of language vitality (e.g. Lewis & Simons, 2010; UNESCO, 2003) and into the structure of attitudinal surveys.

A recent increase in the use of Lombard across online platforms and social media has been providing possible means to potentially break the circle within which the unintelligibility myth operates. An increase in online use spurred by targeted activities organised by the third-sector organisation Far Lombard is giving Lombard speakers the opportunity to gain regular exposure to dialects other than their own, including dialects spoken across relatively large geographical distances. This increased exposure has spurred the beginning of a shift away from the unintelligibility myth and towards the perception that Lombard dialects share a high degree of mutual intelligibility, thus opening up new communicative opportunities. While there is still a long way to go, these initiatives have shown that language myths can be dispelled, and their hold over the emancipation of a language loosened, with some promising results.

Overall, the unintelligibility myth can be an effective tool in preventing the emancipation of a language and should therefore be taken seriously when evaluating regional/minority language situations around the world. I hope that the examples I have provided can help other researchers to identify cases where the unintelligibility myth may be at work so that it can be tackled and ultimately rendered powerless. Following examples from the Lombard situation, the potentially pernicious effects of the unintelligibility myth may be reduced by creating opportunities for cross-dialectal exchanges. It would therefore be good practice for such opportunities to become an integral part of awareness-raising campaigns and for language maintenance efforts to actively encourage expansion of use and growth in communicative opportunities.

Acknowledgements

I would like to thank Simona Scuri, Federico Gobbo and the organisers and audience of the conference NEWCON 2020: New Contexts for the Use of Minoritized Languages/Varieties, where some of the issues discussed in this chapter were originally presented.

Notes

(1) For the sake of brevity, I will refer to all of these as 'regional/minority' languages from this point forward, though I do not intend to suggest they are necessarily the same, nor do I believe that they are. In cases where a distinction needs to be made, I will use the single appropriate term on its own, e.g. 'contested' or 'minoritized', etc.

(2) It is a matter of dispute whether Weinreich himself came up with the phrase. Among the names cited as possible authors are the linguist Antoine Meillet and the literary theorist Viktor Shklovsky.

(3) Article 24, Regional Law, 7 October 2016: 'Promozione della lingua lombarda attraverso le sue varietà locali' (Promotion of the Lombard language through its local varieties).

(4) 'In ogni caso, se proprio si volesse usare il termine "lingua" e non quello di "dialetto", bisognerebbe parlare di "lingue lombarde", perché in Lombardia non esiste un unico "dialetto lombardo"'. See https://accademiadellacrusca.it/it/contenuti/la-salvaguardia-della-lingua-lombarda-in-una-legge-regionale/7402 (accessed July 2023).

(5) 'I dialetti lombardi sono ben differenziati tra quelli a ovest e quelli a est dell'Adda'. See https://accademiadellacrusca.it/it/contenuti/la-salvaguardia-della-lingua-lombarda-in-una-legge-regionale/7402 (accessed July 2023).

(6) 'in Lombardia, si parlano dialetti abbastanza distinti … andrebbero inquadrati in questo orizzonte più ampio, piuttosto che considerarli varietà di una "lingua lombarda"'. See https://accademiadellacrusca.it/it/contenuti/la-salvaguardia-della-lingua-lombarda-in-una-legge-regionale/7402 (accessed July 2023).

(7) 'in Lombardia ci sono molti dialetti tutti diversi fra loro'. *La Repubblica*, 16 January 2016.

(8) 'il lombardo non esiste … i dialetti sono moltissimi'. Radio interview on Rai Radio 3, 19 October 2016.

(9) 'perché tra il bergamasco e il milanese e il varesotto non ci sono meno differenze che tra l'italiano e il portoghese' (https://genova.repubblica.it/cronaca/2017/10/22/news/povera_liungua_italiana_assediata_dai_dialetti_dal_basso_e_dall_inglese-178924011/).

(10) Source: https://it.wikipedia.org/wiki/Discussione%3ALingua_lombarda
(11) 'Dalle mie parti il dialetto non assomiglia per niente a quello parlato a Bergamo, eppure mi trovo in provincia di Bergamo!' (https://www.ecodibergamo.it/stories/bergamo-citta/proposta-lega-incentivi-alle-scuoleche-valorizzano-la-lingua-lombarda_1165715_11/).
(12) 'basta sentir parlare in dialetto un varesino, un bustocco, un bergamasco o un bresciano per verificare come si tratti di "lingue" diverse e assolutamente incomprensibili per il forestiero' (https://www.varesenews.it/lettera/ma-una-lingua-lombarda-non-esiste/).
(13) 'quasi incomprensibili anche a gente che parla lo stesso dialetto a soli 30 chilometri di distanza'.
(14) 'un milanese e a un bergamasco che discutono, immagino occorra un terzo che traduca'.
(15) 'Non esiste la lingua Lombarda! A parte le differenze di suono e di termini, il milanese ed il bergamasco hanno anche diverse coniugazioni'.
(16) 'troviamo una differenziazione enorme nonchè vere e proprie isole linguistiche che demarcano profonde differenze'.
(17) 'ti sfido a parlare con uno di Bagolino (BS) o uno di Cimbergo in Valcamonica e capirci qualcosa'.
(18) 'el andaluz no es una lengua porque no se habla igual en toda Andalucia' (https://0positivo.wordpress.com/)
(19) 'El andaluz tiene una gran diversidad lingüística pues un granadino no habla igual que un sevillano, un gaditano, un cordobés, etc.'
(20) Activities related to TV and film tend to be restricted to Lombard-speaking Switzerland, although some involve collaborations with Lombard speakers in Italy. See Coluzzi *et al.* (2021) for details.

References

Adler, A. (2021) Language, or dialect, that is the question: How attitudes affect language statistics using the example of Low German. *Languages* 6 (1), 40.
Androutsopoulos, J. (2013) Participatory culture and metalinguistic discourse: Performing and negotiating German dialects on YouTube. *Discourse* 2, 47–71.
Baker, C. (1992) *Attitudes and Language*. Multilingual Matters.
Bauer, L. and Trudgill, P. (1998) *Language Myths*. Penguin UK.
Bell, J. (2013) Language attitudes and language revival/survival. *Journal of Multilingual and Multicultural Development* 34 (4), 399–410.
Belmar, G. and Glass, M. (2019) Virtual communities as breathing spaces for minority languages: Re-framing minority language use in social media. *Adeptus* 14, 1–24.
Berthele, R. (2016) Demography vs. legitimacy: Current issues in Swiss language policy. *Cahiers du Centre de Linguistique et des Sciences du Langage* (48), 27–51.
Blommaert, J. (2005) Situating language rights: English and Swahili in Tanzania revisited. *Journal of Sociolinguistics* 9 (3), 390–417.
Brasca, L. (2021a) Mixing methods in linguistic classification: A hidden agenda against multilingualism? In M. Tamburelli and M. Tosco (eds) *Contested Languages: The Hidden Multilingualism of Europe* (pp. 59–86). John Benjamins Publishing Company.
Brasca, L. (2021b) Classification of 'Gallo-Italic': Current Issues in the Literature and Proposals for a Solution. Unpublished PhD thesis, Bangor University.
Carvalho, A.M., Freire, J.L. and Da Silva, A.J. (2010) Teaching Portuguese to Spanish speakers: A case for trilingualism. *Hispania* 93 (1), 70–75.
Coluzzi, P. (2008) Language planning for Italian regional languages ('dialects'). *Language Problems and Language Planning* 32 (3), 215–236.
Coluzzi, P., Brasca, L. and Miola, E. (2019) Writing systems for Italian regional languages. *Journal of Multilingual and Multicultural Development* 40 (6), 491–503.

Coluzzi, P., Brasca, L. and Scuri, S. (2021) Revitalising contested languages. In M. Tamburelli and M. Tosco (eds) *Contested Languages: The Hidden Multilingualism of Europe* (pp. 163–182). John Benjamins Publishing Company.

Dołowy-Rybińska, N. and Soria, C. (2021) Surveying the ethnolinguistic vitality of two contested languages. In M. Tamburelli and M. Tosco (eds) *Contested Languages: The Hidden Multilingualism of Europe* (pp. 125–142). John Benjamins Publishing Company.

Fishman, J.A. (2008) Rethinking the Ausbau-Abstand dichotomy into a continuous and multivariate system. *International Journal of the Sociology of Language* 191, 17–26.

Flórez, S. (2006) A study of language attitudes in two creole-speaking islands: San Andres and Providence (Colombia). *Ikala, Revista de lenguaje y cultura* 11 (17), 119–147.

Gibbons, J. and Ramirez, E. (2004) Different beliefs: Beliefs and the maintenance of a minority language. *Journal of Language and Social Psychology* 23 (1), 99–117.

Hull, G. (1982) The linguistic unity of Northern Italy and Rhaetia. PhD dissertation, University of Sidney West.

Johnson, D.C. and Ricento, T. (2013) Conceptual and theoretical perspectives in language planning and policy: Situating the ethnography of language policy. *International Journal of the Sociology of Language* 219, 7–21.

Kahn, L. (2014) *Colloquial Yiddish*. Routledge.

Kloss, Heinz (1967) 'Abstand languages' and 'ausbau languages.' *Anthropological Linguistics* 9/7, 29–41.

Langan, K. (1996) Issues of ethnic participation in language planning in an age of ethnic empowerment: Observations from Guatemala. In T. Hickey and J. Williams (eds) *Language, Education and Society in a Changing World* (pp. 107–116). Multilingual Matters.

Lawson, R. (2014) *Sociolinguistics in Scotland*. Palgrave Macmillan.

Lee, C. and Barton, D. (2013) *Language Online: Investigating Digital Texts and Practices*. Routledge.

Leonardi, M.M.V. and Tamburelli, M. (2021) The cost of ignoring degrees of Abstand in defining a regional language. In M. Tamburelli and M. Tosco (eds) *Contested Languages: The Hidden Multilingualism of Europe* (pp. 87–103). John Benjamins Publishing Company.

Lewis, M.P. and Simons, G.F. (2010) Assessing endangerment: Expanding Fishman's GIDS. *Revue roumaine de linguistique* 55 (2), 103–120.

Lewis, M.P., Gary, P., Simons, G.F. and Fennig, D.C. (2015) *Ethnologue: Languages of the World* (18th edn). SIL International.

Loureiro-Rodríguez, V., Boggess, M.M. and Goldsmith, A. (2013) Language attitudes in Galicia: Using the matched-guise test among high school students. *Journal of Multilingual and Multicultural Development* 34 (2), 136–153.

Lucas, C. (ed.) (2001) *The Sociolinguistics of Sign Languages*. Cambridge University Press.

Maiden, M. and Parry, M. (2006) *The Dialects of Italy*. Routledge.

Marley, D. (2004) Language attitudes in Morocco following recent changes in language policy. *Language Policy* 3 (1), 25–46.

Matheson, D. (2014) Education in Scotland. In D. Matheson (ed.) *An Introduction to the Study of Education* (4th edn) (pp. 179–201). Routledge.

Moseley, C. (ed.) (2010) *Atlas of the World's Languages in Danger* (3rd edn). UNESCO Publishing.

Nuñez, M.R. (2001) Sociolinguistica Andaluza: Problemas y perspectivas. *Sociolinguistica Andaluza* 12, 21–48.

Olko, J. and Sallabank, J. (eds) (2021) *Revitalizing Endangered Languages: A Practical Guide*. Cambridge University Press.

Pellegrini, G.B. (1995) Il cisalpino e il retoromanzo. In E. Banfi, G. Bonfadini, P. Cordin and M. Iliescu (eds) *Italia settentrionale: crocevia di idiomi romanzi. Atti del convegno internazionale di studi di Trento* (pp. 1–14).

Posner, R. (1996) *The Romance Languages*. Cambridge University Press.
Price, A.R. and Tamburelli, M. (2016) Minority language abandonment in Welsh-medium educated L2 male adolescents: Classroom, not chatroom. *Language, Culture and Curriculum* 29 (2), 189–206.
Romaine, S. (2002) The impact of language policy on endangered languages. *International Journal on Multicultural Societies* 4 (2), 194–212.
Rumsey, A. (1990). Wording, meaning, and linguistic ideology. *American Anthropologist* 92 (2), 346–361.
Sanchez-Alcolea, M.T. (2017) The language situation in Jamaica: A cartographic exploration of language narratives amongst creole-speaking teachers of Spanish. Unpublished PhD Thesis, Federal University of Paraná.
Sanga, G. (1997) Lombardy. In M. Maiden and M. Parry (eds) *The Dialects of Italy* (pp. 253–259). Routledge.
Sealey-Ruiz, Y. (2006) Spoken soul: The language of Black imagination and reality. *The Educational Forum* 70 (1), 37–46.
Tamburelli, M. (2014) Uncovering the 'hidden' multilingualism of Europe: An Italian case study. *Journal of Multilingual and Multicultural Development* 35 (3), 252–270.
Tamburelli, M. (2021) Contested languages and the denial of linguistic rights in the 21st century. In M. Tamburelli and M. Tosco (eds) *Contested Languages: The Hidden Multilingualism of Europe* (pp. 21–39). John Benjamins Publishing Company.
Tamburelli, M. and Brasca, L. (2018) Revisiting the classification of Gallo-Italic: A dialectometric approach. *Digital Scholarship in the Humanities* 33 (2), 442–455.
Tamburelli, M. and Tosco, M. (2021) What are contested languages and why should linguists care? In M. Tamburelli and M. Tosco (eds) *Contested Languages: The Hidden Multilingualism of Europe* (pp. 3–17). John Benjamins Publishing Company.
TNS-BRMB (2010) *Public Attitudes towards the Scots Language*. Scottish Government Social Research.
Tosco, M. (2008) Introduction: Ausbau Is everywhere! *International Journal of the Sociology of Language* 191, 1–16.
Tosco, M. (2021) Democracy: A threat to language diversity? In M. Tamburelli and M. Tosco (eds) *Contested Languages: The Hidden Multilingualism of Europe* (pp. 41–56). John Benjamins Publishing Company.
Trudgill, P. (1992) Ausbau sociolinguistics and the perception of language status in contemporary Europe. *International Journal of Applied Linguistics* 2 (2), 167–177.
UNESCO Ad Hoc Expert Group on Endangered Languages (2003) *Language Vitality and Endangerment*. UNESCO.
Vessey, R. (2016) Language ideologies in social media: The case of Pastagate. *Journal of Language and Politics* 15 (1), 1–24.
Weinreich, Ulrich (1954) Is a structural dialectology possible? *Word* 10, 388–400.
Young, C. (2023) *Unlocking Scots: The Secret Life of the Scots Language*. Luath Press Limited.
Zahn, C.J. and Hopper, R. (1985) Measuring language attitudes: The speech evaluation instrument. *Journal of Language and Social Psychology* 4 (2), 113–123.

3 Focus on Faroese: Digital Insights into the Smallest North Germanic Language Community

Laura Zieseler

Introduction

This chapter presents a case study of how structural and sociolinguistic change manifests itself in the small autochthonous language of the Faroe Islands, and how computer-mediated communication (henceforth CMC) shapes this development. Faced with the challenges of steadily increasing language contact, the Faroese language community needs to adapt to external influences amidst at times clashing notions of top-down linguistic purism vs. bottom-up pragmatism. In this context, the developments observed in Faroese CMC can be considered to be an example of *mediatisation* (Androutsopoulos, 2016).

Linguistic, Historical and Sociocultural Background

Although not featured in the European Charter for Regional or Minority Languages, since it fulfils the criteria of a demographic *and* functional majority language in the Faroe Islands, Faroese still faces many of the challenges encountered by minority languages because of its size and marginality (Sandøy, 1992: 69–70). With ca. 50,000 native speakers living on the archipelago and a further estimated 25,000 mostly residing in mainland Denmark, Faroese is the smallest present-day North Germanic language and has an unusually close-knit community (Leonard, 2016). Due to the equally small size of its online community, it can be regarded as a 'digital minority language' (Knudsen, 2010: 138–139).

Both geographically and structurally, Faroese is located between Icelandic and certain south-western Norwegian dialects (Thráinsson *et al.*, 2004/2012: 369). Like Icelandic, it is classified as Insular

Scandinavian, which is characterised by more grammatical complexity and more lexical conservatism than Mainland Scandinavian languages. Unlike Icelandic, however, Faroese cannot look back on nearly a millennium of written language tradition due to its political history. Having been subject first to the Norwegian crown since the 11th century and later to the Danish crown, including various unions, the Faroe Islands eventually became a Danish *amt* ('province') when the *Løgting* ('Faroese Parliament') was dissolved in 1816. In 1849, they were fully integrated into the Danish Realm. The *Løgting* was reinstituted in 1852, but only regained its former political power with the *Heimastýrislógin* ('Home Rule Act') of 1948 (Lindqvist, 2018: 3–5). The country's long-standing dependence on Denmark fundamentally changed its linguistic setting.

When the Danish Bible was introduced in the Faroes during the Reformation, Danish became the only language of the church. Soon, the last remnants of Faroese literacy were discontinued and Danish became the sole written language. A diglossia emerged with Danish as the high (H) variety and Faroese as the low (L) variety (Lindqvist, 2018: 5–6). Later, Danish conquered other prestigious domains such as law, trade or education. Meanwhile, Faroese was restricted to the private sphere and to traditional professions (e.g. agriculture or hunting), and it became increasingly Danicised, especially in the capital, Tórshavn.

It was only during National Romanticism that Faroese received its modern orthography, which was devised in the 1840s mainly by the *Icelandic* philologist and politician Jón Sigurðsson and the *Danish* philologist N.M. Petersen, and only slightly revised by the *Faroese* theologian V.U. Hammershaimb. Sigurðsson implemented a *historicising* spelling system recreating a hypothetical older language stage. This system is strikingly similar to Icelandic and has a marked gap between graphemes and phonemes, i.e. orthographic depth (Lindqvist, 2001: 13–17). To this day, Hammershaimb is often wrongfully credited as 'the father of the Faroese written language', a founding myth that is of great national significance (Lindqvist, 2018: 193–197). The novel orthography became the official norm in the late 19th century. It was hailed as an expression of emancipation from Danish hegemony *and* criticised for being too difficult for anyone without in-depth knowledge of Old Norse or Icelandic. In the 1890s, an orthophone reform proposal failed (Lindqvist, 2018: 175–188), and the orthography soon became established, but has remained a debated topic until today.

Another consequence of the creation of modern written Faroese was the emergence of linguistic purism in the 1880s, i.e. 'a normative ideology aimed at keeping the language clean of foreign elements … considered to be "impure" … often combined with efforts to substitute foreign elements with native ones, or to adapt them to a native form … most often focused on the lexical [level]' (Brunstad, 2001: 27; transl. L.Z.).

An orientation towards Icelandic regarding lexical purification meant that 'de-Danicisation' was often synonymous with 'Icelandisation' during early Faroese purism. Soon, this strategy also met with criticism that is echoed to this day.

Throughout the late 19th and the 20th century, efforts were made to introduce *genuinely Faroese* neologisms. Many of these failed, often because they were *perceived* as Icelandicisms regardless of their origin. Furthermore, these efforts were regarded as a prescriptive stigmatisation of *actual* language use. From the 1960s onwards, the language created by purist scholars at *Føroyamálsdeildin* ('Faculty of Faroese Language and Literature') therefore came to be denounced as *setursmál* ('university language') by its critics: an elitist, *unintelligible* variety of Faroese present in most of the dictionaries published until the 1990s. Thusly codified, de-Danicised, purist Faroese developed into a written, overtly prestigious H variety, while Danicised, largely uncodified, vernacular Faroese was degraded to a spoken, overtly stigmatised L variety. Thus, after centuries of *interlingual* Danish–Faroese diglossia, a new, *intralingual*, primarily *medial* diglossia has emerged (Lindqvist, 2018). Its linguistic reality has been empirically confirmed (e.g. Clausén, 1978; Jacobsen, 2012; Jacobsen & Steintún, 1992; Pauladóttir, 2008) and is illustrated in Table 3.1.

The Home Rule Act of 1948 recognised Faroese as the country's principal official language, while Danish as its second official language is to be learned 'well and carefully' and can be used in public affairs (Mortensen, 2015: 75). Thus, all Faroese are required to become bilingual: spoken Faroese is acquired at home, written Faroese is taught at school from 1st grade, and spoken and written Danish is obligatory from 3rd to 9th grade (Mortensen, 2015: 84). The average L2 competence is high especially among younger people, who often temporarily move to Denmark for study or work.

English is compulsory from 4th to 9th grade. At upper secondary level, it is the only mandatory language taught besides Faroese (Mortensen, 2015: 84). However, Danish and English are not only

Table 3.1 Medial diglossia in the Faroe Islands (adapted from Lindqvist, 2018: 24)

	Written (conceptual literacy, language of distance)	Spoken (conceptual orality, language of immediacy)
H variety Far. *setursmál* ('university language')	Historicising (and de-Danicised) Faroese	Literacy-based Faroese
	Danish	Standard Danish
Semi-H variety	—	Faroese writing-induced pronunciation of Danish
L variety High Intimacy Language (Leonard, 2016)	—	Faroeised Danish (so-called *gøtudanskt*)
		Danicised Faroese varieties

conveyed 'from above' in institutional settings but also increasingly 'from below' through mass media. In domains such as popular culture, technology or science, English is becoming as important as Danish (Knudsen, 2010). As a result, many Faroese native speakers are more or less trilingual.

In 1985, *Føroyska Málnevndin* ('the Faroese Language Committee') was established as an information and counselling board for public institutions and for the general public, but without legislative power (Mortensen 2015: 78). In 2012/13, it was succeeded by *Málráðið* ('the Language Council'), whose updated mandate made its authority more binding than before (Mortensen, 2015: 78). The Language Council bill of 2012 states that *Málráðið* is 'to cultivate, develop and protect ... Faroese ...', 'to collect and register newly arrived words, ... pronunciations, and other linguistic phenomena ..., to assist in the selection and creation of neologisms', 'to guide, advise, and make decisions on language questions', and 'to determine Faroese spelling' (*Løgtingslóg nr. 59*, 2012/2017, transl. L.Z.). In 2013, *Málráðið* made its first decision by vetoing the inclusion of *c, w, x, z* in the Faroese alphabet (Mortensen, 2015: 82).

The manifesto *Málmørk* (Málstevnunevndin & Mentamálaráðið, 2007) details Faroese language policy, focusing on *málrøkt* ('language cultivation') and *málstøða* ('language status'). The aim is 'to secure the status of Faroese as a fully developed language fit to be used in all social domains', making it 'important to develop and update modern Faroese technical terms' (Málstevnunevndin & Mentamálaráðið, 2007: 6, 11–12, transl. L.Z.). Previously, English had mainly been considered via Danish as its mediating language (Brunstad, 2001: 251, 410). Accelerating digitalisation and globalisation, however, have intensified direct contact with English (Jacobsen, 2012). Due to its growing dominance in various domains, English is considered a threat that is addressed with the terms *økismissi/økisvanda* and *økisvinning* ('domain loss and gain') throughout *Málmørk* (Mortensen, 2015: 83). The focus has shifted from *regressive* – *reclaiming* domains from Danish and removing established Danicisms – to *conservative* purism – *defending* domains by strengthening Faroese against new Anglicisms, internationalisms, and English as a whole (Brunstad, 2001: 410).

Such efforts to strengthen Faroese are visible on *Málráðið*'s website, malrad.fo. On its homepage, a column titled *nýggj orð* ('new words') lists the latest Faroese neologisms, and a prominent link leads to entire *orðalistar* ('glossaries') of such neologisms sorted by domain.

At the beginning of the 21st century, over 130 years of Faroese purism have heavily shaped 'the [country's] ideological climate with regard to language use, language correctness and language planning' (Vikør, 1993/2001: 184). Based on studies on overt language attitudes (Kristiansen & Vikør, 2006), the North Germanic language communities can be ranked along a 'purism continuum' as shown in Figure 3.1.

Purist ―――――――――――――――――――――――――――――――― Liberal

Iceland > Faroe Islands > Swedish-speaking Finland > Norway > Sweden > Denmark

Figure 3.1 North Germanic language communities on the purism continuum (based on Kristiansen, 2009: 100)

The official ideological climate of each community is openly supported by its members, with Iceland being the most and Denmark the least purist one (Kristiansen, 2009: 97, 100–101). And it is between these two extremes that the Faroese have found themselves since the 19th century. Language ideologies 'are conceptualizations about languages, speakers, and discursive practices [and] are pervaded with political and moral interests and are shaped in a cultural setting' (Irvine, 2012). As shown above, the official Faroese language ideology is puristic. Simultaneously, the fact that '[l]anguage ideologies are inherently plural', 'positioned', and hence 'always partial' (Irvine, 2012) can also be observed in the Faroese language community – not least in the context of CMC.

Androutsopoulos (2011: 146) argues that 'digital media enable an expansion of vernacular writing into new domains of practice, and therefore a diversification of ... written language norms. [This] affords vernacular written usage more space, visibility and status than ever before'. Similarly, Grondelaers *et al.* (2016: 130) point out 'the growing importance of ... internet communication', where 'digital language practices fragment the locus of normative authority', thus making CMC 'less sensitive to official language norms' in an age where writing has become an integral part of everyday communication compared to pre-internet times. This last aspect is also stressed by Hårstad (2021: 39; transl. L.Z.), who states that 'a population who keeps writing more and more' is posing a serious challenge to standard norms in many digital areas, so that 'even though the notion of normativity still seems to be standing strong among language users online, the One correct language has gradually become much less dominant than [before]'. As will be shown, the idea of 'One correct/pure language' is also being challenged in Faroese CMC.

Top-down interventions to purify Faroese usually affect all social levels, from the micro- (individual) and the meso- (social sub-groups and domains) to the macro-level (society as a whole). By contrast, the bottom-up pragmatic countermovement is mostly seen in flexible individual micro-choices, which nevertheless often converge to widespread patterns on the meso- and sometimes even macro-level.

In the following section, the complex interplay of the outlined extra- and intralinguistic aspects and their impact on Faroese and its language community will be analysed in relation to a language contact phenomenon: the integration and use of non-native nouns in CMC.

On the Integration of Non-Native Nouns in the Context of CMC – Excerpts from a Study

In their study of traditional written media, Simonsen and Sandøy (2008) ascribe the absence of inflectional forms of certain nouns in their corpus to the language users' reluctance to apply morphological modifications to lexemes with a silent final <-e>, e.g. *interface*, or ending on unstressed -*o*, e.g. *bingo*. My (Zieseler, 2024) study hypothesises that these nouns, contrary to Simonsen and Sandøy's (2008: 21–22) claim, are indeed integrated through both native and non-native analogy not only in spoken but also in written Faroese. My (Zieseler, 2017) previous findings had already indicated the existence of novel integration patterns in the context of CMC, especially in communication forms characterised by *conceptual orality* (Dürscheid, 2016). If the effects of normative linguistic pressure are indeed lower in the digital domain than in traditional media, then novel, non-canonical language phenomena are more likely to occur in CMC than elsewhere. Since Faroese CMC had hitherto not been subject to systematic research, I (Zieseler, 2024) collected the majority of my data online and supplemented selected language material from traditional sources (printed press, literary texts, legal texts, etc.).

The purpose of my study was to investigate the morphological, graphemic, and graphonological integration of a subgroup of non-native nouns in written Faroese amidst a range of language-internal and -external factors. These nouns were chosen according to a formal property that makes them particularly challenging to integrate, i.e. a word-final vocalic element (phonological and/or graphemic). My observations corroborate the emergence of new inflectional paradigms and provide insights into a specific area of contact-induced language change alongside its accompanying metalinguistic discourse (Zieseler, 2024). Some of my findings will be presented here, focusing on non-native feminine nouns on -*a* in order to highlight various challenges and opportunities Faroese is facing as a digital minority language in the 21st century.

Non-native feminine nouns on -*a*: Integration strategies

Faroese pizza and corona

One frequent non-native feminine noun on final unstressed -*a* in Faroese is *pizza/pitsa*(F.):

(1) *eina verri **pitsu**.* 'a worse pizza(F.Acc.Sg.)'.

Nativised *pitsa* is codified in *Føroysk orðabók* (FO, 1998, s.v. *pitsa*) with the gloss 'pizza', while Petersen's *Donsk-føroysk orðabók* (DFO, 1995, s.v. *pizza*) lemmatises non-nativised *pizza* but also mentions the

Far. *gent-a*('girl'F.Nom.Sg.) : Far. *gent-u*('girl'F.Acc./Dat.Sg.)
=
Far. *pizz-a*(F.Nom.Sg.) : X
→ X = Far. *pizz-u*(F.Acc./Dat.Sg.)

Figure 3.2 Native proportional analogy for the integration of Far. *pizza* as a weak feminine noun

variant *pitsa*. All dictionaries categorise it as a weak feminine noun. The graphonological make-up of *pizza* makes it easy to fit in with this particular noun class: its final vowel *-a* can be readily reanalysed as the inflectional class marker, a stem-producing vowel, of a weak feminine noun by the native proportional analogy outlined in Figure 3.2.

This final vowel could also have been reanalysed as the marker of a weak neuter noun in analogy with native *eyga* ('eye(N.)'). But since *pizza* is common gender (CG.) in the mediating language Danish, it is almost certain to become either masculine or feminine in Faroese (Petersen, 2009: chap. 7), as seen in similar borrowings such as *corona*:

(2) minka um **koronuna** 'reduce the corona(F.Sg.Acc.Def.)'

The stem-inflectional paradigm for *pizza/pitsa* is also codified in several dictionaries, and even *korona* is listed as a feminine noun, albeit without an inflectional paradigm. In terms of Natural Morphology, this reanalysis of final unstressed *-a* satisfies *system adequacy* (Wurzel, 1984): with its high native type frequency and stability in Faroese grammar, stem inflection is an unmarked and thus productive pattern. However, an entirely different paradigm can be observed in CMC, too:

(3) hava á **pizza'ina** 'have on the pizza(F.Acc.Sg.Def.)'
(4) **Coronain** hevur heldur ikki 'Neither the corona(F.Nom.Sg.Def.) has'.

This paradigm can be analysed as an instance of contact-induced pattern transference. Danish influence on Faroese is pervasive both on an individual, short-term level – code-switching – and on a collective, long-term one – matter and pattern transference leading to language change (cf. Petersen, 2010).

Unlike Faroese, Danish lacks nominal stem inflection, and instead operates on the word base for all noun classes.[1] The corresponding non-native proportional analogy for Faroese *pizza'ina* looks as in Figure 3.3:

Dan. *pizza*(CG.Sg.) : Dan. *pizza-en*(CG.Sg.Def.)
=
Far. *pizza*(F.Nom.Sg.) : X
→ X = Far. *pizza-ina*(F.Acc.Sg.Def.)

Figure 3.3 Non-native proportional analogy for the integration of Far. *pizza* as a word-based inflecting noun

While such word-based inflection is entirely in keeping with *Danish* morphology, it is marked within native *Faroese* grammar. However, leaving the final vowel unchanged by *not* reanalysing *-a* as a stem suffix ensures higher *formal transparency* through morpheme consistency, which in turn facilitates both encoding and decoding of the underlying form and preserves *semantic transparency* (Wurzel, 1984). This transparency is further increased by placing an apostrophe as a boundary marker between the foreign content morpheme *pizza* and the native grammatical morpheme *-ina*.

The degree of morphonemic opacity engendered by stem inflection as opposed to word-based inflection is encapsulated by the following example:

(5) *pitsuni (pizza'ini) hjá mammu míni.* 'my mum's pizza(F.Dat. Sg.Def.)'.

The two paradigms yield considerably different forms both regarding syllable number (three vs. four), pronunciation ($pits[\upsilon]ni$ vs. $pizz[ajɪ]ni$) and orthography (<ts> vs. <zz>, apostrophe).

Some authors choose a more 'native' way of marking morphemic boundaries in word-based inflection:

(6) *bíløgdu 3 pizzaðir ... pizzaðirnar vóru komnar ... miðan á pizzaðunum* ... 'ordered three pizzas(F.Acc.Pl.) ... the pizzas(F.Nom. Pl.Def.) had arrived ... the centre of the pizzas(F.Dat.Pl.Def.)'

Here, the morpheme boundary has been consistently filled with the grapheme <ð>. Since the non-native spelling <zz> is also preserved, it can be inferred that the author is well aware that <ð> has no etymological basis in the original loanword, i.e. Ital./Dan. *pizzað. I refer to this novel inflectional paradigm as <ð>*-declension*. If the spelling is even further nativised by replacing <zz> with <ts> and <c> with <k>, the resulting forms appear strikingly Faroese:

(7) *Handan pitsaðin ljóðar lekkur.* 'This pizza(F.Nom.Sg.Def.) sounds delicious'.
(8) *so kom hendan Koronaðin* 'then this Corona(F.Nom.Sg.Def.) came'

This <ð>-declension is most commonly found in CMC, but also appears to be spreading into other, more traditional domains offline, including newspapers, magazines, etc. In order to explain this phenomenon, the status of <ð> needs to be examined.

Faroese <ð>

In modern Faroese orthography, <ð> has no phonetic value in most cases (Thráinsson *et al.*, 2004/2012: 20, 104–105) due to the historical sound change ð > Ø. If <ð> occurs intervocalically, the resulting hiatus between the adjacent syllables is filled with epenthetic [j] (*liðug*), [v] (*veður*) or [w] (*suður*) according to a set of complementary distribution rules (Thráinsson *et al.*, 2004/2012: 38–39). Exactly the same phenomenon occurs in 'real' orthographic hiatuses (*fáur*) and with intervocalic <g> (*siga*). In native lexemes, <ð> and <g> can but *need* not appear between a stressed and an unstressed syllable (e.g. homophonous ˈ*fríur* vs. ˈ*fríður*), whereas they *always* appear between two unstressed syllables, e.g. ˈ*mánaður*, ˈ*árligur*.

For non-native lexemes, the situation is quite different – and problematic. When nouns with a final unstressed vowel such as ˈ*pizza* or *co*ˈ*rona* receive a word-based paradigm rather than a stem-inflecting one, a *real* orthographic hiatus emerges between the final non-native vowel and the initial vowel of the inflectional suffix. Since two adjacent *unstressed* syllables are involved, this real orthographic hiatus (<pizzaina>) violates Faroese graphotactics. Word-internal punctuation marks (<pizza'ini>) therefore do not only mark the *morphemic* boundary but also disrupt a *graphotactically inadmissible* hiatus. Inserting <ð> as an orthographic hiatus breaker (<pizzaðini>), however, is even less marked than using punctuation marks.

Currently, <ð>-declension is still a non-canonical inflectional paradigm coexisting with stem inflection. However, it appears to be gaining momentum in more recent loanwords and may eventually become fully established alongside stem inflection. The reanalysis of <ð> as the default grapheme representing hiatus-breaking epenthetic [j; v; w] is further corroborated by the absence of alternative orthophone spellings such as *<pizzajini>, *<Koronajin>.[2]

In CMC, technology-induced *constraints and affordances* (Herring *et al.*, 2013: 7–9) reveal more about the current status of <ð>. A fair bit of Faroese CMC is written on input devices without a dedicated <ð> key, and the convention is to then replace it with <d>. This also affects <ð>-declension, see example (9):

(9) *battarídir* ... *fylgja vid* 'batteries(N.Nom.Pl.) are included'

Here, similar-looking <d> replaces <ð> not only as an orthographic hiatus-breaker (<battarídir> instead of <battaríðir> ← <battaríir>), but also in other positions, as in *<vid> instead of native <við>. This consistent substitution <ð> → <d> indicates that <ð>-declension is not an ad hoc solution, but rather that <ð> is what the authors actually intended to write. This is further strong proof for the recent refunctionalisation of <ð>.

Like apostrophes and hyphens, orthographic hiatus-breaking <ð>/<d> can be regarded as 'innovative separators' and hence as instances of *digital mediation*, a process giving 'rise to graphic variability that is not just a mirror-image of phonic variability but emerges against the backdrop of the orthographic representation of a given linguistic item in a given language' (Androutsopoulos, 2016: 289–290).

Although these non-canonical integration patterns are becoming more common in CMC, they are still not being perceived as part of canonical written Faroese by many language users, as indicated by various metalinguistic elements surrounding said nouns and patterns. Due to its purist ideological climate, the Faroese language community is permeated by metalinguistic (self-)awareness – even in CMC with its comparatively low level of normative sensitivity, as will be shown in the following section.

Metalinguistic discourse
Glosses and scare quotes

Firstly, context glosses can be found quite frequently. In the following examples, the non-native lexemes are indexed with a subscript 'nn', the native ones with 'n', while the term being glossed is marked with 'l' for 'lemma', and the gloss itself with 'i' for 'interpretamentum':

(10) *innan eitt* **tema** *(evni)* 'within a subject$_{nn-l}$ (subject$_{n-i}$)'

This constellation lemma$_{nn}$ – interpretamentum$_n$ represents the prototypical direction of glossing: a newly arrived, largely unknown non-native lexeme is interpreted by means of a well-known native one. But upon closer inspection, many non-native nouns glossed this way are neither entirely new to nor unestablished in the Faroese language community: the internationalism *tema* ('topic, subject(N.)') is codified in several dictionaries and very frequently used, ruling out explication as the main motive behind the native gloss *evni*. Faroese purist language ideology tends to reject non-native lexemes, no matter how well established and integrated. This induces normative pressure: Since transferring oral L-variety elements into the written H variety violates the medial diglossia, the addition of *normative* native glosses such as *evni* signals that 'I am well aware that there (ought to) exist(s) a Faroese term for this non-native lexeme, and this native gloss proves that I am not just too lazy or uneducated to be using it'.

By contrast, there are also instances in which native nouns are glossed with non-native ones, and their function is primarily *explicative*:

(11) *at* **ávíst evni** *(tema)* 'that a particular topic$_{n-l}$ (topic$_{nn-i}$)'

The fact that *tema* is the interpretamentum of the native lemma *evni* could be due to the extensive polysemy of *evni*. Adding *tema* as an interpretamentum helps disambiguation by narrowing down the meaning of *evni* to the sememe 'subject, topic'. In fact, *tema* could be establishing itself to independently denote this sememe, thus contributing to lexical elaboration (see also Clausén, 1978: 136). Thus, *tema* turns out to be less of a 'luxury' (non-catachrestic) loan and more of a 'necessary' (catachrestic) one (Onysko & Winter-Froemel, 2011).

The following aforementioned example involves the same loanword in different variants:

(12) *pitsuni (pizza'ini) hjá mammu míni.* 'my mum's pizza$_{n-l}$ (pizza$_{nn-i}$)'.

Here, less nativised *pizza'ini* is used to explicate fully nativised *pitsuni*. The motivation appears to be that a high degree of integration may render the original lexeme unrecognisable, i.e. that *nativisation* may paradoxically lead to linguistic *alienation*. Therefore, the author adds a less opaque form in which the original non-native morpheme is left unaltered and separated from the native inflectional morpheme by an apostrophe, which aids semantic interpretation through morphological segmentation. Juxtaposing a 'traditional native', codified paradigm with an 'innovative native' one most used in spoken Faroese – and increasingly in CMC – indicates keen metalinguistic awareness.

Other frequent metalinguistic elements are quotation marks. Non-native ad hoc insertions are typically unintegrated and hence often treated like 'citation-forms' from a 'foreign tongue' or a variety perceived as non-standard (Dahlstedt, 1962: 13; transl. L.Z.). The difference between citation words and foreign words is not binary, but rather depends on the linguistic domain, general writing practices, and on the author's attitude towards purism (Dahlstedt, 1962: 13–14). One expression of this attitudinal component are *scare quotes*, i.e. quotation marks used as 'a central and pervasive device ... enabl[ing] speakers to indicate that they distance themselves ... from certain aspects of certain linguistic practices' (Cappelen & Lepore, 2007: 56). Their (perceived) attitudinal value ranges from unease to irony, sarcasm or even hostility, thus adding metalinguistic content (Predelli, 2003: 2–3; Trask, 1997). In Faroese CMC, many quotation marks that initially appear to 'merely' flag citation words also express metalinguistic value, as seen in the next examples:

(13) *einum amerikanskum 'cowboyði.'* 'an American "cowboy(M.Dat.Sg.)"'.
(14) *eftir 'dateina'* 'after the "date"(F.Acc.Sg.Def.)'.
(15) *internet 'meme'ini' eru* 'the internet "memes"(N.Nom. Pl.Def.) are'.

Unlike typical citation words, these lexemes are partly or fully nativised, indicating that they are actually used within the Faroese speech community. But since they are not officially codified, they cause insecurity in the language users, who then simultaneously embrace the 'incorrect' lexeme *and* distance themselves from it through scare quotes. As McArthur (1992: 839) remarks, scare quotes imply 'something like [XY], *as they are often called*'. This 'so-called' is sometimes even spelled out:

(16) *at taka* **sjálvsmynd** *ella eina sokallaða* **'Selfie'** 'to take a self-portrait$_{n-1}$ or a so-called 'Selfie'$_{nn-i}$'

The Anglicism *selfie* is hardly an exotic ad hoc insertion. Instead, it is used as an explicative, disambiguating gloss for *sjálvsmynd* and its broader meaning 'self-portrait'. Nevertheless, the author has decided to flag well-established *selfie* with both scare quotes and *sokallaða*, illustrating the underlying struggle with the rift between spoken vernacular and written purist Faroese.

Metalinguistic reflections

More explicit metalinguistic discourse occurs as well, as seen in the exchange in Figure 3.4.

The first user inflects *pitsa* using word-based <ð>-declension, *pitsaðin*, causing another user to list the entire canonical stem-inflectional paradigm of weak feminine *pitsa*. To further underline their point, the second user juxtaposes non-native *pitsa* with native weak feminine *dunna* ('duck(F.)'), stating that the form *pitsaðin* instead of *pitsan* is as incorrect as the form *dunnaðin* instead of *dunnan*. This analogy implies a common purist fear vis-à-vis language change: if left unchecked, developments in the non-native part of the lexicon may spill over to its native part and lead to language decay (Far. *málspilla*). Eager to prevent such developments, the official language policy sometimes goes overboard, as shown by the next example.

In November 2018, *Málráðið* added several lexemes to the regularly updated list of neologisms on its website. The article in Figure 3.5, published on a news portal, relates this update.

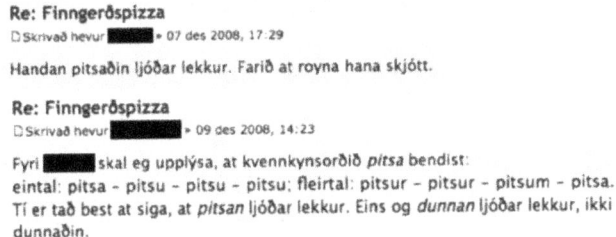

Figure 3.4 Debate over the correct inflection of *pitsa* on Kjak.org

Málráðið hevur talað - # eitur hassjtagg á føroyskum

[...]

NÝGGJ ORÐ (FØ - DA/EN)

Á hesum lista siggjast eisini onnur orð, ið eru føroyskað uttan at stórvegis annað er gjørt við tey enn at broyta stavestingina. Til dømis 'karaóki', sum er føroyska stavsetingin fyri hetta fyribrigdi at syngja til innspældan tónleik, hóast 'karaoke' eisini hevur fingið føroyskt yrði, nevniliga 'sangdubbing' í navnhátti og sagnorðið (at) 'sangdubba', sambært Málráðnum.

'*Málráðið* has spoken ... And 'karaoke' is to be spelled 'karaóki' ... On this list, there are also other words that are Faroeised without there being anything much changed beyond the spelling. For example 'karaóki', which is the Faroese spelling ..., although 'karaoke' already has received a Faroese equivalent, namely 'sangdubbing' ... and ... (at) 'sangdubba', according to *Málráðið*'.

Figure 3.5 Article on *karaoke*

The loanword *karaoke* is challenging to nativise. There are no native Faroese nouns on final unstressed -*e*, and non-native final -*e* is usually changed to -*a* (e.g. Dan. *drone* > Far. *drona*) rather than to -*i*. However, *Málráðið* chose strong neuter *karaóki* (malrad.fo, 'nýggj orð', s.v. *karaóki*) instead of weak neuter or feminine **karaóka*. This choice could be explained as follows:

Firstly, the noun has already been (unofficially) nativised in Icelandic as *karaókí/karíókí* (Wikipedia, s.v. *karaókí*). Since <í> represents monophthongal /i/ in Icelandic but diphthongal /ʊi/ in Faroese, only <ó>[ɔuː] can be sensibly transferred to Faroese. Secondly, ó also indicates main stress, as seen in other nativised nouns such as Far. *per'sónur* ('person(M.)'), while final <i>[ɪ] tends to be centralised to [ə] in many Faroese dialects (Thráinsson *et al.*, 2004/2012: 349–355). Overall, this spelling is therefore more orthophone than it initially appears. Finally, Danish *karaoke*(CG.) is also pronounced in an unnativised way as [kʰæɹəˈoʊkʰi] (DDO, s.v. *karaoke*). Thus, *Málráðið*'s spelling is likely an attempt to codify a Danish-conveyed, Anglicised Japanese internationalism in a partly Icelandic-inspired, partly orthophone fashion. In an embedded Facebook comment below the article, one user reacts to this nativisation as in Figure 3.6.

Focusing on -*o*- → -*ó*-, the user questions *Málráðið*'s grasp of Faroese dialectology. The variable ó has several variants ([œuː], [ɛuː], [auː], [ɔuː]) in different dialects (Thráinsson *et al.*, 2004/2012: 348), while o is pronounced as [oː/ɔ] throughout. The commentator suspects that *Málráðið* favours the variety spoken in the capital Tórshavn (*havnarmálið*), which has <ó>[ɔuː] ≈ General American [oʊ].

Veit Málráðið av at bókstavurin "Ó" hevur ymiska úttalu runt um landið? Virkar meira sum havnarmálið verður tað autoreseraða skriftmálið í Føroyum.

Like · Reply · 3y

'Does *Málráðið* know that the letter "Ó" has various pronunciations throughout the country? Seems more like *havnarmálið* is becoming the authorised written language in the Faroes'.

Figure 3.6 Reaction to *karaóki*

> Sangdubbing..... giiiisus kreist
> Like · Reply · 3y

Figure 3.7 Reaction to *sangdubbing*

Diatopic variety has been treasured in the Faroes since the 19th century, when traditional dialects came to be regarded as a reflection of the 'true', 'unspoiled' origin of Faroese, and thus of the nation itself. All dialects are considered equal, and none has been singled out as the basis for a written standard. Instead, the orthographic depth of the historicising norm is meant to cover *all* modern-day dialects equidistantly (Lindqvist, 2018: 12–13). This would be compromised if the capital's variety were to underpin the 'authorised [= standard] written language'.

The next comment (Figure 3.7) concerns the proposed alternative for non-native *karaoke/karaóki – sangdubbing*.

This creative orthophone Faroese spelling of *Jesus Christ!* <giiiisus kreist> [tʃiːsʊs kɹaist] emulates its English pronunciation [dʒiːzəs kɹaɪst]. It can also be read as a parody of *Málráðið*'s own linguistic creativity behind *sangdubbing*(F.). Firstly, *sangur* ('song(M.)') is derived from Danish *sang* ('song(CG.)'), with the 'correct' native alternative being Far. *songur*. This Danicism is then combined with the (Danish-conveyed) Anglicism *to dub/dubbing*, which is probably also based on native Far. *at dubba* ('to equip, fit') through phono- or rather graphosemantic matching (Sapir & Zuckermann, 2008). The result is not a genuine Faroese coinage, but a Danish-English-Faroese hybrid loan, which is rejected by the normative 'voices from below' (Linn, 2010): neither *karaóki* nor *sangdubbing* appear to be in use online, where uninflected *karaoke* is commonly found instead. Nevertheless, *Málráðið* continues to list both neologisms on its website, making them prescriptive 'paper words' (Clausén, 1978).

When exchanges between voices from above and voices from below keep failing, the latter sometimes turn to each other for linguistic advice instead, as is the case in the public Facebook group *Føroysk rættstaving* ('Faroese orthography').

Færøysk rættstaving

Created in 2010, this group had about 17,000 members in 2023 and keeps growing at a steady pace. It's About page reads as follows:

> Everybody is welcome to discuss and make corrections, observations, reflections, and other things regarding Faroese. All of you who are unsure about how words are spelled or inflected... ask! It is important to know that everybody can make mistakes. The aim is to teach – to help – to support each other in a friendly manner. (*Føroysk rættstaving*; transl. L.Z.)

> Eg skuldi keypa eitt bestemt slag av pitsu, í einum handli og spurdi eina unga damu, um tey høvdu tær pitsairnar. Hon svaraði mær aftur, at tey ikki høvdu tær pitsurnar. Eg bleyv rættaður óbeinleiðis, av einum persóni, ið var 1/3 av mínum aldri og sum hevur fingi stempul á seg, sum vánaligir bendarar. Eg visti væl, at tað eitur pitsur, men hevði gloymt tað, (ringur vani bítur) og bleyv gleðiliga tikin á bóli. Fór út aftur við einum stórum smíli.
>
> Gefällt mir · Antworten · Teilen · 36 Wo.   4

'I wanted to buy a certain kind of pizza [*pitsu*] in a shop and asked a young woman whether they had those pizzas [*pitsairnar*]. She replied that they didn't have those pizzas [*pitsurnar*]. I was corrected indirectly by a person who was one third my age and who had been labelled as someone who was bad at inflection [literally 'bad inflectors']. I knew well that it was called pizzas [*pitsur*], but I had forgotten it (force of bad habit) and was gladly caught in the act. Left the shop with a big smile'.

Figure 3.8 Metalinguistic introspection in *Føroysk rættstaving*

It thus serves as an 'unofficial language council' by taking the motto of the official *Málráðið* literally: *Øll eiga málið* ('The language belongs to everybody'). This group currently represents the hub of online Faroese metalinguistic discourse, including self-reflections as in the post in Figure 3.8.

This user recounts being confronted for their 'incorrect' word-based inflection of *pitsairnar* instead of the codified stem-based inflection *pitsurnar* by a younger speaker who is said to be 'bad at grammar'. But rather than being ashamed, the author stresses their satisfaction with this encounter. The fact that they have internalised the overt normative ideology to such a degree that they *gladly and publicly* stigmatise their own, spontaneous vernacular spoken Faroese as 'bad habit' indicates not only metalinguistic awareness but also linguistic insecurity. In Haugen's (1962) terms, this insecurity induced by the conflicting norms of intralinguistic diglossia can be referred to as *schizoglossia*.

Numerous threads in *Føroysk rættstaving* address *corona*. In one thread dating from October 2020, users argue about the correct morphology of this then newly arrived lexeme (Figure 3.9).

The first user disapproves of KVF's (*Kringvarp Føroya* 'National Faroese Broadcasting Company') inflection of *corona* as a weak feminine noun with the oblique form *coronu* rather than the weak neuter oblique form *corona*. Another user replies that it is indeed a weak feminine inflecting in analogy with native weak feminine *kona* ('woman, wife(F.)'). This prompts a third user to question this 'switch' to feminine, since they thought *corona* was a clipping of neuter *koronavirus* ('coronavirus(N.)'). The first user agrees and quips that '*corona*(N.) is not a woman/ wife (*kona*(F.))'. A fourth user insists that *corona* is an 'ancient word that has always been inflected as a weak feminine'. This last user was a member of *Málráðið* when they wrote this post. Actually, several

Focus on Faroese: Digital Insights into the Smallest North Germanic Language Community   69

Figure 3.9 Discussion thread on the gender of *corona* in *Føroysk rættstaving*

Málráðið-members have been active in this group, as shown in the orthographic discussion in Figure 3.10.

Opening the first thread, a user predicts that the Faroese word of the year 2020 will start with <C>, i.e. *corona*. Another user retorts that <c> is not part of the Faroese alphabet. A third user concludes wryly that without <c> in the alphabet, there is no *corona* pandemic in the Faroes either. In another thread, the first author calls the discussion 'tiring', since those disliking <c> go out of their way to make it an 'un-Faroese' grapheme; they may as well try and prove the non-existence of <i> in Faroese by spelling every word with <y> instead – as humorously illustrated by the author (*<tyl, ykky> instead of <til, ikki>, etc.). Another user claims that *corona* is spelled with <k> in e.g. Danish, Norwegian, and Icelandic, but that the Danes are so heavily Anglicised that they still use <c> despite it being codified with <k>.

This exchange has several noteworthy aspects. Firstly, it highlights how the official orthography evokes polarised reactions ranging from anti-Danish prescriptivism to anti-purist ridicule. Secondly, the arguments made are both *endonormative* and *exonormative*. The first user criticises the arbitrariness of graphemic taboo: The differentiation of <i> and <y> is based on Old West Norse etymology, while from a present-day perspective they are interchangeable due to a historical merger to /i/.[3] By the same historicising logic, replacing <c> with <k> to represent one

Figure 3.10 Discussion threads on the spelling of *corona* in *Føroysk rættstaving*

and the same phoneme, /k/, would obscure the noun's etymology. This endonormative take is countered by an exonormative one: *other* Germanic languages are invoked as role models for integration, while the Danish language community is scathed for being too Anglicised to care about its own official norms. However, while <c> has indeed been substituted with <k> in Norwegian and Icelandic, in Danish, the older lexeme 'stellar corona' is codified with <k>, and re-borrowed 'coronavirus' with <c>. Thirdly, those polar normative stances are defended by two members of *Málráðið*: one liberal (S.H.), the other purist (E.H.). The voices from above have apparently become more diverse and open towards direct exchange with the voices from below.

Conclusion and Outlook

In a globalised world, Faroese is a small 'language at risk' (Sandøy, 1992: 69–70). As a member of the *Løgting* put it during the debate over an orthographic reform:

> The Faroese language must not end up as a curiosity that we have as an ornament while using Danish and English. [It] is the basis and frame of our culture [and] an absolutely decisive part of our identity. Thus, [its] status ... needs to be strengthened ... among other things by allowing [it] to be so spacious and flexible that it can be used in all circumstances. (Skaale, 2009; transl. L.Z.)

Language change through the integration of non-native elements is crucial for such spaciousness, flexibility and hence linguistic vitality, as opposed to turning the language into a purist 'straitjacket' (Sandøy, 1992: 67). Although Faroese can be considered a model of 'successful language planning' (Kattenbusch, 1989; transl. L.Z.), purist intervention has also hurt its own cause: Alienating the language community from the written language and simultaneously making it self-conscious about its spoken language has induced medial diglossia and even *schizoglossia*. Many Faroese language users appear to be very aware of the fact that they fail to meet the prescribed norm. The official normative ideal is internalised, but not all details of the purist norms themselves, which therefore remain mere prescriptions. This 'Janus face' of language cultivation (Sandøy, 2003: 103) may eventually become a greater threat to Faroese than external pressures by facilitating domain abandonment (Mortensen 2015, 91) due to the 'puristic paradox' of whether it is 'worse to write *bad* Faroese than *not* to write Faroese' (Sandøy, 1992: 67, 72). The opposing extralinguistic forces impacting Faroese language use are illustrated in Figure 3.11.

All of these factors can be roughly aligned with the purist or the pragmatic pole of the ideological spectrum. The major cornerstones are spoken vs. written Faroese, L variety vs. H variety, Icelandic vs. Danish, and bottom-up vs. top-down. However, these orientations are neither clear-cut nor static: prestige can be overt or covert, purist corpus planning includes both integration and substitution, prescriptive norms can become successfully internalised, etc.

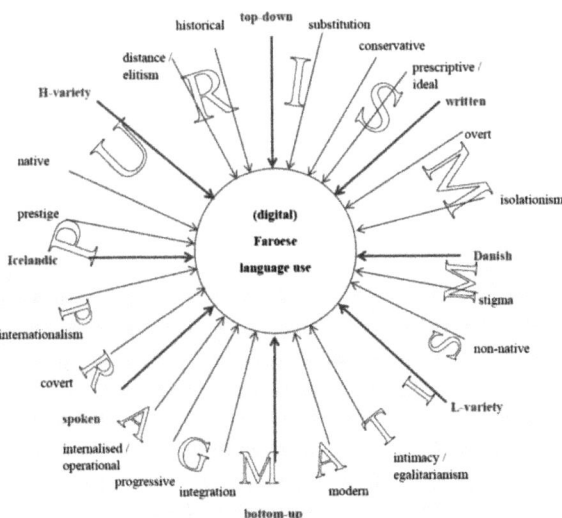

Figure 3.11 Opposing forces in the ideological climate influencing (digital) Faroese language use

The impact of these forces is also reflected metalinguistically, including explicative vs. normative glosses, scare quotes and introspective reflections or explicit criticism, indicating that the average Faroese language user tends to critically judge both their own normative competence and that of others (Vannebo, 1980: 9). Since spoken Faroese is a high-intimacy language with high emotional value (Leonard, 2016), its informally internalised norms are particularly resistant to top-down prescriptivism. Instead, new written norms are being established through informal, non-institutionalised 'bottom-up Faroeisation'.

I have described the integration of non-native nouns on final vowels to illustrate such contact-induced change 'from below'. Contrary to purist fears, the novel word-based <ð>-declension does not simplify Faroese nominal morphology, but rather increases its overall functional complexity. The nativisation strategies follow systematic rather than random patterns. The recurring use of punctuation marks and particularly <ð>/<d> as orthographic hiatus-breakers is an instance of 'semiotic materialisation' or 'secondary mediation' of technology-dependent communication (Androutsopoulos, 2016: 287–288). This bottom-up Faroeisation catalysed by CMC is now gradually spreading to other communication forms, text genres and registers across different domains and media online and offline.

In 1992, Sandøy (72) stated that '[a] Faroese cannot live in the Faroes today without knowing Danish, whereas a Dane can live there without understanding Faroese'. Nowadays, this can be restated as 'with knowledge of Danish or English, it is possible to live in the Faroes without understanding Faroese'. One way of successfully organising this 'necessary trilingualism' (Sandøy, 1992: 72) involves consolidating Faroese by overcoming its intralingual medial diglossia, which is precisely what bottom-up Faroeisation might achieve as shown in Table 3.2.

The nativisation strategies analysed here indicate that parts of the language community have started to adapt written Faroese so as to better reflect the reality of *actual* language use. In the future, written,

Table 3.2 Potential diglossic reorganisation due to ongoing bottom-up Faroeisation

	Written (conceptual literacy, language of distance)	Spoken (conceptual orality, language of immediacy)
H variety	Historicising (and de-Danicised) Faroese	Danicised, internationalised Faroese varieties
	Danish	Standard Danish
Semi-H variety	– speech-oriented Danicised, internationalised and 'bottom-up Faroeised' Faroese	(Faroese writing-induced pronunciation of Danish)
L variety	– colloquial speech-oriented Danicised, internationalised and 'bottom-up Faroeised' Faroese **(primarily used in CMC)**	(Faroeised Danish (so-called *gøtudanskt*))
		Danicised, internationalised Faroese varieties

colloquial speech-oriented Danicised, internationalised and 'bottom-up Faroeised' Faroese could potentially be elevated from an L to a semi-H variety, and eventually become a spoken H variety alongside Standard Danish through consistent, widespread use beyond CMC. Thus, it would replace prescribed, literacy-based spoken Faroese as the H variety, which has never really been adopted by the language community, but has been shunned as a contrived 'paper variety'. Such a destigmatisation of non-purist Faroese would make the language more elaborate and flexible, and subsequently more resistant to domain loss.

The actual outcome ultimately depends on whether the language community *as a whole* embraces this development. While the normative voices from below and from above often used to disagree, they are now starting to meet at eye level: Thanks to the conceptual immediacy and informality of CMC, some members of *Málráðið* do not act as language officials in the Facebook group *Føroysk rættstaving*, but rather 'blend in with the crowd', although most Faroese are likely aware of their professional status. The high intimacy of a tight-knit and not just 'imagined community' (Anderson, 1983/1996) offline is also manifest online. At best, *Málráðið's* grass-roots approach may be beneficial, at worst, divisive.

The internet has facilitated linguistic liberation from deeply ingrained, all-pervasive ideological pressure and enabled the normative voices from below to actively shape the metalinguistic discourse. In Androutsopoulos' (2016: 294–295, 298) terms, this is a result of *mediatisation*, a 'metaprocess of social and cultural change through the development of communications media', which encompasses 'the circulation and diffusion of linguistic features[, particularly] semiotic innovations in the digital age'. It remains to be seen whether this process will contribute to a lasting shift in the country's official ideological climate.

Notes

(1) A few exceptions include certain loanwords as well as vowel alternation in some native nouns.
(2) Comparable spellings can be found in Jakobsen's (1892) basically orthophone writing system.
(3) In <ei>[ai(ː)/a/ɔ] and <ey>[ɛiː/ɛ], however, they are *not* interchangeable.

References

Anderson, B. (1983/1996) *Imagined Communities* (revised edn). Verso.
Androutsopoulos, J. (2011) Language change and digital media: A review of conceptions and evidence. In T. Kristiansen and N. Coupland (eds) *Standard Languages and Language Standards in a Changing Europe* (pp. 145–159). Novus.
Androutsopoulos, J. (2016) Theorizing media, mediation and mediatization. In N. Coupland (ed.) *Sociolinguistics. Theoretical Debate* (pp. 282–302). Cambridge University Press.
Brunstad, E. (2001) *Det reine språket. Om purisme i dansk, svensk, færøysk og norsk*. Nordisk institutt ved Det historisk-filosofiske fakultet.

Cappelen, H. and Lepore, E. (2007) *Language Turned on Itself. The Semantics and Pragmatics of Metalinguistic Discourse.* Oxford University Press.
Clausén, U. (1978) *Nyord i färöiskan. Ett bidrag till belysning av språksituationen på Färöarna.* Almqvist & Wiksell.
Dahlstedt, K.-H. (1962) Vad är främmande ord? In K.-H. Dahlstedt, G. Bergman and C.I. Ståhle (eds) *Främmande ord i nusvenskan* (pp. 1–31). Bonniers.
DDO = Hjorth, E. and Kristensen, K. (eds) (2003–2021) *Den Danske Ordbog.* Det Danske Sprog- og Litteraturselskab (ed.). Gyldendal. See https://ordnet.dk/ddo (accessed October 2021).
DFO 1995 = Petersen, H.P. (1995) *Donsk-føroysk orðabók. 3. utg. Red. av Hjalmar P. Petersen med hjelp av Marius Staksberg.* Føroya Fróðskaparfelag. See https://sprotin.fo/dictionaries (accessed October 2021).
Dürscheid, Chr. (2016) Nähe, Distanz und neue Medien. In H. Feilke and M. Hennig (eds) *Zur Karriere von ‚Nähe und Distanz'. Rezeption und Diskussion des Koch-Oesterreicher-Modells* (pp. 357–385). De Gruyter.
FO 1998 = Poulsen, J.H.W., Simonsen, M., Jacobsen, J. í L., Johansen, A. and Svabo Hansen, Z. (eds) (1998) *Føroysk orðabók.* Føroya Fróðskaparfelag/Vestmanna: Sprotin. See https://sprotin.fo/dictionaries (accessed October 2021).
Føroysk rættstaving. See https://www.facebook.com/groups/185932738087033/about (accessed October 2022).
Grondelaers, S., van Hout, R. and van Gent, P. (2016) Destandardization is not destandardization: Revising standardness criteria in order to revisit standard language typologies in the Low Countries. *Taal en Tongval* 68 (2), 119–149.
Haugen, E. (1962) Schizoglossia and the linguistic norm. In E.D. Woodworth and R.J. DiPietro (eds) *Monograph Series on Languages and Linguistics* 15 (pp. 63–69). Georgetown University.
Herring, S.C., Stein, D. and Virtanen, T. (2013) Introduction to the pragmatics of computer-mediated communication. In S.C. Herring, D. Stein and T. Virtanen (eds) *Pragmatics of Computer-Mediated Communication* (pp. 3–33). De Gruyter Mouton.
Hårstad, S. (2021) Digital skriving under den sosiolingvistiske lupen: Har det skjedd en språklig revolusjon? In L. Jølle, A.S. Larsen, H. Otnes and L.I. Aa (eds) *Morsmålsfaget som fag og forskningsfelt i Norden* (pp. 21–45). Universitetsforlaget.
Irvine, J.T. (2012) Language Ideology. *Oxford Bibliographies.* See https://www.oxfordbibliographies.com/display/document/obo-9780199766567/obo-9780199766567-0012.xml (accessed January 2023).
Jacobsen, J. í L. (2012) *Ærligt talt, who cares? En sociolingvistisk undersøgelse af holdninger til og brug af importord og afløsningsord i færøsk.* Novus.
Jacobsen, L.G. and Steintún, M.N. (1992) Hvørji orð verða nýtt í føroyskum í dag? *Málting* 6, 35–41.
Jakobsen, J. (1892) *Føriskar vysur.* S. L. Møllers Bogtrykkeri.
Kristiansen, T. (2009) Åbne og skjulte holdninger til engelskindflydelsen – hvad kan sprogpolitikken påvirke? *Sprog i Norden* 2009, 95–112.
Kristiansen, T. and Vikør, L.S. (eds) (2006) *Nordiske språkhaldningar. Ei meinings-måling.* Novus forlag.
Kattenbusch, D. (1989) Die Färöer – Ein Beispiel für eine vorbildliche Autonomie und gelungene Sprachplanung. *Europa Ethnica* 46, 164–172.
Knudsen, K.J.L. (2010) Language use and linguistic nationalism in the Faroe Islands. *International Journal of Multilingualism* 7 (2), 128–146.
Leonard, S.P. (2016) A 'high-intimacy' language in the Atlantic: Radio and purism in the Faroe Islands. *Journal of Anthropological Research* 72 (1), 58–76.
Lindqvist, Ch. (2001) *Skandinavische Schriftsysteme im Vergleich.* Niemeyer.
Lindqvist, Ch. (2018) *Untersuchungen zu den Gründungsdokumenten der färöischen Rechtschreibung: Ein Beitrag zur nordischen Schriftgeschichte.* Benjamins Publishing Company.

Linn, A. (2010) Voices from above – voices from below: Who is talking and who is listening in Norwegian language politics? *Current Issues in Language Policy* 11 (2), 114–129.
Løgtingslóg nr. 59 (2012/2017) See https://logir.fo/Logtingslog/59-fra-15-05-2012-framalrad (accessed April 2019).
Málstevnunevndin and Mentamálaráðið (2007) *Málmørk: Álit um almennan málpolitikk.* See https://d3b1dqw2kzexi.cloudfront.net/media/2481/m%C3%A1lm%C3%B8rk-%C3%A1lit-um-m%C3%A1lpolitikk.pdf (accessed October 2021).
Málráðið (2021) *Málráð.fo.* See http://malrad.fo/ (accessed October 2021).
McArthur, T. (1992) *The Oxford Companion to the English Language.* Oxford University Press.
Mortensen, B. (2015) Policies and attitudes towards English in the Faroes today. In A. Linn, N. Bermel and G. Ferguson (eds) *Attitudes towards English in Europe* (pp. 71–96). De Gruyter.
Onysko, A. and Winter-Froemel, E. (2011) Necessary loans – luxury loans? Exploring the pragmatic dimension of borrowing. *Journal of Pragmatics* 43 (6), 1550–1567.
Pauladóttir, M. (2008) Skiftismæli í føroyskum? *Fróðskaparrit* 56, 63–96.
Petersen, H.P. (2009) *Gender Assignment in Modern Faroese.* Verlag Dr. Kovač.
Petersen, H.P. (2010) *The Dynamics of Faroese-Danish Language Contact.* Winter.
Predelli, S. (2003) Scare quotes and their relation to other semantic issues. *Linguistics and Philosophy* 26, 1–28.
Sandøy, H. (1992) Faroese – a minority language or a national language? The socio-political problem of becoming and being a fully-fledged small national language. In G. Blom, P. Graves, A. Kruse and B.T. Thomsen (eds) *Minority Languages: The Scandinavian Experience* (pp. 57–74). Nordic Language Secretariat.
Sandøy, H. (2003) Purisme i færøysk. In H. Sandøy, R. Brodersen and E. Brunstad (eds) *Purt og reint. Om purisme i dei nordiske språka* (pp. 85–109). Høgskolen i Volda.
Sapir, Y. and Zuckermann, G. (2008) Icelandic: Phonosemantic matching. In J. Rosenhouse and R. Kowner (eds) *Globally Speaking: Motives for Adopting English Vocabulary in Other Languages* (pp. 19–43). Multilingual Matters.
Simonsen, H. and Sandøy, H. (2008) Tilpasning af importord i det færøske skriftsprog. In H. Omdal and H. Sandøy (eds) *Nasjonal eller internasjonal skrivemåte? Om importord i seks nordiske språksammfunn* (pp. 49–76). Novus.
Skaale, S. (2009) Uppskot til samtyktar um klassiska latínska alfabetið. See https://www.logting.fo/files/casestate/9223/016.09%20Uppskot%20um%20alfabet.pdf (accessed August 2018).
Thráinsson, H., Petersen, H.P., Jacobsen, J.íL. and Svabo Hansen, Z. 2004/2012) *Faroese. An Overview and Reference Grammar* (2nd edn). Føroya Fróðskaparfelag.
Trask, L. (1997) Scare quotes. In L. Trask *Guide to Punctuation.* University of Sussex. See http://www.sussex.ac.uk/informatics/punctuation/quotes/scare (accessed June 2019).
Vannebo, K.I. (1980) Om språkvitenskapens normbegrep. *Tijdschrift voor Skandinavistiek* 1, 3–23.
Vikør, L.S. (1993/2001) *The Nordic Languages: Their Status and Interrelations* (3rd edn). Novus.
Wikipedia (2019) Karaóki. See is.wikipedia.org/w/index.php?title=Kara%C3%B3k%C3%AD&oldid=1654632 (accessed November 2019).
Wurzel, W.U. (1984) *Flexionsmorphologie und Natürlichkeit.* Akademie-Verlag.
Zieseler, L. (2017) Hey nørdar! Investigating Faroese-English language contact in computer-mediated communication. *Fróðskaparrit* 64, 35–66.
Zieseler, L. (2024) *On the Integration of Non-Native Nouns in Faroese.* Winter.

Examples and Figures

(1) See https://www.facebook.com/pg/Hj%C3%A1-Rafik-771338082988231/reviews/ (accessed January 2019).

(2) See https://dimma.fo/grein/danir-minka-um-koronuna/ (accessed April 2021).
(3) See https://www.ebenezer.fo/Default.aspx?pageid=7552&NewsItemID=24107 (accessed May 2017).
(4) See http://www.vp.fo/news/tad-gloymda-ambassaduparid (accessed April 2021).
(5) See http://www.kjak.org/viewtopic.php?f=17&t=1038&p=21434&hilit=pitsuni+pizza%27ini+#p21434 (accessed May 2017).
(6) See https://www.facebook.com/pg/Hj%C3%A1-Rafik-771338082988231/reviews/ (accessed January 2019).
(7) See http://www.kjak.org/viewtopic.php?f=17&t=1038&p=19599&hilit=pitsa%C3%B0in#p19599 (accessed May 2017).
(8) See http://sinnisbati.fo/Tilt%C3%B8k/soega/ (accessed April 2021).
(9) See http://www.dals.fo/ambod+av+ollum+slag+ambod+maskinur+og+byggitilfar+rotikassin+1386630141.html (accessed May 2018).
(10) See https://www.setur.fo/fo/utbugving/bachelor/folkaskulalaerari/skeidslysingar/?educationYearId=0&courseId=7486.17 (accessed March 2018).
(11) See https://logir.fo/Kunngerd/102-fra-26-06-2001-um-studentaskular-og-stakgreinalestur-a-studentaskulastigi-sum-seinast-broytt-vid-kunngerd (accessed March 2018).
(12) See http://www.kjak.org/viewtopic.php?f=17&t=1038&p=21434&hilit=pitsuni+pizza%27ini+#p21434 (accessed May 2017).
(13) See http://www.kjak.org/viewtopic.php?f=9&t=4084&p=90334&hilit=%27cowboy%C3%B0in#p90334 (accessed May 2017).
(14) See https://www.brudleyp.fo%2Fvetrarbrudleypid-hja-totu-kristinn%2F&usg=AOvVaw0E26pYkAi1YljKyyU4WR6y (accessed July 2019).
(15) See http://www.gaming.fo/index.php?mod=board&action=thread&where=650 (accessed December 2018).
(16) See https://kvf.fo/roddin/greinar/2015/05/12/soleidis-tekur-tu-eina-raetta-sjalvsmynd (accessed June 2018).
Figure 3.5 See http://www.kjak.org/viewtopic.php?f=17&t=1038&p=19599&hilit=pitsa%C3%B0in#p19599 (accessed May 2017).
Figures 3.6, 3.7, 3.8 See https://portal.fo/dagur-10302/malradid-hevur-talad---eitur-hassjtagg-a-foroyskum.grein (accessed July 2018).
Figure 3.9 See https://www.facebook.com/groups/185932738087033/posts/3275948495752093/?comment_id=3276250112388598 (accessed August 2021).
Figure 3.10 See https://www.facebook.com/groups/185932738087033/permalink/3874211395925797/ (accessed August 2021).
Figure 3.11 See https://www.facebook.com/groups/185932738087033/posts/3260972410583035 and https://www.facebook.com/groups/185932738087033/posts/3269366619743614 (accessed August 2021).

4 Breton in the Online Context: A New Speaker Community?

Merryn Davies-Deacon

Introduction

Breton

Breton is a member of the Brythonic branch of the Celtic family of languages, historically spoken in the region of Brittany in north-west France. While the language has experienced a gradual decline in usage since as long ago as the 10th century (Abalain, 2000: 46), initially due to invasions and then as a result of the growing prestige of French, its endangerment began in earnest in the early 20th: the separation of church and state in France in 1905, population shift as a result of the First and Second World Wars and the subsequent turn towards industrialisation even in rural areas were all factors that encouraged the rapid decline in use of Breton. Consequently, by the 1940s, the typical patterns of language shift could be observed, with those in towns, of higher social classes, and younger and female speakers preferring to use French (Broudic, 2013: 14–16). Over 1 million people, three quarters of the population of the western part of Brittany, known as *Breizh-Izel* ('Lower Brittany') and roughly delineated by an eastern border running from Saint-Brieuc in the north to Vannes in the south, used Breton as their preferred language of everyday communication in 1900 (Broudic, 2013: 9); just under 200,000 people were estimated to speak it by 2007 (Broudic, 2009: 62).

Since the early 20th century, however, a language revitalisation movement has gradually gained prominence in Brittany, marked by several milestones such as the opening of the first Breton immersion schools in the 1970s (Abalain, 2000: 80) and the gradual adoption of bilingual street and road signs since the 1980s (Abalain, 2000: 87). While many parents began to stop passing Breton on to their children, some of those who had not been exposed to the language in childhood began to learn it, initially by seeking out existing speakers and later by availing themselves of a small but growing number of pedagogical resources. In a wider context, recent scholarship on autochthonous minority languages has defined this type of speaker as *new speakers*, in opposition to *traditional speakers* who acquire languages 'through their home and community environments' (Bermingham, 2018: 112). The specific definition of the new speaker tends to vary depending on the research context and methodology employed: some work stresses a need for the language acquired not to be the common language of the wider community, while other research suggests that its not being spoken in the family is sufficient; some scholars insist on the positive attitude of the new speaker towards the language, at odds with its typical lack of prestige among traditional speakers. Taking a broad approach to the new speaker, Hornsby (2015: 108) defines the category with reference to 'transmission, attitude and origin': the new speaker has acquired the language through means other than uninterrupted intergenerational transmission, is positively disposed towards it and need not originate from the same community as traditional speakers.

This type of sociolinguistic research on new speakers dates back only a few years: Grinevald and Bert (2011: 51) refer to the 'neo-speaker', but note that 'this type of speaker has not been referenced in the literature yet'; more recently, a more substantial literature on the topic has developed (e.g. O'Rourke & Pujolar, 2019; Smith-Christmas *et al.*, 2018). However, in the specific context of Breton, the concept of the new speaker is present in research dating back significantly further, with the term *néo-bretonnant* (literally 'new speaker of Breton') first appearing in the work of Jones (1995, 1996, 1998). In the past, scholarly work has often taken an unfavourable attitude to these speakers, preferring a position of 'native authenticism', which ascribes greater value to traditional speaker practices (Hornsby & Quentel, 2013: 78).

Néo-bretonnants are typically associated with a number of characteristics that differentiate them from traditional speakers: they are said to be young, middle-class, well-educated, urban, located all over Brittany, proud of their Breton identity and militant in their use of Breton, using it in as many contexts as possible. Traditional speakers, on the other hand, are depicted as elderly, working-class, poorly educated and unable to read and write in Breton, rural, located exclusively in *Breizh-Izel*, indifferent towards the concept of pan-Breton identity and ashamed of their ability to speak Breton, with the effect that they speak it only with close friends and family members within their local communities. Work on Breton and its speakers has tended, not always uncritically, to repeat some or all of these stereotypes: see, for example, Jones (1995: 428–9, 1998: 132–3), Abalain (2000: 76), Timm (2001: 454, 2003: 34, 42), German (2007), Adkins (2013: 58–9), Hornsby and Quentel (2013: 75–76), Le Dû and Le Berre (2013: 53), Le Nevez (2013: 92) and Rottet (2014: 212–3). However, more recently, some work has called attention to the problematic nature of this discourse and emphasised the need for a more nuanced approach (see Hornsby, 2021).

Stereotypes relating to the type of language used by the *néo-bretonnants* are equally prevalent. As they are characterised as L2 speakers of Breton, structural elements of their language, such as word order in spontaneous speech and phonology, are said to be heavily influenced by French (Timm, 2003: 42). On the other hand, those parts of language more easily consciously modified, such as word order in more measured speech and lexicon, are claimed to be deliberately distanced from French (German, 2007: 153). *Néo-bretonnants*, we are told, thus tend to make efforts to use VSO (the typical unmarked word order in traditional Breton), while traditional speakers frequently depart from this for stylistic reasons; *néo-bretonnants* are also said to favour neologisms based on Celtic lexical roots over the French-derived borrowings that traditional speakers will often make use of (Jones, 1998: 134).

Another linguistic attribute of the *néo-bretonnants* is their supposed preference for standard language. Traditional speakers typically use dialectal forms of Breton, i.e. local varieties of the language that can be grouped into four main regional dialects corresponding with the former bishoprics of *Breizh-Izel*. *Néo-bretonnants*, it is claimed, instead use a standard form based mostly on the Leoneg[1] dialect, the geographically most distant from, and hence structurally least influenced by, French: this standardised variety is that found in grammars such as Hemon (1964). There is no officially prescribed standard form of Breton that has been comprehensively codified, but, as later sections of this chapter will show, institutional use of the language tends to employ this standardised Leoneg-based variety, tending moreover towards the use of Celtic-derived neologisms in preference over French borrowings, which follows the stereotypical *néo-bretonnant* practice. This de facto standard typically encompasses the use of a particular orthography, referred to as *peurunvan* ('supraunified'). However, other orthographic systems co-exist: the two other most widely used supradialectal orthographies are known as *skolveurieg* ('university spelling') and *etrerannyezhel* ('interdialectal'). Abalain (2000: 85) reports that in the late 20th century, 73.4% of those who wrote in Breton preferred *peurunvan*, while 14.6% used *skolveurieg*, showing that at least in orthographic terms, there is in fact some room for departure from the standard.

Breton on the internet

Here, we focus on the use of Breton in online contexts, with the intent to determine whether these are populated by a community of stereotypical new speakers. This chapter therefore offers a case study of contemporary Breton speakers who use their language in online settings, offering insights into the way language on the internet may conform to or reject the supposed linguistic features used by new speakers. In the case of Breton, the web is indeed a context where we would expect this type of speaker to be prevalent, based on the supposed attributes of *néo-bretonnants* seen in the previous section: their youth, higher social class and proximity to urban centres are all factors that would imply they are more likely internet users than the traditional speaker population. Additionally, given that much online content is in written form, if traditional speakers are unable to read and write Breton this precludes them from using the language in this context. Finally, the fact that traditional speakers are said to restrict their use of Breton to intimate settings implies that even if they had access to the internet and were literate in Breton to a degree that would enable them to use it in this manner, they would not wish to do so. The web thus appears to be a context where we would expect the majority of content, particularly that in written form, to be produced by new speakers, and hence by stereotypical *néo-bretonnants*, if we are to accept the claims of earlier research.

Breton has a modest but visible presence online. It can be observed in official contexts, such as the websites of the regional council of Brittany and of the five[2] departmental councils within the region: many of these offer a few pages in or about Breton, while the regional council allows visitors to view the entire site through the language.[3] Breton is additionally identifiable on social networking sites: *Indigenous Tweets* indicates that it ranks within the top 20 of the world's minoritised languages in terms of the number of tweets sent on an all-time basis.[4] On Facebook, beyond use on personal profiles, a number of groups specifically encourage interaction in Breton; the largest of these, *Facebook e brezhoneg!*, will be discussed below.

Examining the online use of Breton can be instrumental in investigating the stereotypes about new speakers of the language. If all new speakers are *néo-bretonnants*, who supposedly use a standardised form of Breton, we would expect to see this form of Breton in a dominant position in online contexts. If this is not the case, and we see the use of other varieties, it would seem either that not all users of Breton online are new speakers, or that not all new speakers identify with the stereotypical *néo-bretonnant* category and with standard language. Either of these findings would thus suggest that there may be more fluidity among speaker types than some research has suggested, with a number of speakers not fitting neatly into one of the two opposing categories. Moreover, if this is found to be the case, speakers who use Breton in these contexts must negotiate their use of language to communicate with others who may use Breton in diverse ways, potentially leading to a wider range of communicative practices on an intraspeaker level offline as well as online as an example of mediatisation (see Androutsopoulos, 2016).

Research Design

Contexts examined

In order to examine the online presence of Breton and the forms that it can take, this chapter highlights three contexts from the web: one standard, one non-standard and the third heteroglossic, an example of user-generated 'unregimented writing' (Androutsopoulos, 2016: 287) where individual contributors may choose to use either standard or non-standard varieties.

First, it will concentrate on the website of *Ofis publik ar brezhoneg* ('The public office of the Breton language', OPAB), the authority with overall responsibility for Breton language planning, investigating the way it depicts Breton and its varieties. There follows a brief discussion of the presence of non-standard Breton in online contexts. After this, the bulk of the analysis concentrates on the use of Breton in the Facebook group *Facebook e brezhoneg!*,[5] drawing from a sample of posts from the group gathered in 2017. Features of the orthography, lexicon, and dialectal qualities of the sample are highlighted in order to illustrate the diversity of Breton users' linguistic practices, and to give an indication of how the use of Breton in this online context can differ from its use in other more traditional media settings.

For this work, *Facebook e brezhoneg!* was systematically sampled and analysed as part of a larger research project concentrating on the use of lexicon in Breton media. The information given about OPAB's website and examples of non-standard Breton contextualises the heteroglossic *Facebook e brezhoneg!*, worthy of more in-depth analysis because of this multiauthorship and increased 'interactive potential for individual speakers' (Reershemius, 2017: 37), allowing us further insight into the wider online speaker community in a way that is characteristic of the performance era of media for autochthonous minority languages (see the Introduction, this volume).

OPAB's website is investigated due to its status as the official body responsible for Breton language planning, and hence as a presumed first port of call for individuals wishing to learn about the language. This supplies us with an online example of standard Breton; cases of non-standard language use online are harder to find due to their lack of official status, and those drawn from in this chapter were found through observation of Breton-language social media, noting which sites were linked to by users. For an appropriate social media context, *Facebook e brezhoneg!* was selected due to its high levels of activity. As well as being the most popular social network in France at the time of data collection,[6] Facebook is more suited to sustained conversation than its largest competitor, Twitter. On Twitter, many of the accounts using Breton are operated on behalf of organisations rather than individuals; tweets are often used to link to content on other websites rather than inciting a conversation within Twitter itself; and at the time of data collection each tweet was limited to 140 characters. This meant that Facebook was a more suitable source for gathering data in the format of a conversation between two or more individuals and provided a greater insight into how the online speaker community is formed.

A number of Facebook groups relating to Breton exist for different purposes, including general discussion, learning the language, and more militant groups encouraging the use of Breton in public contexts. *Facebook e brezhoneg!* is the largest and most active of these, as well as one of the longest established, created in 2012. Its original purpose was as a campaign group pressuring Facebook staff to allow the site's interface to be translated into Breton; after this goal was achieved in late 2014, the group became a general message board for Breton speakers (see also Heyen's discussion of 'breathing spaces', this volume, highlighting the importance of this type of community for autochthonous minority language speakers). At the time of data collection, there were over 10,000 members, including Breton speakers, learners, researchers and authority figures such as dictionary compilers and members of OPAB staff. As an 'open group', anyone can view posts and search the group without requiring a Facebook account, while any logged-in Facebook user can join the group and leave comments without prior moderation. Given that *Facebook e brezhoneg!* was and remains the largest and most active Facebook group for Breton speakers, it was deemed the most suitable context for investigating the 'virtual community' (Belmar & Glass, 2019) of Breton speakers and determining whether this can be considered a community of stereotypical new speakers, bearing in mind the caveat that any conclusions drawn relate to members of this group specifically and not necessarily to the wider population of Breton-speaking internet users.

Breton is the most frequently used language on *Facebook e brezhoneg!*, but French is also common, given that all Breton speakers within Brittany also speak French. French is often used by learners requesting linguistic help, or in translations appended to posts written in Breton. This is done despite group administrators' apparent efforts to construct the group as a Breton-only space: its header image, in place since 2016,[7] informs users, in both French and Breton, that posts should be written in Breton. However, based on the posts sampled, the use of French does not seem to attract any negative attention (see also Reershemius, this volume, on the comparative lack of language policing in more recent social media contexts). Language is a frequent subject of discussion, but so is news, particularly on political topics, from both within Brittany and beyond. The group is also used to advertise events such as Breton classes and conversation circles; unlike the Facebook group examined by Zieseler (this volume), while the question of neologisms and borrowings is salient for the analysis presented here, *Facebook e brezhoneg!* does not deal exclusively with the Breton language itself.

Data sampling and analysis

A sample of around 11,000 words was taken from *Facebook e brezhoneg!*, comprising posts written between November 2016 and March 2017; 99 different users are represented in the sample. A small number of criteria were developed in order to determine which posts would be included: the subject matter of the original post had to be non-linguistic to minimise chances of including vocabulary or orthographies not normally employed by the writer; the first post in each thread had to be made up of text rather than a link or uncaptioned photo, to ease analysis; and at least 50% of the post had to be in Breton. Moreover, posts were sampled only if they had at least one top-level response in Breton from a different user, to ensure that their content was accepted as valid Breton by interlocutors.

Usernames and other potentially identifying information were removed, and the sample was encoded according to the Text Encoding Initiative[8] in a way that preserved the nested comment structure of Facebook posts. This enabled statistical analysis of the sample and comparison with data from other sources. For the wider research project, which focused on the lexicon in order to determine whether the users of Breton in this and other media contexts fit the stereotypical attributes of new speakers, a systematic method was used to tag specific lexemes for statistical comparison across contexts (for details, see Davies-Deacon, 2020: 55–60). Items of orthographic interest also emerged while tagging the data by hand, and while less relevant to the wider research, are also discussed here as they contribute to the understanding of how new speakers use Breton in these online contexts and whether this conforms with the standard variety.

Research questions

The wider project from which the *Facebook e brezhoneg!* data are taken was primarily concerned with whether features attested in Breton-language media support or challenge the traditional academic perception of *néo-bretonnants* and their language, i.e. that they tend to use a more standard linguistic variety. For the purposes of this chapter, focusing on online contexts and bringing in additional websites for contextualisation and comparison, we can ask: does the online context more broadly, based on the sites examined, reflect these supposed features of new speakers of Breton, and can it therefore be considered a new speaker community? How do new speakers of Breton in the online context

84 Part 1: Shifting Ideologies

communicate with a potentially diverse group of interlocutors, while using language in a way that expresses their own specific identity?

Standard Breton Online: OPAB

The role of OPAB

As noted above, language planning for Breton is the responsibility of OPAB. Set up in 1999 as *Ofis ar brezhoneg*, the organisation became a public body in 2010 as a result of regional and departmental legislation (Cadot, 2010). Since then, it has been accountable to the regional government of Brittany and the councils of the five departments of the historical region of Brittany, receiving funding from them as well as from the French state. Its headquarters are located in Carhaix, situated in inland Finistère, the part of the region with the highest population of traditional speakers of Breton. However, OPAB is decentralised, with further offices located in the other four departments so as to cover the entire cultural territory of Brittany.[9]

OPAB is involved in all elements of language planning for Breton: status planning, acquisition planning and corpus planning. In terms of status planning, it works with regional and departmental councils to ensure representation of Breton in the public space, such as road signs, and encourages municipal councils and private businesses to sign up to the charter 'Ya d'ar brezhoneg' ('Yes to Breton') as official proof that the town or organisation is inclusive of the language. Its involvement with acquisition planning entails the compilation of statistics on enrolment in immersion and bilingual schools, and the provision of details on where such schools are located, as well as information on classes for adults and the creation of advertising campaigns to encourage members of the public to sign up for these classes. For corpus planning, OPAB maintains a database of recommended terminology, known as TermOfis,[10] actively developed by a small team of researchers based in its Rennes office. Other linguistic services it provides through its website include a database of place names, KerOfis,[11] that lists the official Breton form of each, and a historical corpus of Breton including words from sources ranging in publication date from the 11th century to today. It also offers a professional translation service, which markets itself as applicable to diverse contexts: 'panelloù, teulioù melestradurel, kazetennoù, levrioù, lec'hiennoù Internet ...' ('signs, administrative documents, magazines, books, websites').[12] Moreover, it provides recommendations on the use of specific vocabulary and orthography, thus presenting itself as an authority on the use of standard Breton.[13]

Another resource provided on OPAB's website is a crowd-sourced terminology database,[14] which lists two or three French terms per month and invites users to suggest and then vote on suitable Breton translations, alerting them via mailing list. While the precise features of this service deserve more discussion than is available here, it is worth noting its existence as a tangible example of how the internet can be harnessed in a way that has direct impact on the language standardisation process. Expansion of the Breton lexicon is a key focus of OPAB, with a dedicated staff maintaining their database of officially advised terminology. The words proposed in this 'forom termenadurezh' ('terminology forum') are often connected to contemporary issues, with recent examples of French words proposed for translation including *flambée des prix* ('explosion in prices') and *arme à sous-munitions* ('cluster bomb'). Giving speakers the chance to propose and vote on terms thus implicates them directly in the standardisation process, touching on one of the central themes of this volume. Questions must be raised here around how representative these suggestions are of the wider speaker community, and it is hoped that future research will be able to investigate this more thoroughly.

Discourse around standard Breton

OPAB's presentation of Breton on its website, available in both Breton and French, is worth examining to gain insight into how the standard variety commonly associated with *néo-bretonnants* is depicted. Generally, this section of the site places emphasis on the language's historical background, as well as on its fitness for use in the modern era. We are told that Breton is 'talvoudus he glad skrivet' ('significant in written heritage'),[15] and various examples of written Breton are mentioned, going back as far as the oldest known manuscript, from the 8th century, and ending with recent dictionaries and work on terminology. This emphasis on the continued presence of written Breton in some form over more than a millennium has the effect of stressing the historical legitimacy not only of the language as a whole, but also of the standard variety specifically, pointing out that codification and work towards the creation of a standard language are not recent phenomena but the continuation of a far longer tradition.

These pages also emphasise the fact that Breton is a Celtic language, giving a map of the territories of the Celtic languages and noting that Breton is most closely related to Cornish and Welsh, thus highlighting its typological distance from French. Indeed, this point is used to emphasise the historical grounding of Breton: 'ur yezh indezeuropek eo ar brezhoneg; komzet e vez abaoe ouzhpenn 1500 vloaz' ('Breton is an Indo-European language; it has been spoken for over 1500 years').[16] An emphasis on the continuity of Breton in some form over a large period is thus again made, with the assertion that Breton is 'Indo-European' also alluding to this historicity, and its place among the other languages of Europe. This, along with the emphasis on the literary tradition noted above, confers legitimacy on the status of Breton as a result of its historical roots and distance from French.

Later on, information is provided that specifically relates to the traditional dialects and standard variety of Breton. This stresses the intercomprehensibility of the dialects, noting first that it may be more appropriate to divide them into a western group and an eastern group rather than the traditional division along the lines of the four bishoprics, and thus implying that the number of dialectal differences may be smaller than suggested elsewhere. This is also suggested in the presentation of information about the structural differences among the dialects:

> N'eo ket ken bras-se an diforc'hioù ha sellet a reont dreist-holl ouzh an taol-mouezh hag an distagadur. N'eus ket nemeur a ziforc'hioù a-fet geriaoueg ha yezhadur. Peurvuiañ e c'haller kompren mat an eil egile, ha hep tamm diaezamant ebet zoken evit an dud a oar lenn ha skrivañ. ('The differences are not so large, and have to do mostly with tonic accent and pronunciation. There are hardly any differences with respect to vocabulary and grammar. The vast majority of people can understand each other well, and, for those who can read and write, even with no difficulty at all' https://www.brezhoneg.bzh/55-istor.htm, accessed November 2021)

This page thus strongly downplays the differences among the dialects. Academic sources tend to be more nuanced on this issue, with some scholars suggesting that while this may be the case in linguistic terms, there is nonetheless a conceptual stumbling block in the minds of many traditional speakers that prevents them from communicating with speakers of other dialects (German, 2007: 153).

This presentation of Breton by OPAB therefore points to a natural evolution towards modern standard Breton, involving the convergence of the dialects over time, largely independent of French influence. It does, however, acknowledge the role of intentional standardisation:

> Diazezet eo bet ar brezhoneg modern gant yezhadurourien ha geriadurourien, da gentañ adalek ar XVIIvet kantved (an Tad Maner) hag an XVIIIvet kantved (Gregor Rostrenenn) ha dreist-holl en XIXvet hag XXvet kantved, gant luskad Gwalarn pergen (1925) a roas lañs da vat d'al lennegezh vodern e brezhoneg. ('Modern Breton has been standardised by grammarians and lexicographers, starting in the 17th century (Père Maunoir) and the 18th century (Grégoire de Rostrenen), and particularly in the 19th and 20th centuries, especially by the Gwalarn movement (1925), which truly gave rise to modern literature in Breton' https://www.brezhoneg.bzh/55-istor.htm, accessed November 2021)

Again, though, this passage highlights the historical roots of standard Breton by citing early examples of standardisation, and links the standard to the earlier evocation of Breton's literary heritage, suggesting that its creation was necessary in order to ensure the continuation of that heritage. Standardisation is thus at once presented as a natural, inevitable process, resulting in a language that would not be too far removed from the traditional dialects, and as a necessary one, creating a language suitable for the modern world. Indeed, the final paragraph of the page characterises modern Breton as 'ur yezh skoueriekaet evit gallout en em dennañ e kement degouezh a vefe hag evit bezañ gouest da vont diouzh emdroadur an teknologiezhioù er bed a vremañ' ('a standardised language in order to deal with any situation that may arise, and to be capable of responding to the evolution of technologies in the modern world')[17] – the implication is that without standardisation, this would not be possible. OPAB thus suggests that the historical evolution of Breton has led to a single, uncontested standard variety, best equipped both to respect the language's prestigious written history and to take it forward into the future. This is the perspective we would expect the stereotypical new speaker to hold, suggesting that OPAB staff form part of the *néo-bretonnant* community and expect readers of these pages to be sympathetic to this presentation of the language.

OPAB does not discuss the standardisation of Breton orthography in any detail, nor the fact that competing supradialectal orthographies continue to exist. Its preference for the de facto standard spelling system, *peurunvan*, is evident from the fact that the basic Breton-French machine translation service it offers[18] does not recognise words spelt in other orthographies. In the domain of lexicon, however, this tool appears to tolerate a greater range of variation, correctly rendering translations of some well-known items of dialectal vocabulary, such as Leoneg *kouer* ('farmer', standard *peizant*) and Gwenedeg *get* ('with', standard *gant*) and *doc'h* ('to, from, at', overlapping in meaning with standard *ouzh, diouzh,* and *eus*). It also recognises some cases of non-standard borrowed vocabulary such as *telefon*, a borrowing from French *téléphone* (standard *pellgomzer*). This indicates a desire to include speakers whose lexis does not match the standard, at least in the cases of these well-known non-standard words. However, this inclusion is restricted to the implicit, with no overt acknowledgement of any debate over the lexicon. In summary, OPAB presents Breton as a fully standardised and largely homogeneous language, and therefore seems to cater more for the stereotypical *néo-bretonnant* than any other type of speaker.

Non-standard Breton online

Online spaces that make use of non-standard varieties of Breton can be identified, but tend not to represent official bodies and are hence much less visible than contexts such as OPAB's website. Moreover, when these online spaces are maintained by small voluntary groups or individuals, they are constantly at risk of sudden deletion if the owner loses the interest, time, or resources required. One example, *Brezhoneg Digor*, which provided recordings and transcriptions of traditional Breton speakers, was deleted suddenly in 2018, with its maintainer leaving the following message:

> J'ai commencé ce travail, transcrire et élaborer le dictionnaire du centre-Bretagne, dans le but d'avoir le niveau nécessaire pour parler et être compris des bretonnants natifs, ce but est dorénavant atteint. ... Mais devant le peu d'intérêt qu'il suscite, si je me fie au nombre ridiculement bas de commentaires postés sur le blog et/ou sur Youtube depuis 11 ans, j'ai donc décidé de me délester de cette charge de travail qui n'est, pour moi, plus une nécessité. ('I started this work, transcribing and annotating the dictionary of the central Breton dialect, with the aim of reaching a level sufficient for speaking to and being understood by native Breton speakers; this goal has since been achieved. ... But given the lack of interest it attracts, if I go by the ridiculously low number of comments posted on the blog and/or on YouTube over the past eleven years, I have therefore decided to relieve myself of this workload, which is no longer necessary for my own purposes' https://web.archive.org/web/20181220035637/https://brezhoneg-digor.blogspot.com/, accessed October 2021)

The same individual continues to upload recordings of conversations with traditional speakers to YouTube, but without the additional linguistic resources formerly provided.[19] It can be noted that by setting himself apart from 'native Breton speakers', the maintainer of this resource appears to fall into the new speaker category, but that his alignment with traditional dialectal varieties distances him from the theorised community of new speakers who use a standardised variety of Breton: this is a case of a new speaker of Breton using the technological tools at his disposal, but certainly not in the sense of contributing to a 'new speaker community' as we would understand the term.

Another example of online non-standard Breton investigated for this research is loeizherrieu.fr,[20] an informational portal dedicated to the life and work of early 20th-century Breton writer Loeiz Herrieu, praised by the website as 'celui qui a certainement fait le plus pour que la langue bretonne vive dans le Pays Vannetais' ('the person who was surely the most responsible for the survival of Breton in the Gwenedeg dialect area').[21] Accordingly, his use of the Gwenedeg dialect is presented on the site as a central characteristic of his work.

As well as information on Herrieu's life and work, the site also presents information on Gwenedeg in general. In contradiction of OPAB's website, it presents dialectal differences in Breton as significant to the point of non-comprehension, quoting from the work of Breton scholar Fañch Morvannou:

Peurvuian e vez diaes d'ar vrezhonegerion KLT lenn gwenedeg kozh, ha diaessoc'h c'hoazh komz gwenedeg. Ken diaes ail e vez moarvad da vrezhonegerion Bro-Wened lenn KLT, ha ken diaes ail komz. Ha kementman en desped d'ar strivoù a zo bet gwraet ewid tostaad dre skrid an daou rummad parlantoù an eil douzh egile. ('For the most part, it is hard for KLT [non-Gwenedeg] Breton speakers to read old Gwenedeg, and harder still for them to speak Gwenedeg. Conversely, it is of course as hard for most Breton speakers from the Gwenedeg area to read KLT, and as hard to speak it. And this is despite the work that has been done to bring the two groups of dialects together in written form' http://loeizherrieu.fr/wwww/tests/tournures.html, accessed November 2021)

This passage is written in standard Breton, albeit in Morvannou's preferred *etrerannyezhel* orthography rather than *peurunvan*. However, the most visible examples of Breton on the site take the form of menu links and page headers, which can be seen on every page. These are bilingual, with the Breton versions written in Gwenedeg, using traditional Gwenedek orthography rather than, for example, *peurunvan* or *etrerannyezhel* with Gwenedek variants and vocabulary. Other parts of the site use different dialects and orthographies: song examples from collections made by Herrieu are reprinted in their original versions, either Gwenedeg in the traditional orthography or another dialect using traditional KLT orthography. Excerpts of Herrieu's writing are kept in their original form, i.e. Gwenedeg with traditional Gwenedek orthography. Other excerpts from materials originally written in standard Breton are kept in their original form, while many pages contain no Breton at all other than in headers and the menu bar. The one page that appears to contain Breton passages not reprinted from another source uses the *etrerannyezhel* orthography with Gwenedek vocabulary.[22]

The use of Breton on the site is therefore minimal: it is mostly restricted to reprints from other sources rather than having been composed specifically for use here. Where the small amount of Breton specific to the site is concerned, it is interesting to note the difference in orthographies between menu items and headers and actual content: the latter, serving a more communicative purpose, uses a modern orthography, while menu items and headers, contributing more to the site's visual identity (and accompanied by a French version in all cases), use the more identifiably Gwenedek traditional orthography. While non-standard Breton is used in both cases, the more non-standard of the two kinds is reserved for these more presentational, less information-rich contexts. This highlights the fact that non-standard Breton has the semiotic advantage of conveying a more localised identity than the standard is able to do, but equally that this comes at the risk of inhibiting comprehensibility. The distribution of orthographies on loeizherrieu.fr shows a pragmatic response to this dilemma: in contexts where communication is more important, a more standard version prevails; where identity can be prioritised, the Breton used is less standard.

While OPAB's website and loeizherrieu.fr provide examples of different uses to which Breton is put online, and the way its form varies accordingly, static websites of this kind tell us little about the speaker community: there is often no way of telling whether other speakers engage with the content of the site. While this shows that non-standard varieties of Breton can be seen online, we need to turn to a social networking site to determine whether such non-standard forms are actually employed in communicative contexts on the internet, and whether these contexts suggest an online presence of the typical 'new speaker community' that research on Breton[23] suggests will exist.

Breton on Facebook: *Facebook e brezhoneg!*

Theoretical considerations

Gathering data from social media is subject to a number of methodological issues that must be borne in mind during the analysis of such data. The ever-changing nature of social media platforms means that it is important to consider the fact that data gathered from these sources function as a snapshot only of the time at which they were produced, and may not be as relevant to our understanding of how the language community has evolved since, even at a distance of only a few years. Moreover, it is crucial to be aware of difficulties in making assumptions about offline communities based on the language practices we observe in online settings. Blommaert and Szabla (2017: 11) note that online communication is a 'complex game' where speakers rely on diverse resources to mitigate for the lack of nonverbal contextualisation cues. To researchers viewing such communications after the fact, these resources can be difficult to identify and interpret, and we should be cautious in taking online language use at its face value, especially in the case of autochthonous minority languages, where identity construction is particularly important, as noted in the introduction to this volume.

Similarly, it is important not to consider the online community a substitute for offline ones. In the context of autochthonous minority languages, where speakers can be prevented from using their language in their local surroundings due to practical constraints such as the lack of a critical mass of speakers, it is tempting to view online contexts as a solution to some of these problems. However, speakers interviewed for the wider research project from which these data are drawn pointed out the drawbacks of relying on these virtual spaces, with one noting:

> je pense que c'est très positif, c'est très important d'utiliser la langue bretonne sur Facebook [...] mais il faut faire attention, je pense, de n'y pas construire une sorte de mirage, d'avoir l'impression qu'il y a une

vraie société bretonne [...] c'est bien, avoir une société bretonne virtuelle, une société en langue bretonne virtuelle, mais il ne faut pas non plus abandonner l'objectif d'avoir une vraie société bretonne avec des gens qu'on rencontre vraiment dans la rue, pour parler la langue dans les magasins, pour acheter des choses et cetera, et il ne faut pas perdre la vue de cet objectif-là aussi. Et le temps qu'on passe sur Facebook tout seul devant son ordinateur, on ne passe pas à avoir des activités ou à faire des choses avec de vraies personnes en parlant cette langue-là ('I think it's very positive, very important to use Breton on Facebook ... but I think we need to be careful not to make it into a kind of mirage, to think there's a real Breton-speaking society ... it's good to have a virtual Breton-speaking society, but we mustn't abandon the goal of a real Breton-speaking society with people that we meet physically in the street, where we can speak Breton in shops when we're buying things and so on, we mustn't lose sight of this objective either. And the time we spend on Facebook alone in front of our computers is time we're not using to participate in activities or do things with real people speaking Breton')

As a result, we must be cautious in applying any conclusions drawn about the online context to the community of Breton speakers and their language use in general; as the remainder of the chapter will show, the language used in this context can often go beyond a merely communicative function, perhaps to a greater extent than in offline settings. Because of this, similarly, it is important to be aware that quantitative analysis alone is insufficient for interpreting the nuances of the highly context-dependent data found on Facebook. The findings I present in this chapter mostly relate to individual cases of language use that suggest certain attitudes were present among users of the group at the time of data collection, and are not intended to contribute to claims about the speaker community as a whole; indeed, my aim is to demonstrate that making such general claims in the first place fails to understand the complex and heterogeneous nature of autochthonous minority language communities.

Orthographies and dialects

While *Facebook e brezhoneg!* is not a context specifically dedicated to non-standard Breton, it nonetheless contains examples of orthographic conventions other than the de facto standard *peurunvan*. Among modern supradialectal orthographies, *peurunvan* is the most frequently used in the sample, but *etrerannyezhel* and *skolveurieg* can also be identified, showing that despite their general lack of use at institutional level, these continue to be used by individuals. There are also examples of dialectal orthographies: one user writes *berman* ('now') and *berton* ('Breton') instead of standard *bremañ* and *breton*, indicating their alignment with the Gwenedeg dialect, while another writes *brezouneg* ('Breton language') instead of standard *brezhoneg*, a marker of the Leoneg dialect. These minor adaptations of standard orthographies allow the expression of a dialectal identity, while remaining comprehensible to users of other dialects or standard Breton; indeed, they attract replies from users of dialects other than their own, showing that these minor variations are no detriment to intelligibility. A small number of posts in the sample are written entirely in the distinctive Gwenedek orthography: they, on the other hand, receive only replies that are also in Gwenedeg, suggesting that speakers of other varieties may be unable or unwilling to engage with them.

Variable orthographic decisions are also made in the case of brand names. In a discussion of the board game Scrabble, two users keep the standard spelling of the game's name, but another two adapt it to a Breton-style orthography, writing *Skrabell*. This adaptation of a brand name, uncommon in major world languages, may indicate a more stereotypically *néo-breton* position, where neologisms are favoured over borrowings, and where unavoidable borrowings are adapted to fit the conventions of Breton to the greatest possible extent. Both versions seem to be considered acceptable to readers, however: no user comments on another's orthographic choice. *Facebook e brezhoneg!* thus appears to be an inclusive space in this respect, where users' different linguistic decisions are generally respected despite the divergent ideologies that are likely to motivate them. Likewise, while posts written in strongly dialectal varieties may not be engaged with by users of the standard, neither are they criticised.

Another orthographic feature seen on Facebook is the use of contractions to mark colloquial language. The unusual nature of much computer-mediated communication as a medium that is written in form but contains many characteristics of speech means that features of this type are uniquely prevalent in the research context of social media, particularly when compared with traditional media forms such as magazines. Thus in the sample from *Facebook e brezhoneg!* we see the phrase 'deuz ar henta' (the *skolveurieg* equivalent of *peurunvan* 'deus ar c'hentañ', meaning 'until next time') rendered as ''z ar henta'. Non-standard uses of orthography thus convey not only allegiance to a particular dialect, or alignment with one side or the other of the new/traditional speaker divide, but in this case, also to a more colloquial linguistic register: in the online context in particular, 'spelling variants can be socially meaningful' (Androutsopoulos, 2016: 289).

Borrowings and neologisms

As the introduction to this chapter states, the lexicon of Breton is one particularly visible domain in which *néo-bretonnants* are said to differ from traditional speakers of the language. Previous research has asserted that especially for the expression of new concepts for which no word existed in Breton prior to the onset of widespread community bilingualism with French, *néo-bretonnants* are said to prefer Celtic neologisms, thus avoiding French influence as much as possible, while traditional speakers are more willing to employ French borrowings (German, 2007: 153). Thus we are told that traditional speakers will prefer words such as *magazin* ('shop', < French *magasin*), *rezen* ('reason', < French *raison*) and *boulangerezh* ('bakery', < French *boulangerie* with a Breton suffix), while new speakers will prefer *stal*, *abeg* and *baraerezh*, which are presented as adaptations of existing Breton words through semantic expansion, or in the case of *baraerezh*, a new derived form (*bara*, 'bread', + *-er*, an agentive suffix, + *-ezh*, a suffix denoting an activity). The preference for neologism has hence become associated with contemporary standard Breton, and indeed neologisms tend to take precedence over borrowings in TermOfis (Davies-Deacon, 2020: 113). Moreover, as we have suggested, the stereotypes around new and traditional speakers of Breton suggest that Facebook should be a community populated exclusively by the former, i.e. by stereotypical *néo-bretonnants* and standard language. If all these stereotypes hold true, we would therefore expect borrowings, beyond long-established examples, to be limited in this context.

Again, however, this is not the case, and we do find numerous examples in *Facebook e brezhoneg!* of words wholly or partly borrowed from French, including some cases that appear to be one-off borrowings: *teleferik* ('cable-car', < French *téléphérique*), *seksist* ('sexist', < French *sexiste*) and *reptilianed* ('reptiles', < French *reptile* plus a Breton plural suffix) are all attested in the sample, instead of standard *fungarr*, *revelour* and *stlejviled*. In these examples, the users appear to be deliberately distancing themselves from standard lexemes that have been created during the 20th century following the neologistic model, and thus going against the stereotypical *néo-bretonnant* alignment, again suggesting that there is room in the social media context for non-standard Breton and a range of speaker perspectives and identities. The examples of *teleferik* and *seksist* also show that a degree of respelling is often necessary in these one-off borrowings: like *Skrabell*, they are altered to comply with Breton orthographic conventions, suggesting in these cases that a degree of alignment with standard Breton is nonetheless maintained.

While the fairly small size of the sample (around 11,000 words) does not lend itself to detailed statistical analysis at the level of the lexeme, some basic statistical methods can be used to investigate choices relating to the question of borrowings versus coinages in more depth. A small number of terms relating to the media were investigated for their rate of occurrence, along with words meaning 'thank you', a commonly cited

Table 4.1 Borrowings and neologisms on Facebook

		Borrowing		Neologism		TermOfis recommendation
		# Tokens	# Unique users	# Tokens	# Unique users	
'radio'	radio	4	3	skingomz	0	0	radio except in some phrases
'telephone'	telefon	0	0	pellgomz	5	3	pellgomz
'internet'	internet	9	8	kenrouedad	2	2	kenrouedad except in some phrases
'television'	tele/TV	1	1	skinwel	1	1	skinwel
'thank you'	mersi	6	4	trugarez	6	6	trugarez

(Blanchard *et al.*, 2013: 150; German, 2007: 186; Lossec, 2013: 26; Rottet, 2014: 240) case where a result of recent semantic expansion coexists with a borrowing considered to be favoured by traditional speakers. The occurrence of these words in the corpus is summed up in Table 4.1, along with the recommendations found in TermOfis.

In most cases, TermOfis recommends a Celtic-derived term, as expected in standard, *néo-bretonnant*-aligned Breton. Where it recommends a borrowed word, in the case of *radio*, this is the only term we find in the corpus: the neologism *skingomz* appears to have been deemed excessive, even by OPAB. Where TermOfis recommends a neologism, attitudes vary among users: *pellgomz* appears to be universally accepted, while the options for 'television' and 'thank you' show a roughly equal divide between users, although this is based on a very small sample size in the former case. For 'internet', *internet* occurs noticeably more frequently than *kenrouedad*, showing in this case of a much more recent term how the borrowing may have become established in the community before the official neologism was decided on. Overall, these data show that in a number of cases, there is no consensus among speakers on which of the two options should be used, showing again that for various items of vocabulary, individual Facebook users have different opinions on whether borrowings or coinages should be used, and that they do not all fit the *néo-bretonnant* stereotype of preferring neologism.

In comparison with other media contexts examined for the same research, *Facebook e brezhoneg!* displays some characteristics that go further in developing our understanding of the specificities of the online setting. Despite the cases of non-standard language discussed above, in comparison with a range of radio programmes and printed media publications (two magazines and a newspaper), the Facebook data were found to exhibit the highest use of neologisms over borrowings, suggesting a higher overall adherence to *néo-breton*. This contradicts general findings relating to linguistic register, which suggested that higher registers of language tended to use more standard and typically more *néo-breton* vocabulary. As an example of computer-mediated communication, we would expect the Facebook context to fall between the others in terms of its register, and indeed it can be judged to do so, going by criteria such as the morphosyntactic complexity of the data produced in this context. It is therefore surprising that the use of neologisms in the Facebook sample occurs at a higher rate than elsewhere, rather than in an intermediate position.

This information can also be contrasted with the fact that the Facebook data also show the highest use of terms not advised in TermOfis, as well as exhibiting a higher use of terms with meanings not attested in standard dictionaries of Breton. This suggests that language is used on Facebook in an innovative, perhaps even playful way, not surprising when 'more than other media, digital communication has been associated with humour, joking, language play, role play, and other nonserious communication' (Vandergriff, 2010: 235; see also Arendt & Stern, this volume). This finding raises an important point about the difference between standard Breton and *néo-breton*: the use of Breton in this context is often highly *néo-breton* but not standard, showing that these two terms cannot be equated. While this deserves further investigation, it shows from the outset that based on linguistic practices, the question of who is a new speaker, a *néo-bretonnant*, or a user of standard Breton is more complex than it may seem, especially in this highly performative online setting.

Conclusion

This chapter has considered a variety of online contexts in which Breton is used: the official website of OPAB, some websites maintained by individuals that make use of non-standard vocabulary, and a heteroglossic social media context. It has shown, in general, that despite OPAB's prioritisation of the standard, non-standard and dialectal Breton have an identifiable online presence, both in dedicated spaces such as loeizherrieu.fr and, to a lesser extent, on Facebook. The Facebook data also show a certain degree of resistance to the typical decision in standard Breton to use Celtic-derived neologisms rather than French-derived borrowings, with various examples of such non-standard borrowings attested. While users of Breton online may or may not be new speakers in the strict sense, the extent to which they engage with stereotypical new speaker practices varies.

Comparing the orthography of the three contexts, it can be seen that different practices are available and index multiple ways of signalling allegiance with standard or dialectal varieties of Breton. OPAB's website makes no mention of the fact that orthographies other than *peurunvan* have ever been available; contrastingly, loeizherrieu.fr uses the original orthographies of quoted texts, resulting in a multiplicity of orthographies. For links and headers, as noted, it employs the Gwenedek dialectal orthography in a symbolic fashion, always side-by-side with French, which allows the site to avoid any issues of comprehension caused by using this lesser-known spelling system; in doing so, it also signals an ideological non-alignment with OPAB, whose website presents Breton as fully standardised. *Facebook e brezhoneg!*, as a heteroglossic context, shows a range of orthographic practices, but mostly conforms to the de facto standard *peurunvan*, suggesting that in terms of this particular linguistic feature, most of its users do fit the new speaker stereotype.

The analysis of the lexicon, however, shows that Facebook users employ considerable variation with regard to the use of borrowings and neologisms, sometimes not exhibiting the attributes we might expect of new speakers in their use of non-officially advised borrowings, while at other times taking a more purist approach than even the official standard. While OPAB relies on standard vocabulary – unsurprisingly as it is the arbiter of that standard – Facebook users employ multiple practices with the result that their lexicon is particularly diverse. This again relates to the heteroglossic nature of this context, but also shows that users of Breton on Facebook engage with the language in multiple ways that show a complex relationship with the language that does not always match expectations. Instead of assuming that new speakers form a homogeneous *néo-bretonnant* community, we should be receptive to the idea that many of them will diverge from the linguistic traits expected. While this study has observed such divergence in the specific context of Facebook, its occurrence raises questions around speaker practices in other domains: those used to communicating with others who may have different backgrounds and different beliefs about the role of Breton, manifesting themselves in diverse linguistic repertoires, may find themselves at ease with navigating a wider speaker community in other spaces including the offline context. Further study is required to discern the potential effects of this mediatisation process (see Androutsopoulos, 2016; Introduction, this volume).

In answer to this chapter's first research question, which asks whether the online context can be considered a new speaker community in terms of whether it conforms with the linguistic characteristics that we would expect of typical new speakers, we can conclude that a diversity of practices can be observed and that while the community may be made up of a majority of new speakers according to other characteristics such as greater access to technology and willingness to use Breton outside intimate contexts, this does not necessarily result in a 'new speaker community' in the sense of a community whose linguistic production is restricted to stereotypically *néo-bretonnant* forms. Indeed, as shown in the way Facebook users bring in dialectal features, the expression of identity takes an important role, and it is perhaps this that we should associate with new speakers of Breton more than any specific linguistic characteristics, given that identity construction has previously been identified as a primary motivation among new speakers (Nance *et al.*, 2016).

This brings us to the second research question, which asked how users of Breton in online contexts are able to balance communication with the expression of identity: the different functions and authorships of the websites in question are also important here. In the case of OPAB, the text is presented on behalf of a public body, while on loeizherrieu.fr, it represents the amateur enthusiasm of one or more anonymous members of the Breton-speaking community for Loeiz Herrieu's writing; the roles played by contributors to these sites are sharply differentiated from each other. On *Facebook e brezhoneg!*, the balance between identity and communication is carefully struck in the use of minor orthographic adaptations to convey allegiance to specific dialects, while the ludic and metalinguistic qualities of much of the language used show that users of the site are acting as private individuals, using language in a more familiar and relaxed way than would be appropriate in the other contexts examined. Therefore, it would be incorrect to assume that contributors to OPAB's website are set apart from other speakers by their use of a more standard linguistic variety; instead, we should consider the possibility that they use standard language in this official context but may not always do so elsewhere. The specific role of each online setting and the capacity in which speakers use language clearly have an effect on the linguistic results, and different speakers are able to employ different registers and styles of language in different situations. The proliferation of different choices around vocabulary on *Facebook e brezhoneg!* speaks to the fact that new speakers of Breton have complex, multifaceted identities, and, depending on the interaction, they can use language in various ways so as to bring out the aspect of their identity that is most salient.

This chapter's discussion of online uses of Breton has shown that it would be incorrect to assume that all users of Breton in these contexts are stereotypical *néo-bretonnants* who favour the standard language and the neologisms that may be associated with it. Either there are more traditional speakers using the internet than we are told, or a significant number of new speakers do not conform to the linguistic stereotypes they have been assigned. Either way, categorising Breton speakers according to a binary division and assuming that all of them meet a number of associated criteria would seem to be an oversimplification, failing to acknowledge that there are a number of potential motivations and ideologies that may underpin the Breton revitalisation movement, which may indeed be heightened by the possibilities provided by the internet (see Kelly-Holmes, this volume). Instead of assuming that online settings are populated by a community of stereotypical new speakers, we should recognise the complexity of Breton use in these contexts and support the continued growth of a diverse community of speakers who use Breton for various reasons and in various ways, making use of the opportunities provided by the internet to overcome some of the drawbacks of being a small, geographically diffuse community. The availability of these online contexts can enable speakers to minimise these practical difficulties, but it should not lead researchers to perpetuate oversimplified and outdated stereotypes.

Notes

(1) This chapter uses Breton names in preference over French where appropriate. For the names of dialects and languages, it follows the Breton rule of using the suffix -*ek* where these occur adjectivally, and -*eg* where they are used as nouns or in conjunction with the word *language/dialect*.
(2) The administrative region of Brittany comprises four departments, but a fifth, Loire-Atlantique, is part of the historical region, contributes to financing the Breton language office, and is typically recognised as part of Brittany by Breton speakers.
(3) See https://www.bretagne.bzh/br (accessed January 2023).
(4) See http://indigenoustweets.com (accessed October 2021).
(5) See https://www.facebook.com/groups/334727793245979 (accessed January 2023).
(6) See http://www.ouest-france.fr/high-tech/facebook-un-francais-sur-deux-actif-sur-le-reseau-3653032 (accessed January 2017).
(7) See https://www.facebook.com/photo/?fbid=10208135488737208 (accessed January 2023).
(8) See https://tei-c.org (accessed November 2021).
(9) See https://www.brezhoneg.bzh/163-bureviou.htm (accessed October 2021).
(10) See https://www.brezhoneg.bzh/87-termofis.htm (accessed January 2023).
(11) See https://www.brezhoneg.bzh/91-kerofis.htm (accessed January 2023).
(12) See https://www.brezhoneg.bzh/69-trein.htm (accessed November 2021).
(13) See https://www.brezhoneg.bzh/177-divizou-hag-erbedadennou-ar-chuzul-skiantel.htm (accessed November 2021).
(14) See https://www.brezhoneg.bzh/89-forom-termenadurezh.htm (accessed April 2022).
(15) See https://www.brezhoneg.bzh/55-istor.htm (accessed November 2021).
(16) See https://www.brezhoneg.bzh/54-ar-brezhoneg.htm (accessed November 2021).
(17) See https://www.brezhoneg.bzh/55-istor.htm (accessed November 2021).
(18) See https://www.brezhoneg.bzh/69-trein.htm (accessed October 2021).
(19) See https://www.youtube.com/c/BrezhonegBew/videos (accessed October 2021).
(20) See http://loeizherrieu.fr (accessed January 2023).
(21) See http://loeizherrieu.fr/www/tests/biographie.html (accessed November 2021).
(22) See http://loeizherrieu.fr/www/tests/ressources.html (accessed November 2021).
(23) See the discussion of *néo-bretonnants* in the introduction to this chapter for a list of works that invoke this distinction between new and traditional speakers of Breton.

References

Abalain, H. (2000) *Histoire de la langue bretonne* (2nd edn). Gisserot.
Adkins, M. (2013) Will the real Breton please stand up? Language revitalisation and the problem of authentic language. *International Journal of the Sociology of Language* 223, 55–70.
Androutsopoulos, J. (2016) Theorizing media, mediation and mediatization. In N. Coupland (ed.) *Sociolinguistics: Theoretical Debates* (pp. 282–302). Cambridge University Press.
Belmar, G. and Glass, M. (2019) Virtual communities as breathing spaces for minority languages: Reframing minority language use in social media. *Adeptus* 14. https://doi.org/10.11649/a.1968.

Bermingham, N. (2018) Double new speakers? Language ideologies of immigrant students in Galicia. In C. Smith-Christmas, N.P. Ó Murchadha, M. Hornsby and M. Moriarty (eds) *New Speakers of Minority Languages: Linguistic Ideologies and Practices* (pp. 111–130). Palgrave Macmillan.

Blanchard, N., Calvez, R. and Thomas, M. (2013) Signe et sens en balance: Le breton affiché dans la ville de Brest. *International Journal of the Sociology of Language* 223, 137–152.

Blommaert, J. and Szabla, M. (2017) Does context really collapse in social media interaction? Paper presented at Moving Texts: Mediations and Transculturations (Aveiro, 12–14 July). URL: https://www.academia.edu/33672243/Does_context_really_collapse_in_social_media_interaction.

Broudic, F. (2009) *Parler breton au XXIe siècle : Le nouveau sondage de TMO Régions*. Emgleo Breiz.

Broudic, F. (2013) Langue bretonne: Un siècle de mutations. *International Journal of the Sociology of Language* 223, 7–21.

Cadot, M. (2010) Arrêté préfectoral portant création de l'établissment public de coopération culturelle « Ofis publik ar brezhoneg – Office public de la langue bretonne ».

Davies-Deacon, M. (2020) New speaker language and identity: Perceptions and practices around Breton as a regional language of France. Unpublished PhD thesis, Queen's University Belfast.

German, G. (2007) Language shift, diglossia and dialectal variation in western Brittany: The case of southern Cornouaille. In H.L.C. Tristram (ed.) *The Celtic Languages in Contact: Papers from the Workshop within the Framework of the XIII International Congress of Celtic Studies* (pp. 146–192). Universitätsverlag Potsdam.

Grinevald, C. and Bert, M. (2011) Speakers and communities. In P.K. Austin and J. Sallabank (eds) *The Cambridge Handbook of Endangered Languages* (pp. 45–65). Cambridge University Press.

Hemon, R. (1964) *Dictionnaire breton-français* (3rd edn). Al Liamm.

Hornsby, M. (2015) The "new" and "traditional" speaker dichotomy: Bridging the gap. *International Journal of the Sociology of Language* 231, 107–125.

Hornsby, M. (2021) Breton. In L. Grenoble, P. Lane and U. Røyneland (eds) *Linguistic Minorities in Europe Online*. URL: https://doi.org/10.1515/lme.14813147.

Hornsby, M. and Quentel, G. (2013) Contested varieties and competing authenticities: Neologisms in revitalised Breton. *International Journal of the Sociology of Language* 223, 71–86.

Jones, M.C. (1995) At what price language maintenance? Standardisation in modern Breton. *French Studies* 49 (4), 424–438.

Jones, M.C. (1996) The role of the speaker in language obsolescence: The case of Breton in Plougastel-Daoulas, Brittany. *French Language Studies* 6, 45–73.

Jones, M.C. (1998) Death of a language, birth of an identity: Brittany and the Bretons. *Language Problems and Language Planning* 22 (2), 129–142.

Le Dû, J. and Le Berre, Y. (2013) La langue bretonne dans la société régionale contemporaine. *International Journal of the Sociology of Language* 223, 43–54.

Le Nevez, A. (2013) The social practice of Breton: An epistemological challenge. *International Journal of the Sociology of Language* 223, 87–102.

Lossec, H. (2013) *Ma Doue benniget ! Histoires drôles en brezhoneg et en français*. Ouest-France.

Nance, C., McLeod, W., O'Rourke, B. and Dunmore, S. (2016) Identity, accent aim, and motivation in second language users: New Scottish Gaelic speakers' use of phonetic variation. *Journal of Sociolinguistics* 20 (2), 164–191.

O'Rourke, B. and Pujolar, J. (eds) (2019) *From New Speaker to Speaker: Outcomes, Reflections and Policy Recommendations from COST Action IS1306 on New Speakers in a Multilingual Europe: Opportunities and Challenges*. IAITH: Welsh Centre for Language Planning.

Reershemius, G. (2017) Autochthonous heritage languages and social media: Writing and bilingual practices in Low German on Facebook. *Journal of Multilingual and Multicultural Development* 38 (1), 35–49.

Rottet, K.J. (2014) Neology, competing authenticities, and the lexicography of regional languages: The case of Breton. *Journal of the Dictionary Society of North America* 35, 208–247.

Smith-Christmas, C., Ó Murchadha, N.P., Hornsby, M. and Moriarty, M. (eds) (2018) *New Speakers of Minority Languages: Linguistic Ideologies and Practices*. Palgrave Macmillan.

Timm, L.A. (2001) Transforming Breton: A case study in multiply conflicting language ideologies. *Texas Linguistic Forum* 2, 447–461.

Timm, L.A. (2003) Breton at a crossroads: Looking back, moving forward. *e-Keltoi: Journal of Interdisciplinary Celtic Studies* 2, 25–61.

Vandergriff, I. (2010) Humour and play in CMC. In R. Taiwo (ed.) *Handbook of Research on Discourse Behaviour and Digital Communication: Language Structures and Social Interaction* (pp. 235–251). Information Science Reference.

Part 2
Digital Tools and Practices

5 Language, Education and Community in a Digital Age: A Welsh Digital Resources Case Study

Rhian Hodges and Cynog Prys

Introduction

This chapter attempts to address two of the overarching themes of this volume by exploring which innovative digital teaching tools and methods are emerging in various autochthonous minority language contexts, and how digital communication is taken into account by policymakers. Therefore, the purpose of this chapter is to provide a digital resources case study focusing on two digital teaching and language revitalisation projects within the spheres of education and the community in Wales. The two resources are *A Toolkit for Promoting the Use of the Welsh in the Community* (Hodges & Prys, 2017) and a *Sociology Multimedia Resources Pack* (Prys et al., 2018). Education, community and the digital sphere are three language use domains which are considered important by the Welsh Government as they attempt to double the numbers of Welsh speakers to 1 million by 2050 (Welsh Government, 2017a). This ambitious target represents a concerted effort to revitalise the Welsh language over the last decade with various language planning agents at the forefront of the revitalisation agenda. Both digital language revitalisation projects reported in this chapter reflect the key typologies of language planning which are outlined by as status, corpus, acquisition (Cooper, 1989) and prestige planning (Haarmann, 1990). The projects discussed within this chapter, while limited in scope and budget, contribute to all four typologies, and influence the Welsh Language corpus, afford new opportunities to use Welsh in the field of education, community and the digital sphere, while also impacting the status and prestige of the Welsh language within higher education. This chapter also highlights the importance of digital content in providing key opportunities for language use and language normalisation for minority languages.

Language policy and planning is a complex field of study which often occurs at various levels across society. According to Baldauf (2006), language planning takes place on three societal levels. These represent the macro-, meso- and micro-levels, where language polices are created and implemented. Liddicoat and Baldauf (2008) propose that governments and their agencies represent macro-level language planners where language policies are administered and implemented on a top-down basis. Indeed, macro-level language planning highlights the traditional field of language planning that emphasises government-led planning and policymaking (Ricento, 2003). Meso-level language planning represents the level at which mediation takes place between the macro, structural level of language policy and planning, and the micro-level language use by individual actors (Pennycook, 2010). While the meso-level can at times be hard to define (Hodges & Prys, 2019), this level can be interpreted as agencies who are tasked with implementing government language polices within various contexts, such as health agencies (Prys *et al.*, 2021), community organisations and educational institutions (Musk, 2010). Finally, micro-level language planning acknowledges the important work of social actors on the ground in implementing language planning through language practices and behaviours (Hodges & Prys, 2019).

In this chapter, we draw upon Baldauf's (2006) framework and propose that language planning in Wales occurs within macro-, meso- and micro-language planning levels. We assert that language planners and policymakers need to pay further attention to meso-level language planning as a crucial lynchpin in the language policy and planning process in Wales. Moreover, this will be illustrated by the meso-level projects highlighted within this chapter.

This chapter will draw on two recent examples of digital research projects designed by meso-level actors to implement macro-level language policy and planning strategies on a micro-community level. The meso-level is represented by the authors of this chapter, who are academic lecturers within a university context. The authors worked alongside two other meso-level actors on the projects outlined in this chapter, the Coleg Cymraeg Cenedlaethol, who are a national Welsh language college tasked with promoting the use of Welsh within higher education in Wales, and Mentrau Iaith Cymru, who are an organisation who work on a national level to promote the use of Welsh in the community. We argue that meso-level language planning represents a key research area for language planners to develop their understanding of how language policy is often complexly negotiated and put into practice on a day-to-day level. Furthermore, this chapter discusses how government language strategies focusing on education and digital platforms can be implemented by meso-level agents.

Welsh Language Context

The 2021 Census states that the Welsh Language is spoken by an estimated 538,000 people, 17.8% of the population, this is a decrease of approximately 23,700 speakers since the 2011 Census (Office for National Statistics, 2022). Language use is beyond the remit of the Census, but recent research highlights that 10% of the Welsh population use the language daily (Welsh Government, 2021) which causes concern in terms of the sustainability and vitality of the Welsh language. Indeed, UNESCO has categorised the Welsh language as a 'vulnerable' language (Moseley, 2011). Despite its vulnerable status, the Welsh language has been pioneering in terms of language revitalisation largely due to Welsh-medium immersion education (Hodges, 2012; Thomas & Williams, 2013). Despite a decline in the number of speakers within the 5–15-year age category (from 40.3% in 2011 to 34.3% in the 2021 Census), the 5–15-year-old category continues to represent the highest age group percentage of Welsh speakers in Wales (Welsh Government, 2022a).

Devolution has also played a crucial role in the Welsh language policy context in Wales. The transfer of policymaking from a centralised to a devolved government highlighted a policy paradigm shift of note. Language policy was integrated within mainstream social policy for the first time in Wales (Lewis & Royles, 2018). The Welsh Government is a key player in creating, administering and implementing language policies across Wales. The Welsh Government's current Welsh Language Strategy, Cymraeg 2050: a million Welsh speakers, ambitiously aims to create 1 million Welsh speakers by 2050 (Welsh Government, 2017a). Forecasting data highlights that by 2050 there will be 666,000 Welsh speakers (Welsh Government, 2017b: 5), 21% of the population. This charts a growth of 100,000 speakers since the 2001 Census, but highlights there will be a shortfall of approximately 334,000 speakers by 2050 (Welsh Government, 2017b: 5). Cymraeg 2050 highlights the importance of education, the community and digital domains in reaching this target as the three are seen as strategic priorities and will be prioritised within this chapter.

Welsh in the community

The community is an all-important language use sphere and can be described as a 'language planning crossroads' (Hodges & Prys, 2019: 1) where many language use spheres such as education, the family and the workplace often meet. The sustainability of minority language communities is an important discussion point regarding language use and the normalisation of language behaviours and ideologies (Williams & Morris, 2000).

While Welsh is a minority language in Wales, the linguistic composition of communities differs from region to region. Communities containing higher densities of Welsh speakers are usually found in west Wales, while the eastern half of Wales contains communities with a lower density of Welsh speakers (Office for National Statistics, 2022). The community with the highest percentage of Welsh speakers was found in Gwynedd (86.3%) and the community with the lowest percentage of Welsh speakers was found in Blaenau Gwent (3.8%) (Welsh Government, 2022a). Such localities would require very different community language planning strategies as their linguistic makeups differ greatly. Both the 2011 and 2021 Censuses reported a decrease in the number of speakers in areas of Wales which previously contained high percentages of Welsh speakers (Office for National Statistics, 2012, 2022). As a result, there are concerns regarding the community use of Welsh within communities across Wales and it can be argued that the linguistic map of Wales is changing as the Welsh speaking heartlands of the west of Wales diminish.

In their study of six communities in west Wales on behalf of the Welsh Government, Hodges and Prys found that opportunities to use Welsh were still prevalent within the communities' studied; however, gaps existed in opportunities to use Welsh socially in some of the communities studied (Welsh Government, 2015). Opportunities for younger people and older people were outlined as areas were opportunities to use Welsh were limited. Furthermore, the study also highlighted a lack of opportunity to use Welsh while accessing formal services, while shopping or accessing public services (Welsh Government, 2015). Furthermore, the Covid-19 pandemic has also caused difficulties for community groups who provide activities to the public through the medium of Welsh. Of the groups studied only 20% managed to adapt their activities to operate online during the first UK lockdown in March 2020 (Welsh Government, 2020a). This finding raises further questions about the ability to maintain community language use, especially during a time of social crisis.

Welsh in education

Minority language education is often described as the centrepiece of language revitalisation efforts as it creates new speakers of minority languages often where language transmission within families and language use within communities have been weakened (Hornsby, 2015; O'Rourke, 2018). However, challenges remain for speakers of minority languages to use these languages within a community setting beyond education (Baker, 2011; Hodges, 2021).

Welsh is a compulsory subject within the national curriculum for pupils up to 16 years of age since the Education Reform Act 1988 and features prominently within the new education curriculum for Wales (Welsh Government, 2022b). It is taught either as a first language in Welsh-medium or bilingual schools or as a second language in English-medium schools. Sixteen percent of pupils in Wales attend Welsh-medium schools, with a further 10% attending schools that are bilingual, dual-medium or English-medium schools with significant Welsh provision (StatsWales, n.d.a). Despite this measure of success, the education system also faces criticisms relating to the lack of Welsh language use by Welsh speakers within the community (Hodges & Prys, 2019). Factors relating to limited confidence, fluency, language ownership and Welsh-speaking identity all impact upon the daily language use beyond the education system (Hodges & Prys, 2019, Price & Tamburelli 2019). Moreover, the education system has been criticised for its lack of linguistic progression between educational sectors. Decreases in the numbers of Welsh speakers are seen between the primary sector (3–11 years of age), secondary sector (11–18 years old), further education sector (16–18 years of age) and higher education (18+ years of age) (Jones, 2019; Welsh Government 2017a). This pattern was also evident in the 2021 Census, were the Welsh language skill of 5–15-year olds was reported to be 34.3%. This decreased to 27.5% among 16–19-year olds. In turn, these decreases could impact the community sustainability of Welsh. However, the 2021 Census reported some increases within the percentages of 16–19-year olds and 20–44-year olds who spoke Welsh compared to the 2011 Census. This could suggest modest progress was made in retaining Welsh speakers post compulsory education.

Since its inception in 2011, the Coleg Cymraeg Cenedlaethol, a national virtual learning college, invests in the creation of Welsh-medium subject specific resources to normalise the study of Welsh-medium education (Ifan & Hodges, 2017). Despite there being approximately 1000 courses and 150 student scholarships available to students to study through the medium of Welsh (Coleg Cymraeg Cenedlaethol, 2021) the numbers of students studying subjects through the medium of Welsh within higher education are comparatively low. Higher education seems to be a constant battleground for competing language choices (Davies & Trystan, 2012). According to the Welsh Government (StatsWales, n.d.bc) there are approximately 4.3% (5,195 students of the total student population of 136,370) of all students across higher education institutes in Wales studying through the medium of Welsh. These statistics include students studying varying amounts of their curriculum through the medium of Welsh, from one module to their entire degree programme. Many factors could be linked to the low student numbers such as linguistic confidence, course preferences, studying beyond Wales and the availability of Welsh-medium resources (Jones, 2010). However, there is little to no research specifically addressing the topic of Welsh language resources in Wales which needs to be addressed to better understand the language planning challenges associated with various educational sectors. This chapter presents innovative learning resources developed for the study of Welsh.

Welsh in the digital age

Language use within digital domains offers an important area for minority languages to remain relevant within contemporary society (Crystal, 2014). However, concerns regarding language use on digital domains increasingly appear within the field of language policy and planning. Soria (2015) suggests that the lack of language use within the digital domain can pose a risk to linguistic communities as speakers move to use other languages within this key domain. This can lead to negative consequences for language communities, and even what Kornai (2013) calls digital language death. The growth of digital communication contains challenges for speakers of minority languages, such as Welsh (Evas, 2014).

Several studies into the use of Welsh online suggest that, while Welsh faces a challenging digital landscape, the language is used within various digital contexts. The use of Welsh on social networking sites suggests that Welsh is used on Facebook in a variety of contexts (Cunliffe *et al.*, 2013). Nonetheless, issues including fluency, confidence and linguistic composition of speakers' communities were raised as key factors for language use online. For those who live in communities with a lower percentage of Welsh speakers, Facebook offers a valuable opportunity for speakers of Welsh to access Welsh speaking networks and practice their Welsh outside of an educational setting. Research by Jones *et al.* (2013) into the use of Welsh on Twitter also found that Welsh is used on the platform and facilitates communication between members of Welsh speaking communities. While Welsh is used on social media platforms, McAlister *et al.* (2013) found that the use of Welsh on traditional websites was lower. Nonetheless, a more recent study by Pritchard (2021) reported that speakers made use of Welsh within a wide variety of digital contexts, including on digital applications. One key area regarding the use of the Welsh language online was Welsh language educational resources (Pritchard, 2021) with 61.5% of Welsh speaking respondents noting that they utilise Welsh language educational applications, such as digital dictionaries and educational resources for children. This significant finding not only points to the availability of Welsh language digital provision, but also suggests that the Welsh speaking public make use of these digital resources. These three domains feature prominently in the Welsh Government's language strategy, Cymraeg 2050 (Welsh Government, 2017a) which is discussed in the next section.

Cymraeg 2050

The Welsh Government's current Welsh Language strategy, Cymraeg 2050: a million Welsh speakers, aims to create 1 million Welsh speakers by 2050. To achieve this, the strategy is based on three strategic themes: increasing the number of Welsh speakers, increasing the use of Welsh, and creating favourable conditions (infrastructure and context) for Welsh to flourish (Welsh Government, 2017a). Within the strategy, the sustainability of Welsh-speaking communities and increasing the use of Welsh are clear strategic priorities. The Welsh Government have set a target within this strategy of increasing the percentage of the population using the Welsh language daily to 20% by 2050 (Welsh Government, 2017a: 48). This is an ambitious target as the most recent data suggests that only 10% of the population in Wales use the language daily (Welsh Government, 2021). Nonetheless, many challenges exist in terms of encouraging the social use of Welsh, such as the confidence and fluency of speakers and the opportunities available to use the language (Hodges & Prys, 2019).

The Welsh Government (2017a) also note that it is vitally important to invest in the development of Welsh language digital technology to enable speakers of Welsh to use their language in as many contexts as possible. Particular attention is paid to the connection between Welsh language resources within the field of education, the workplace and within informal social settings. As a result, a key aim within the strategy is to 'ensure that the Welsh language is at the heart of innovation in digital technology to enable the use of Welsh in all digital contexts' (Welsh Government, 2017a: 71). To achieve these ends, the Welsh Government have invested £651,000 in language technology between 2018 and 2021, including Welsh language speech-to-text facilities, development of a virtual assistant, and working with global companies like Microsoft to produce Welsh language interfaces for their software packages (Welsh Government, 2020b).

The role of education features prominently within the strategy, especially the need to develop opportunities for young people to use Welsh, and the importance of supporting new speakers of Welsh to use the language within a variety of contexts. The strategy also highlights the need to create a linguistic progression between statutory education and post-compulsory education to create speakers with a command of the Welsh language. According to Cymraeg 2050, 'One of the main objectives of this strategy therefore is to ensure that fewer young people lose their Welsh language skills when moving from statutory education to further/higher education, and that more reach their mid-twenties with a command of the language' (Welsh Government, 2017a: 31). A crucial component of Welsh medium education is providing access to Welsh-medium teaching resources for educators and students alike. Thus, Cymraeg 2050 emphasises the need to 'develop a growing workforce able to teach Welsh and teach through the medium of Welsh' (Welsh Government, 2017a: 31).

Two Digital Language Revitalisation Projects

It is against this language planning and policy backdrop, that the authors undertook two distinct digital language revitalisation projects to assist in the promotion and normalisation of Welsh within the key language use domains outlined in the Cymraeg 2050 strategy, the community, education and the digital domain. These projects focus on the community use of Welsh (A Toolkit for Promoting the Welsh Language in the Community), and use of Welsh within the educational sphere (Sociology Multimedia Resource Pack). Both projects are digital resources and react to the priority areas outlined by the Welsh Government. Moreover, both projects can be interpreted as meso-level agents (university lecturers), working with other stakeholders (e.g. funders), to enact, on a practical level, the macro-level language planning agenda outlined by the Welsh. Meso-level language planning strategies are an important piece of the language planning jigsaw that interact between the macro- and the micro-levels and often contribute to status and prestige planning. Moreover, the importance of finding practical, everyday solutions to language planning challenges is of increasing importance within the field. According to Darquennes (2013: 1), 'the practical side of language policy and planning' sits alongside 'the history of the field, language practices in different domains of society and ideas and beliefs about language' and is an integral part of achieving holistic language policy and planning goals. Furthermore, these practical aspects are often overlooked within language planning as an academic field and are pertinent to be discussed as part of this chapter. Both language revitalisation projects included within this chapter emphasise the importance of practical language planning resources when discussing language use, language behaviour patterns and attempting to reverse language shift. While both language revitalisation projects are limited in size and budget, we argue that they represent innovative examples of meso-level language planning strategies by agents implementing macro-level language planning agendas on a micro-community level. It could also be claimed that these projects contribute, in part, and side by side with other initiatives, to key language planning typologies such as status and prestige planning along with corpus and acquisition planning.

A Toolkit for Promoting the Welsh Language in the Community (2017)

Hodges and Prys were commissioned by the Welsh Government to undertake an evaluation of the previous Welsh Language Strategy,

A Living language: a language for Living (Welsh Government, 2012). This research, Welsh Language Use in the Community: Research Study (Welsh Government, 2015) emphasised the complexity of assessing the community vitality of the Welsh language in various communities across Wales. The study highlighted various challenges facing the Welsh language within the sample communities in Wales. These challenges included examples of language shift from Welsh to English in some communities, gaps in provision for activities for older children, lack of social usage of Welsh outside the classroom, and barriers facing new speakers of Welsh within their communities (Welsh Government, 2015).

Following this commission, Hodges and Prys developed a digital resource to share good practice found within the communities studied.[1] Hodges and Prys received funding from the Bangor University ESRC Impact Acceleration Account to explore key research themes further and offer some practical, micro-level language planning practices and solutions for those interested in promoting the use of Welsh in the community. A Toolkit for Promoting the Welsh Language in the Community (Hodges & Prys, 2017) was developed and published, in partnership between Bangor University and Mentrau Iaith Cymru, a national organisation that facilitates the community use of Welsh across Wales. Mentrau Iaith Cymru, who are funded by the Welsh Government, work with a network of 22 local Welsh language initiatives across Wales by supporting local language planning agents with marketing and communication, training and lobbying. The purpose of the toolkit is to facilitate knowledge transfer between language planners at Bangor University and grassroots, micro-level, organisations involved in language revitalisation in the community.

The digital toolkit is hosted by Mentrau Iaith Cymru on their national website and is accessible to all community groups and individuals involved in communities and language promotion.[2] It is possible to access the toolkit to learn of good practice and gain some inspiration in terms of the types of Welsh medium community activities held across Wales. For example, a new parent could access the toolkit to discover the types of Welsh-medium activities available to them and their children. Similarly, a new business could utilise the toolkit to find ways to increase the use of Welsh within their business or develop new business networks.

A key aim of the toolkit is to bridge the gap that often exists between academic research and practical activities taking place within individual communities (Hodges & Prys, 2017). The toolkit offers many examples of community activities and resources through the medium of Welsh, that could be adapted and adopted by other communities across Wales and within an international context. It can be utilised by individuals, community level organisations and national governments to facilitate a more holistic approach to language planning which aims to include the macro-, meso- and micro-levels. Indeed, the examples provided within the toolkit were based on the following themes: Parents with Young Children, Young People, Leisure, Welsh Language Learners, Shops and Businesses, Public Services and Technology, Resources and Equipment. These themes include key aspects involving the community, education, and digital domains respectively.

Within this chapter, we will include three toolkit examples that focus on the relationship between technology and the community/education.

Toolkit theme: Young people

The use of Welsh among young people was a key theme from the original research conducted by Hodges and Prys on behalf of the Welsh Government (Welsh Government, 2015). The study found evidence that gaps appeared in the provision of Welsh and bilingual community activities for older young people within the communities studied. To address this research finding, the toolkit included an innovative example of a grassroots activity that provides a key digital language use domain for older young people. Our first example from the toolkit is a YouTube Video Games Club, called 'Yn Chwarae' (Playing') by Menter Caerffili which allows young people to play and stream video games with each other through the medium of Welsh. It provides much needed social opportunities to use Welsh within a non-formal context beyond the education system. Included within the toolkit is the following comment from two young people who regularly use this activity:

> The 'Yn chwarae' YouTube channel by Menter Caerffili...is important because we need to advertise the language and video games are a good way of reaching a lot of young people like us in our communities. It is important to find an activity that's relevant to us that happens in Welsh. (Hodges & Prys, 2017: 100).

Caerffili is a locality with a lower percentage of Welsh speakers compared to the national average where daily opportunities to use Welsh within the community can be limited outside of the educational domain (Hodges, 2021). Digital platforms have developed to become important spaces for speakers of Welsh to socialise and share Welsh language content online (Cunliffe et al., 2013) and for young people to use Welsh in a normalised context (Cunliffe & ap Dyfrig, 2013). This takes on extra significance as digital platforms such as YouTube represent an important part of current youth culture.

Toolkit theme: Technology, resources and equipment

Cymraeg 2050 outlines the importance of linguistic infrastructure, including corpora, dictionaries, and terminology to the revitalisation of Welsh (Welsh Government, 2017a). The toolkit created by Hodges and Prys (2017) also refers to the role that language technologies and digital recourses play in enabling the use of Welsh on a community level. The role of social media for promoting Welsh language and bilingual events was seen as an important way of reaching the Welsh speaking community (Welsh Government, 2015). The use of electronic dictionaries and spellcheckers were also seen as useful tools for enabling individuals to use their written Welsh with confidence on social media accounts (Hodges & Prys, 2017).

The following example was given by a community member within the toolkit.

> The app has been very useful in giving me more confidence to write in Welsh! I find that I am writing so much more in Welsh these days, in everyday situations (such as on Facebook and Twitter) as well as in more formal situations, such as writing job applications. I also use the Cysgliad package which corrects my written work like a Welsh spellchecker. (Hodges & Prys, 2017: 147)

This example refers to linguistic infrastructure projects which are funded by the Welsh Government and the Coleg Cymraeg Cenedlaethol, which have been developed by the Language Technology Unit at Bangor University. The Ap Geiriaduron (Dictionary App) is a free app which includes the Cysgair Welsh language electronic dictionary. This can be seen as an example of the Welsh Government's investment in digital linguistic infrastructure being used by the public and enabling the use of written Welsh in the online domain. The example is also noteworthy as it provides evidence of how digital linguistic infrastructure projects, funded by the Welsh Government, impact upon the language practices of individuals in both formal and informal language use domains.

The next example from the toolkit focuses on the role of social media in raising awareness of the Welsh language events and services, on digital platforms is the Welsh language Twitter hour; Yr Awr Gymraeg (The Welsh Hour) on Twitter. Yr Awr Gymraeg is the first Twitter hour in Welsh. It is held between 8 and 9pm every Wednesday evening and is an opportunity to promote Welsh-medium events, networks, businesses and services. Through the hashtag #yagym, Yr Awr Gymraeg, promotion and marketing messages reach around 6 million timelines and over 1 million accounts every week and is a familiar brand for Twitter users in Welsh. According to Huw Marshall, Founder of Yr Awr Gymraeg:

> The influence of #yagym is effective on several levels. Our messages are shared internationally, throughout Wales and on a community level. Indeed, the community influence is especially effective, not only for promoting the Welsh language but also in helping to develop Welsh networks at a very local level. (Hodges & Prys, 2017: 148)

This example emphasises the importance of social media in terms of marketing Welsh language projects, businesses and services on a local, national and international level. It could be argued that this example also demonstrates the importance of an online community that contributes to community language activities and networks (online communities have been particularly relevant during the Covid-19 global pandemic). This example was included in the toolkit as it has been an innovative and popular method for businesses and organisations to increase their following and raise awareness of the services and goods they offer through the medium of Welsh. The Welsh language Twitter hour also plays a significant role in disseminating information about upcoming Welsh language community events, for Welsh speakers and learners of Welsh. As a result, it could be suggested that it leads to the development of language skills of individuals, and the maintenance and creation of Welsh language social networks.

While the three examples mentioned within this chapter represent interventions and programs which are limited in size and scope, we suggest that the toolkit represents an innovative example of how meso-level actors can work together with micro-level community actors to create digital resources to assist in the revitalisation of a minority language. Since its publication, the digital toolkit has been used by project partners and community language planning agents, Mentrau Iaith Cymru, as a resource to help community actors develop their own initiatives to promote Welsh within individual communities across Wales.

Pecyn Adnoddau Amlgyfrwng Cymdeithaseg (Sociology Multimedia Resource Pack)

The second project included within this chapter is a project to create Welsh language digital resources for secondary school students. In this case, the project developed a digital resource pack for 16- to 18-year olds who study sociology through the medium of Welsh. The Welsh Government (Welsh Government, 2017a) outline the importance of post-compulsory education in reaching the target of creating a million Welsh speakers by 2050 and in doing so prioritise this age group within their language strategies. Central to this aim is ensuring linguistic pathways that help young people continue to use Welsh, and develop Welsh language skills, between statutory education and the workplace. Thus, this project represents an example of meso-level actors implementing macro-level language policy and educational policies in Wales. The Welsh Government represent the macro-level language policy and planning, while the authors of the paper (university lecturers) and the Coleg Cymraeg Cenedlaethol (Welsh National College) represent the meso-level who are tasked with providing additional content and resources to enable social actors to use Welsh within the educational sphere.

The Coleg Cymraeg Cenedlaethol, funded by the Welsh Government, are tasked with the key role of developing Welsh medium post-compulsory education within the sector. Their Academic Plan (Coleg Cymraeg Cenedlaethol, 2017: 17) outlines the need to create opportunities for speakers of Welsh to study in a wide variety of subject areas in universities across Wales. For the next decade, the Coleg Cymraeg Cenedlaethol (2017: 13) outline the importance of developing a Welsh medium study infrastructure and call for the development of online digital teaching technologies, flexible learning opportunities, expanding accessibility to Welsh language provision and offering new learning pathways for studying through the medium of Welsh. Furthermore, they emphasise the dramatic developments of educational technologies during recent years and the need for Welsh medium education to be at the forefront of these developments.

As a result, the authors were commissioned by the Coleg Cymraeg Cenedlaethol to produce a series of Welsh language resources for the teaching of sociology through the medium of Welsh. The aim of the resource pack was to create attractive digital multimedia teaching tools that are freely available to teachers and students who teach and study sociology though the medium of Welsh.[3] The project was conceived, and funded, against the context of the low numbers of secondary school pupils (11–18 years) studying sociology through the medium of Welsh, and the impact this had on the language choices and pathways of pupils as they moved into post-compulsory education. The project also worked to develop Welsh language terminology within the field of sociology.

The resource packs were designed to fulfil the specification for the A Level Sociology examination which school pupils can undertake as an elective subject during their final two years of schooling. Furthermore, the resource packs were also designed to offer a Welsh language introduction to the subject area for students starting social science degree programs at universities in Wales. This also helped develop a clear pathway for students who study sociology within secondary school to maintain their Welsh language skills and continue to study sociology through the medium of Welsh at university level. Thus, the project was designed to reach as wide an audience as possible, and by doing so, maximising the reach and impact of the initiative. The completed resources have been placed on the Coleg Cymraeg Resource Portal and are available free of charge to the public across Wales and beyond.[4]

The resource packs themselves were produced in the form of e-books and contained two key features. Firstly, the project commissioned a professional cartoonist to produce attractive, bespoke artwork for the eBook. The use of cartoons was adopted as a pedological tool to help explain key, and often complex, sociological concepts in a visual and entertaining way. The use of humour was also an important feature and was used as a way of attracting an audience and helping students remember key points. The use of cartoons within a minority language context was also an attempt to use a medium which could be defined as 'cool'.

The use of cartoons to transmit ideas is used by educators in various disciplines (Mediouni *et al.*, 2019). Their study found that using educational cartoons was favourably received as a teaching tool by faculty and students alike (Mediouni *et al.*, 2019). According to Schacht and Stewart (1990) cartoons, and the use of humour, is an effective method to lessen anxiety and improve the learning environment. Within the field of sociology, the use of cartoons as a pedological teaching tool is well established. Hall and Lucal (1999) note that sociology instructors do not need to follow conventional teaching approaches and that it is possible to use visual art in the form of comic books as innovative techniques to teach the subject in the classroom.

Example 1: Focus group interviews

Figure 5.1 appeared in the first e-book which focuses on research methods. A chapter within the e-book introduces the use of focus group interviews as a method of collecting data from a group of

Figure 5.1 'To start, how about we go around the circle and share our name and some dark secret from our past'
Source: image copyright, Huw Aaron.

participants. The strengths and weakness of this methodology are discussed, alongside the ethical dilemmas which are raised by collecting data via this method. One key point for students to understand while learning about the usage of focus groups is that the group nature of data collection impacts the privacy of participants. As a result, care must be taken if selecting this data collection method as focus group participants may not wish to share any private opinions or experiences with the group. The above example uses both a visual representation of a focus group, and the use of humour, to make this crucial point.

Example 2: Imbedded videos and YouTube channel

The second key element of the resource pack included the use of embedded videos as additional digital resources to help explain key sections of the A Level Sociology curriculum. Using the cartoon's images produced within the e-books, short video clips were recorded by the authors and embedded (see Figure 5.2). These video clips offered an added multimedia dimension to the project and enabled students and school pupils to use the resource as revision aids outside of the formal classroom setting. Furthermore, these video clips were placed on a YouTube channel, and social media accounts associated with the project, to increase the amount and visibility of sociology resources on these popular platforms. This content also acted as a means of advertising the e-book to the public, as links and information regarding the resources were included on these key digital platforms.

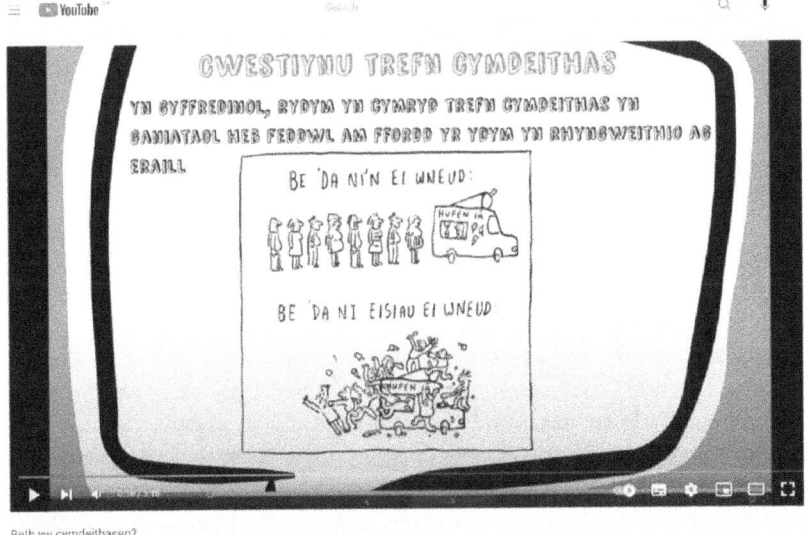

Figure 5.2 What is sociology? Questioning social order

Terminology standardisation

One further element that was developed during this project was the standardisation of Welsh language terminology within the field of sociology and other related disciplines. The standardisation of terminology is a key element of corpus planning (Cooper, 1989) and media can play an important role in the dissemination and visibility of new terminology in the digital sphere (Honeycutt & Cunliffe, 2010, and see the introduction chapter for a further introduction). While some, albeit limited, Welsh language sociology materials were available, much of the terminology had been developed in an ad hoc manner, over several decades. As a result, there was a lack of clarity regarding the correct Welsh terms for many sociological concepts, even though sociology is taught through the medium of Welsh within the national educational sector. This led to inconsistency in the terminology used in current Welsh language resources. As a result, a key component of this project was the creation of new terminology for sociological concepts, and to standardise terminology for existing terms.

The authors worked with a team of professional terminologists from Canolfan Bedwyr (Bangor University) to develop this element of the project. The team of terminologists are funded by various Welsh Government projects and work to develop Welsh language terminology in various academic subject areas, at all levels of the education sector (Prifysgol Bangor University, n.d). Professional terminologists are often linguists who research, define and standardise new terminology. They make use of digital corpora and databases including current terms used within various disciplines. Interestingly, professional terminologists are not necessarily subject specialists, therefore, the authors worked with subject specialists from other institutions, including schoolteachers who teach sociology at A Level in Welsh, and lecturers who teach sociology through the medium of Welsh at undergraduate level. The authors also consulted with practitioners who work within key community groups to advise on appropriate terminology for use with their communities. Consulting with subject specialists and practitioners, along with terminology specialists, was invaluable in developing new terminology or standardising current terminology for sociology through the medium of Welsh. Examples of the new sociology terminology developed by the authors are terms such as, 'tan ddosbarth' (underclass) when discussing social class and socioeconomic backgrounds. Interestingly, the term 'is-ddosbarth' (lower class) had been informally used by schoolteachers in Wales for a significant period. However, this term was deemed to be an incorrect translation of the concept as the underclass is defined as a class that is situated below the working class. Therefore, the Welsh language term for underclass was standardised as a part of the project as the 'tan ddosbarth'.

Figure 5.3 Samplu Caseg Eira (snowball sampling)
Source: image copyright, Huw Aaron.

The Welsh language term for snowball sampling (see Figure 5.3) was also standardised within the research methods e-book. The concept of snowball sampling represents a method of recruiting participants for a study by growing your sample size by recruiting individuals through the social network of previous participants. Examples were found in previous Welsh language literature of the use of 'samplo pelen eira', which is a literal translation of snowball sampling. However, the standardised Welsh language term for a snowball that is thrown and a snowball that is grown by rolling differ. Within the field of sociology, a snowball sample represents the growing of a population of participants for a study, the term 'caseg eira' (snow horse) was selected and standardised within sociological terminology. Furthermore, the concept was illustrated by a cartoon combining the literal and sociological meaning of snowball sampling.

All new terms were included into the national Terminology Portal, Porth Termau Cenedlaethol Cymru.[5] Furthermore, the terminology developed during the project has also been used within other pioneering projects funded by the Coleg Cymraeg Cenedlaethol such as the Deunyddiadau Dysgu Digidol Project (Digital Teaching Resources Project). This project provides innovative Welsh-medium digital learning resources for university students on subjects including contemporary Welsh society and sociological theory. Terminology developed during the project also plays an integral part in the Esboniadur (Glossary) project which was also funded by the Coleg Cymraeg Cenedlaethol and provides definitions and annotated biographies on key sociology and social policy concepts. The resources are also utilised by students and educators within different disciplines. For example, the Research Methods e-book is used within the fields of education, history, music, geography and psychology, highlighting its multidisciplinary value.

While the above project features innovative and useful teaching tools for the teaching of sociology through the medium of Welsh, and in doing so, the promotion of Welsh within the education sector, their reach is limited to these domains. Nonetheless, we argue that this project represents a practical example of a digital project which enables the use of Welsh by individual social actors within the educational sector (e.g. students and teachers). This aligns with the Welsh Government's aim of developing pathways for the use of Welsh within schools and universities in Wales, as outlined by their current Welsh language strategy (Welsh Government, 2017a). Moreover, the project illustrates a successful example of different levels of language planning actors (the macro, meso and micro) interacting to develop new resources to help achieve language planning objectives outlined by the Welsh Government, implemented by meso-level actors.

Discussion

The Welsh Government represent macro-level language planning agents in Wales and are involved in what Cooper (1989) defines as status, corpus and acquisition planning. The projects featured within this chapter also deal with the four typologies of language planning in an attempt to contribute on a practical level to the revitalisation of Welsh. This could also reflect what Darquennes (2013: 1) refers to as a 'practical side of language policy and planning' as both projects are designed to positively impact language use in the respective domains. We propose that both projects contribute, in part, to the status and prestige of the Welsh language by promoting the use of Welsh within key domains, such as the community, education and digital platforms. This chapter represents two examples of meso-level language planning interventions that focus on the interplay between key language planning agents.

It could be argued that there is need for a greater understanding of the role played by meso-level language planners in implementing macro-level language policy, as they are often tasked with creating day-to-day opportunities for social actors to use their language(s) within key language use domains.

This chapter has focused on two examples of meso-level digital interventions within the Welsh language context, where there has been a concerted effort to revitalise Welsh within the community and through educational policies by macro-level policymakers. We argue that the toolkit contributes to normalising Welsh language activities by providing community actors with good practice which can be emulated within other communities across Wales and beyond. The community language planning toolkit offers practical examples for community language planners and social actors to incorporate Welsh medium activities into their daily lives. Since its publication, the toolkit has been utilised by Mentrau Iaith Cymru (a national organisation that supports a network of 22 local Welsh language initiatives across Wales and employs over 300 staff) (Mentrau Iaith, n.d) as part of their staff training programme. Discussions are also underway about providing post-graduate level language planning training to Mentrau Iaith staff following this partnership. As the toolkit represents good practice as noted by community members and key stakeholders themselves, it is hoped that it will inspire micro-level social actors to think of innovative ways to revitalise Welsh in their communities. While the original focus of the toolkit was communities in Wales, since its publication, the authors have received inquiries from Corsica, Germany, Ireland and the USA which could highlight the potential future collaboration within this field. While the impact of the toolkit is difficult to measure, the use of this resource by a variety of organisations suggests the usefulness of resources that share good practice and empower micro-level social actors who are involved in the language planning process.

The Sociology Multimedia Resources Pack represents another example of an innovative digital teaching tool designed to encourage the use of Welsh within education and thus contributing to the broader revitalisation context of minortised languages. It is aimed at enabling teachers of Sociology to teach through the medium of Welsh by providing quality digital Welsh language resources. The resources are also aimed at learners within the education system to enable Welsh speakers to study the sociology curriculum through the medium of Welsh. Digital teaching and learning platforms have been particularly important during the Covid-19 global pandemic and the resources pack has been a timely contribution. The resources have been viewed or downloaded 7000 times (at time of publication) on the Coleg Cymraeg Cenedlaethol website where they are located (Coleg Cymraeg Cenedlaethol, n.d.). Furthermore, in 2023 the resource pack was awarded the prestigious national award for Outstanding Welsh Medium Resource, which highlights its contribution to the field. This highlights the resource pack's contribution to the field of digital teaching and learning of Sociology through the medium of Welsh. The resources also aim to remove barriers that might impede the linguistic journeys of learners (such as lack of Welsh medium sociology resources) as they move from secondary school to higher education. The Sociology Multimedia Resources Pack also contributes to corpus and acquisition planning through the development of Welsh language educational materials and Welsh language terminology. Following their publication, these digital resources are used by students and teachers across Wales, and contribute, in part, to the normalisation of the use of Welsh within the educational sector. The use of these resources, by pupils and educators, demonstrate the impact of the project in developing the digital ecosystem of Welsh language provision within the educational sector.

The digital resources showcased within this chapter provide examples of creating innovative, digital teaching and revitalisation projects through the medium of Welsh. Indeed, both projects are particularly noteworthy as they contribute to the digital vitality of the Welsh language within the community and education. They reflect what Crystal (2014) states is the importance of the digital sphere for minority languages so that they remain relevant to contemporary society. Both projects attempt to contribute to the Welsh Government's ambitious target of achieving 1 million Welsh speakers by 2050 by normalising the use of Welsh in the community, education, and digital domains. Furthermore, these projects could also be useful language revitalisation tools for other minority languages within an international context. For example, there could be scope to create a European minority languages toolkit that brings together key activities, resources and projects from a number of minority languages facing similar and different challenges.

The language revitalisation projects discussed within this chapter highlight the role of meso-level actors, in this case university lecturers and their project partners, as meso-level agents in the language planning process. It can be argued that these projects react to government language policy strategies and attempt to implement these strategies by bridging the macro-, meso- and micro-level of language planning. The authors of this chapter bridge all three language planning levels in their work as meso-level language planning agents who implement macro-policy on a practical micro-level. Furthermore, it could be noted that the authors were part of a triumvirate of meso-level organisations co-working and co-producing digital resources that could contribute to language revitalisation and reversing language shift. Indeed, Bangor University, Mentrau Iaith Cymru and the Coleg Cymraeg Cenedlaethol are organisations that receive funding from the Welsh Government but also work closely with individual communities or organisations to implement macro-level plans for social actors on a micro-community level. Creating the toolkit and resources pack afforded key opportunities to implement Welsh Government Welsh language strategies while reimagining them for particular social actors in communities with different linguistic compositions. While the projects reported upon within this chapter are limited in scope, they can be interpreted as an attempt by meso-level agents, the authors and their partners, to implement and interpret the macro-level policies, such as those published by the Welsh Government (Welsh Government, 2017a).

Conclusions

This chapter attempts to address two of the overarching themes of this volume by exploring which innovative digital teaching tools and methods are emerging in various autochthonous minority language contexts, and how is digital communication taken into account by policymakers. Digital resources such as those discussed within this chapter can contribute to the revitalisation process of minority languages. They play a role in both teaching minority languages and normalising their use within the educational sector and within the community at large. The resources discussed within this chapter contain examples of good practice that can be adopted by autochthonous minority languages beyond Wales. Indeed, the resources pack is a useful example of how digital technologies influence the learning and teaching of minority languages by producing contemporary and relevant resources that fit the current digital needs of its learners. Additionally, the toolkit could be a useful template for autochthonous minority languages to follow as they aim to contribute to the vitality of their languages both within a geographical and online capacity. Both resources are useful starting points from which to begin further discussions about the importance of investing in digital teaching methods and digital community resources so autochthonous minority languages are included within digital domains, side-by-side with the more dominant languages.

While the impact of these resources is difficult to measure, we argue there is a need to create more resources to normalise digital language use within the field of autochthonous minority languages, and the teaching of various subjects through the medium of such languages. Digital teaching technologies have shaped the learning experiences of young people during recent times and so it is crucial that these experiences are strengthened by resources in minority languages. Similarly, as many community activities are held in an online capacity and online communities become more prominent, it is all important that digital resources written in a minority language exist to raise awareness of such activities.

Looking to the future, we suggest that there should be a more prominent emphasis on the partnership between meso- and macro-level language planning agents in the co-production of digital teaching and community resources. Indeed, national governments and those tasked with implementing language policies on a practical level should work in partnership to embrace the digital technologies needed by autochthonous minority languages and their speakers moving forward.

Notes

(1) https://www.mentrauiaith.cymru/wp-content/uploads/2017/08/pecyncymorth_terfynol-1.pdf.
(2) Y Mentrau Iaith | Cryfhau'r Gymraeg yn y Gymuned.
(3) Both authors teach sociology through the medium of Welsh at undergraduate and postgraduate level.
(4) https://www.porth.ac.uk/cy/collection/paac-pecyn-adnoddau-amlgyfrwng-cymdeithaseg.
(5) http://termau.cymru/.

References

Baker, C. (2011) *Foundations of Bilingual Education and Bilingualism* (5th edn). Multilingual Matters.

Baldauf, R.B. (2006) Rearticulating the case for micro language planning in a language ecology context. *Current Issues in Language Planning* 7 (2–3), 147–170.

Coleg Cymraeg Cenedlaethol (2017) *Coleg Cymraeg Cenedlaethol Academic Plan*. Coleg Cymraeg Cenedlaethol. See https://www.colegcymraeg.ac.uk/en/media/main/2015colegcymraeg/dogfennau/TheColegCymraegCenedlaethol-AcademicPlan.pdf (accessed December 2021).

Coleg Cymraeg Cenedlaethol (n.d.) PAAC Pecyn Adnoddau Amlgyfrwng Cymraeg (Sociology Multimedia Resources Pack). See https://www.porth.ac.uk/cy/collection/paac-pecyn-adnoddau-amlgyfrwng-cymdeithaseg (accessed November 2023).

Coleg Cymraeg Cenedlaethol (2021) *Setting The Pathways of Success: The Coleg Cymraeg Cenedlaethol's Strategic Plan 2020/2021 to 2024/2025*. The Coleg Cymraeg Cenedlaethol.

Cooper, R.L. (1989) *Language Planning and Social Change*. Cambridge University Press.

Crystal, D. (2014) *Language Death*. Cambridge University Press.

Cunliffe, D. and ap Dyfrig, Rh. (2013) The Welsh language on YouTube: Initial observations. In E.H Gruffydd Jones and E Uribe-Jongbloed (eds) *Social Media and Minority Languages* (pp. 130–145). Multilingual Matters.

Cunliffe, D, Morris, D. and Prys, C. (2013) Young bilinguals' language behaviour in social networking sites: The use of Welsh on Facebook. *Journal of Computer-Mediated Communication* 18 (3), 339–361.

Davies, A.J and Trystan, D. (2012) 'Build it and they shall come?' An evaluation of qualitative evidence relating to student choice and Welsh-medium higher education. *International Journal of Bilingual Education and Bilingualism* 15 (2), 147–164.

Darquennes, J. (2013) Current issues in LPP research and their impact on society. *AILA Review* 26, 11–23.

Evas, J. (2014) The Welsh Llanguage in the digital age. META-NET. See https://orca.cardiff.ac.uk/48988/1/10006110_4950.pdf (accessed January 2023).

Ifan, G. and Hodges, R. (2017) Creative collaboration in higher education: A *Coleg Cymraeg Cenedlaethol* case study. In D.M. Palfreyman and C. van der Walt (eds) *Academic Biliteracies: Multilingual Repertoires in Higher Education* (pp. 142–159). Multilingual Matters.

Hall, K.J. and Lucal, B. (1999) Tapping into parallel universes: Using superhero comic books in sociology courses. *Teaching Sociology* 27 (1), 60–66.

Haarmann, H. (1990) Language planning in the light of a general theory of language: A methodological framework. *International Journal of the Sociology of Language* 95, 109–129.

Hodges, R. (2012) Welsh-medium education and parental incentives–the case of the Rhymni Valley, Caerffili. *International Journal of Bilingualism and Bilingual Education* 15 (3), 355–373.

Hodges, R. (2021) Defiance within the decline? Revisiting new Welsh speakers' language journeys, *Journal of Multilingual and Multicultural Development* 1–17.

Hodges, R and Prys, C. (2017) Pecyn Cymorth Hybu'r Gymraeg yn y Gymuned/ A Toolkit Promoting the Welsh Language in the Community Prifysgol Bangor a Mentrau Iaith Cymru. See https://www.mentrauiaith.cymru/wp-content/uploads/2017/08/pecyncymorth_terfynol-1.pdf (accessed June 2022).

Hodges, R. and Prys, C. (2019) The community as a language planning crossroads: Macro and micro language planning in communities in Wales. *Current Issues in Language Planning* 20 (3), 207–225.

Honeycutt, C. and Cunliffe, D. (2010) The use of the Welsh language on Facebook: An initial investigation. *Information, Community & Society* 13 (2), 226–248.

Hornsby, M. (2015) The 'new' and 'traditional' speaker dichotomy: Bridging the gap. *International Journal of the Sociology of Language* 2015 (231), 107–125.

Jones, G.R (2010) Factors influencing choice of higher education in Wales. *Contemporary Wales* 23 (1), 93–116.

Jones, Rh., Cunliffe, D. and Honeycutt, C. (2013) Twitter and the Welsh language. *Journal of Multilingual and Multicultural Development* 34 (7), 653–671.

Jones, S.L. (2019) Perspectives and attitudes towards Welsh-medium study at post-compulsory level among 15–16-year-old students in the South Wales valleys. *International Journal of Bilingual Education and Bilingualism* 25 (1), 261–271.

Kornai, A. (2013) Digital language death. *Plos One* 8 (10), 1–11.

Lewis, H. and Royles, E. (2018) Language revitalisation and social transformation: Evaluating the language policy frameworks of sub-state governments in Wales and Scotland. *Policy & Politics* 46 (3), 503–529.

Liddicoat, A.J. and Baldauf Jr, R.B. (2008) Language planning in local contexts: Agents, contexts and interactions. In A.J. Liddicoat and R.B. Baldauf Jr (eds) *Language Planning and Policy: Language Planning in Local Contexts* (pp. 3–17). Multilingual Matters.

McAlister, F., Blaunt, A. and Prys, C. (2013) Exploring Welsh speakers' language use in their daily lives. BBC Cymru Wales/S4C/Welsh Government. See https://www.s4c.cymru/abouts4c/corporate/pdf/e_daily-lives-and-language-use-research-report.pdf (accessed June 2022).

Mediouni, M., Schlatterer, D.R and Khoury, A. (2019) Revisiting an old strategy: Cartoons in medical education. *Journal of Visual Communication in Medicine* 42 (1), 26–30.

Mentrau Iaith Cymru (n.d.) See https://mentrauiaith.cymru/en/mentrau-iaith-cymru/ (accessed April 2022).

Moseley, C. (2011) *Atlas of the World's Languages in Danger*. UNESCO Publishing.

Musk, N. (2010) Bilingualism-in-practice at the meso level: An example from a bilingual school in Wales. *International Journal of the Sociology of Language* 2010 (202), 41–62.

Office for National Statistics. (2012) 2011 census: Key statistics for Wales, March 2011. See https://www.ons.gov.uk/peoplepopulationandcommunity/populationandmigration/populationestimates/bulletins/2011censuskeystatisticsforwales/2012-12-11#:~:text=our%20language%20skills.-,The%20usually%20resident%20population%20of%20Wales%20was%203.1%20million%20in,higher%20than%20any%20England%20region (accessed January 2023).

Office for National Statistics (2022) Welsh Language, Wales: Census 2021. See https://www.ons.gov.uk/peoplepopulationandcommunity/culturalidentity/language/bulletins/welshlanguagewales/census2021 (accessed January 2023).

O'Rourke, B. (2018) Just use it! Linguistic conversion and identities of resistance amongst Galician new speakers. *Journal of Multilingual and Multicultural Development* 39 (5), 407–418.

Pennycook, A. (2010) *Language as a Local Practice*. Routledge.

Price, A. and Tamburelli, M. (2019) Welsh-language prestige in adolescents: Attitudes in the heartlands. *International Journal of Applied Linguistics* 30 (2), 195–213.

Prifysgol Bangor University (n.d) Canolfan Bedwyr: about us. See https://www.bangor.ac.uk/canolfanbedwyr/amdanom.php.en (accessed November 2021).

Pritchard, S. (2021) Y Gymraeg o fewn y byd digidol: profiadau ac agweddau siaradwyr Cymraeg yng Ngwynedd o ddefnyddio apiau Cymraeg neu ddwyieithog. (The use of Welsh in the digital world: the experiences and use of Welsh language and bilingual apps by Welsh speakers in Gwynedd). Unpublished PhD thesis, Bangor University. See https://research.bangor.ac.uk/portal/files/37476151/2021PritchardSMPhD.pdf (accessed June 2022).

Prys, C., Hodges, R. and Aaron, H. (2018) Pecyn Adnoddau Amlgyfrwng Cymdeithaseg (Sociology Multimedia Resources Pack). Coleg Cymraeg Cenedlaethol. See https://www.porth.ac.uk/en/collection/paac-pecyn-adnoddau-amlgyfrwng-cymdeithaseg (accessed June 2022).

Prys, C., Hodges, R. and Roberts, G.W. (2021) Rhetoric and reality: A critical review of language policy and legislation governing official minority language use in health and social care in Wales. *Minorités linguistiques et société / Linguistic Minorities and Society* 15 (16), 87–110.

Ricento, T. (2003) Historical and theoretical perspectives in language policy and planning. *Journal of Sociolinguistics* 4 (2), 196–213.

Schacht, S. and Stewart, B.J. (1990) What's funny about statistics? A technique for reducing student anxiety. *Teaching Sociology* 18 (1), 52–56.

Soria, C. (2015) Towards a notion of digital language diversity. In *Linguistic and Cultural Diversity in Cyberspace*. Proceedings of the 3rd International Conference (Yakutsk, Russian Federation, 20 June–July, 2014).

StatsWales (n.d.a) Number of Pupils in primary, middle and secondary school classes by local authority and Welsh category. See https://statswales.gov.wales/Catalogue/Education-and-Skills/Schools-and-Teachers/Schools-Census/Pupil-Level-Annual-School-Census/Welsh-Language/pupilswelshclasses-by-localauthority-welshcategory (accessed December 2021).

StatsWales (n.d.b) Students in Wales with teaching through the medium of Welsh by institution. See https://statswales.gov.wales/Catalogue/Education-and-Skills/Post-16-Education-and-Training/Higher-Education/Welsh-Medium/studentsinwaleswithteachingthroughthemediumofwelsh-by-institution (accessed December 2021).

Thomas, H. and Williams, C.H. (2013) *Parent, Personalities and Power: Welsh-medium Schools in South-east Wales*. University of Wales Press.

Welsh Government (2012) A living language: A language for living: Welsh language strategy 2012-17. Cardiff: Welsh Government. See https://gov.wales/sites/default/files/publications/2018-12/welsh-language-strategy-2012-to-2017-a-living-language-a-language-for-living.pdf (accessed December 2021).

Welsh Government (2015) Welsh Language Use in the Community. Cardiff: Welsh Government. See https://dera.ioe.ac.uk/24483/1/151007-welsh-language-use-community-research-study-en.pdf (accessed December 2021).

Welsh Government (2017a) Cymraeg 2050 - A million Welsh Speakers. Cardiff: Welsh Government. See https://gov.wales/sites/default/files/publications/2018-12/cymraeg-2050-welsh-language-strategy.pdf (accessed December 2021).

Welsh Government (2017b) Technical report: Projection and trajectory for the number of Welsh speakers aged three and over, 2011 to 2050. Cardiff: Welsh Government. See https://gov.wales/sites/default/files/publications/2018-12/welsh-speaker-estimates-2011-to-2050-technical-report.pdf (accessed December 2021).

Welsh Government (2020a) The effects of Covid-19 on Welsh language groups – survey findings. Cardiff: Welsh Government. See https://gov.wales/sites/default/files/statistics-and-research/2020-12/the-effects-of-covid-19-on-welsh-language-community-groups-survey-findings_1.pdf (accessed December 2021).

Welsh Government (2020b) Welsh language technology action plan: Progress report 2020. Cardiff: Welsh Government. See https://www.gov.wales/sites/default/files/publications/2020-12/welsh-language-technology-action-plan-progress-report-2020.pdf (accessed November 2023).

Welsh Government (2021) Welsh Language Use in Wales (initial findings): July 2019 to March 2020. Cardiff: Welsh Government. https://www.gov.wales/welsh-language-use-wales-initial-findings-july-2019-march-2020-revised-html (accessed November 2023).

Welsh Government (2022a) *Welsh Language in Wales (Census 2021): Census 2021 Data about the Welsh Language Skills (Ability to Understand Spoken Welsh, Speak Welsh, Read Welsh, and Write Welsh) of People Aged Three Years or Older Living in Wales.* Welsh Government.

Welsh Government (2022b) Curriculum for Wales: Language, literacy and communication. See https://hwb.gov.wales/curriculum-for-wales/languages-literacy-and-communication/designing-your-curriculum#:~:text=Welsh%20is%20a%20mandatory%20requirement,to%20learning%20and%20teaching%20Welsh. (accessed January 2023).

Williams, G. and Morris, D. (2000) *Language Planning and Language Use: Welsh in a Global Age.* University of Wales Press.

6 Teaching a Regional Language in Online Courses: A Learner-Oriented Perspective on Agency, Practices and Evaluation

Birte Arendt and Ulrike Stern

Introduction

This chapter[1] focuses on the connection between mediatisation and teaching/learning, describes the potential for the acquisition of autochthonous minority languages (in the following, 'AML') and discusses aspects of target group adequacy. We are convinced that online language courses can make a decisive contribution in this area, especially for AML, and that the model presented here could also be transferred to other small languages. From a learner-oriented perspective, we want to describe how online teaching can be made functional in a way that comes close to the interactivity of face-to-face teaching, including the horizontal dimension (student-to-student) and how this offer addresses the particular needs of adult AML speakers, termed the 'doubly excluded generation'. In doing so, this chapter will focus on digitally mediated language learning opportunities by examining examples from online courses for learning the regional language Low German (see Reershemius, in this volume). The case study aims to analyse the feasibility and success of online delivery for new speakers of a smaller language in terms of agency, practices and speaker-centred evaluation.

Low German is a non-standardised West Germanic variety that today has many similarities with High German due to language affinity and a constant language contact situation, as well as regionally and historically determined differences at all linguistic-systematic levels (Stellmacher, 2000). The historical variety of Middle Low German was the lingua franca of the Hanseatic League of Merchants in Europe from the 13th to 16th centuries. From the 17th century onwards, the pejorification of the variety began to displace it from written communication domains and gradually led to its marginalisation and a loss of communication domains to the dominant standard language High German (Peters, 2015) as well as a loss of intergenerational transmission. Low German is currently regarded both as a dialect used primarily for private oral communication in the local area and as a state-recognised regional language (Arendt, 2021). The language area in Germany comprises eight northern federal states. The number of competent speakers is low and declining. According to recent surveys, for example GETAS in 2007 or INS in 2016, about 15% of the population in the language area can speak Low German well to very well (cf. Adler *et al.*, 2016; Möller, 2008: 12). Thus, Low German is considered vulnerable according to the *UNESCO Atlas of the World's Languages in Danger* and in 1999 it was recognised by the *European Charter for Regional or Minority Languages* (1992). Low German now has high prestige and the desire to learn the language or to speak it better is particularly high in the adult generation, which usually still understands Low German well but does not really have a background of interfamilial acquisition (Arendt, 2021; Adler *et al.*, 2016). In order to preserve the language, Low German is now increasingly integrated into kindergartens and schools (Arendt & Langhanke, 2021) with the aim of teaching active language skills and creating new – mainly young – speakers. The current generation of adults is doubly excluded from possible language learning opportunities; they cannot participate in interfamilial transmission, nor can they take advantage of school-based opportunities. In this respect, these adults can be seen as a 'doubly excluded generation' of AML semi-speakers with special needs.

The concept of mediatisation assumes that social, inter- and intra-individual practices increasingly refer to media, especially digital media. This also applies to learning practices. Basically, learning – in a socio-cognitive perspective – is an individual, cognitive appropriation process that cannot be implemented by digital tools but can most certainly be supported. In the following, we assume that digitalisation in particular can open up alternative ways of using and learning the language for new speakers of autochthonous minority languages, especially adults. The effects of digital mediatisation are manifold (Reershemius, 2017) and raise the question of whether and how Web 2.0 can lead to new learning opportunities (e.g. Crystal, 2006; Kelly-Holmes & Atkinson, 2017). At the same time, digitally supported learning is still afflicted with many negative prejudices, which lead to statements such as 'digitally you only reach young people', 'nobody does that anyway', 'in online courses you train passivity, you can only read and listen as a passive consumer' and 'cooperative learning is not possible online and anyway only something for advanced learners'. Using online courses for Low German as an example, we will therefore discuss these prejudices as well as the learning possibilities from the participants' point of view.

In doing so, we consider the following three research topics and questions:

(1) **Agency:** Who uses digitally mediated language learning services and why? Can they support the 'doubly excluded generation'?
(2) **Practices:** What teaching/learning practices and what normative actions are established by learners and teachers? Can online courses promote interactive learning or just passive consumption?
(3) **Evaluation:** How do the participants evaluate the online courses? Do they judge these courses to be helpful for their particular needs?

First of all, the chapter presents the theoretical concepts. Then, after introducing the data basis on online courses for Low German in Mecklenburg-Western Pomerania since 2019, it goes on to present the findings on participants, their teaching/learning practices and their evaluation of the courses. Finally, the potential of online courses for language maintenance is discussed.

Theoretical Framework

Combining sociolinguistic and didactic approaches, the chapter takes as its basis the theoretical concepts of (1) mediatisation, (2) interactive computer-assisted language learning and (3) new speakers and ambivalent norm concepts of AML.

(1) Androutsopoulos (2016) develops a complex understanding of mediatisation (see Reershemius & Arendt, this volume), of which the two aspects of *space* and *practices* are relevant for the present chapter. The first aspect asks how media can open up spaces – in our sense, possible learning spaces.

> [D]igital technologies provide infrastructure by which virtual spaces for interaction and discourse are semiotically constructed by institutions and publics. [...] Space does not just refer to the physical site of co-present viewing. In online communication, the metaphor of space connotes movement, presence, interaction, and agency. People go to and act in virtual spaces [...]; people move in virtual spaces through their avatars [...]; and they discursively construct these spaces by means of mediational tools, including those that enable the production of digital written language. (Androutsopoulos, 2016: 287)

As a hypothesis of this chapter, we can add the following to the above quote: '*People act in virtual spaces and construct these spaces by means of mediational tools, including those that enable the learning of AML*'. These virtual spaces fundamentally activate translocal communications and thus can potentially facilitate learning-enhancing interactions between spatially separated learners. They can connect them in a virtual space to form a learning community. The second aspect relevant to us is the focus on practices (Androutsopoulos, 2016: 295; *nexus-of-practice approach*) that constitute digital communication. The central question here seems to be whether and how digital practices can promote the acquisition or teaching of AML. Do possible language use practices in digitally constituted spaces have the potential to stimulate acquisition and interactive language learning? By focusing on such practices, the above-mentioned prejudices which assume passive consumption can be questioned, as can the possibilities for cooperative learning.

(2) Furthermore, this chapter is based on theoretical approaches to interactive computer-assisted language learning (CALL). The core thesis is that mediatisation and, more specifically, digitalisation can change learning opportunities. Numerous different technologies for communication (cf. Schroeder, 2017; Thurlow *et al.*, 2012) have become established and enable translocal (Kytölä, 2015) communicative networking beyond spatial boundaries. This is particularly useful for speakers of AML, whose geographical distribution can present an obstacle to communication. At the same time, a co-constitutive design of technology and pedagogy takes place, as in the CALL approach (Schmidt & Blume, 2016; Warschauer, 2004). This integrative approach is based on a sociocognitive view of language learning as a dynamic, interaction-driven, self-organised mental activity of learners (Warschauer, 2004: 22). Central aspects of this learner- and interaction-centred approach (cf. also task-based learning, Caruso & Hofmann, 2018) are adequate teacher feedback to support learners (Meskill & Anthony, 2015; Schmidt & Blume, 2016; Seljan *et al.*, 2004), gamification-based methods (Biebighäuser, 2016; Gee, 2007; Jones, 2016; Stieler-Hunt & Jones, 2019; Zichermann & Cunningham, 2011), large amounts of input with different speakers as models, many opportunities to practise, and a stress-free environment (Schmidt & Blume, 2016). Interactivity is therefore considered a quality feature of the CALL approach. Digital development can thus enable both direct synchronous interaction analogous to typical face-to-face classroom interactions (in the following, 'f2f') and translocal multimodal communication in online courses. The question nevertheless remains as to how the learners, in other words the participants in online courses, shape the learning opportunities in their communicative practices.

(3) New speakers and ambivalent norm concepts are relevant speaker- and language-centred features of many AML. According to the sociolinguistic perspective-changing centre-periphery dynamics (Pietikäinen *et al.*, 2016), learners of Low German are typical 'new speakers' (cf. Hornsby & Vigers, 2018; Jaffe, 2015; O'Rourke, 2018; Puigdevall *et al.*, 2018). This means individuals who acquired their language in contexts other than the home, such as through immersion or

other bilingual education or as an adult, and who now use the language competently (Cenoz, 2009; Nic Fhlannchadha & Hickey, 2018: 39). This group has special attributes. Firstly, this group is characterised by very heterogeneous language skills, as they lack systematic interfamilial language acquisition. These skills can be fruitfully integrated and networked in cooperative learning, which is why this chapter also focuses on these learning opportunities. Second, for many adult learners of AMLs, despite their desire to learn offline, there are few learning opportunities because of the focus of language policies on kindergartens and schools (Arendt, 2021; Reuter, 2021). Thirdly, due to the employment of adults, time resources for learning are limited and teaching must be flexible. These adults – as already mentioned above – form a 'doubly excluded generation' of AML speakers with special needs, who can be reached with online courses. They are key social actors who can establish, shape or prevent the process of language maintenance through their linguistic practices. For this reason, the chapter focuses on these actors in terms of agency and evaluation and attempts to reconstruct their characteristics and motives for learning and also examines their assessment of the course(s). Low German is a variant-rich, highly internally differentiated variety which is only partly standardised and is now being taught in traditionally strongly normative and standard-oriented teaching/learning contexts. Norm conflicts can therefore occur both in relation to the language itself and its variants and to communicative practices. This raises questions about the underlying norms and their negotiation, as well as about bilingual practices such as code-switching (Auer, 1998; Gumperz, 1982; Woolard, 2004) and translanguaging (cf. García & Li, 2014) in online courses.

Teaching Low German in Online Courses

Starting at the end of 2018 in cooperation with the *Länderzentrum für Niederdeutsch Bremen* (Regional Centre for Low German Bremen), online courses became an essential part of the work and teaching concept of the Competence Centre for the Teaching of Low German at Greifswald University (CCTLG), even before online learning became necessary and common due to the Covid-19 pandemic. The courses offer a primarily oral, synchronously organised learning environment (cf. Meskill & Anthony, 2015: 8) with numerous parallels to f2f classrooms. The aim is to create an extracurricular learning space, primarily for the purpose of teachers' continuous professional development. At the same time, the courses are available to all interested parties free of charge and as such are an open educational resource. They are offered for beginners or for advanced learners.

Eleven courses with a total of 118 participants, six for beginners and five advanced, took place from 2019 to the end of April 2021 and form

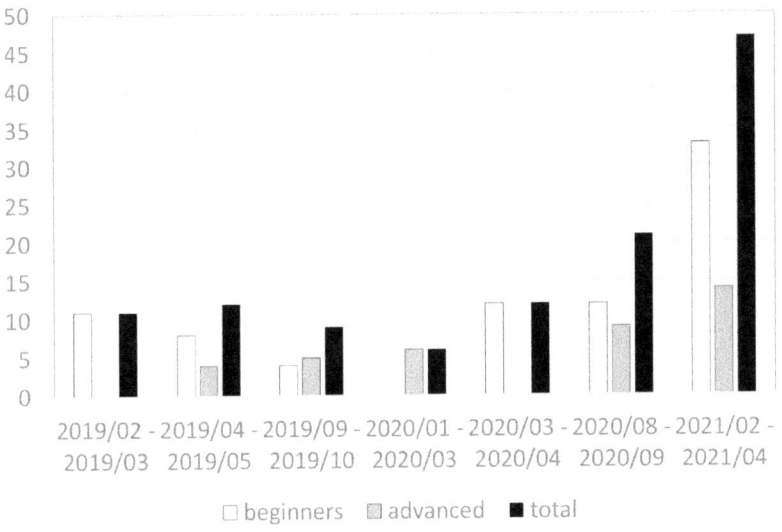

Figure 6.1 Number of participants

the data basis for this study. As Figure 6.1 shows, there was an increase in the number of participants over time.

Each course comprises eight sessions lasting around 60 minutes. The aim is to offer variety while practising all the competences needed for communicating in the target language (cf. Council of Europe, 2001): reading aloud, reading comprehension, listening comprehension, writing, speaking and translating. In both courses, care is taken to create interactive practice spaces and to consistently increase the level of difficulty. The beginners course focuses on teaching the basic vocabulary and grammar, whereby use of the language is gently but constantly encouraged. Topics are based on experiences in daily life. Within the framework of these topics, grammar is discussed, such as verb and noun use. The different varieties of Low German are also reviewed and examples from Low German literature are presented (Figure 6.2).

A typical advanced course focuses on learners using vocabulary while revising grammar. Although the course is short, the thematic frame is built by a 'simulation globale', a roleplay designed in France in the 1970s (cf. Debyser, 1984; Jones, 2016; Maak, 2011) as a typical part of gamification approaches (cf. Jones, 2016). The participants create their own world, working in a process-oriented way, creatively and interactively. In their avatar role, participants can interact freely and practise using the language meaningfully in different contexts (Biebighäuser, 2016; Jones, 2016). This creative, open and learner-oriented digital mode makes it attractive for participants to attend

134 Part 2: Digital Tools and Practices

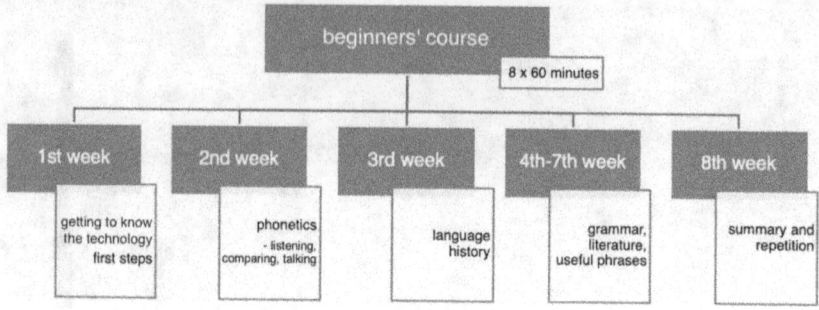

Figure 6.2 Sequence of the beginners' course

the course several times. In this way, a mediatised virtual space for sustainable and lasting language acquisition and practice can be created.

Data and Method: Questionnaire on Learner Perspectives and Authentic Interactions in Online Courses

The article is an explorative case study where we look at the extracurricular teaching of AML to adults as new speakers in online courses using the example of Low German in Germany.

As Figure 6.3 shows, the analysis is based on two data sets, written questionnaires from four courses, and interaction observation of a selection of online courses. Learner characteristics, motives for participation and the evaluation are based on a written survey with open and closed questions that was conducted in four courses in 2020 and 2021. Of the 59 total participants, 22 completed the questionnaire, which corresponds to a 37% response rate. Simple quantitative analyses of the questionnaire responses were performed to determine percentage distributions. Due to the comparatively small number of cases and the explorative nature of the study, statistical significance tests were not used. The scope of the results is limited in two ways, namely quantitatively and qualitatively. Since only a good third of the

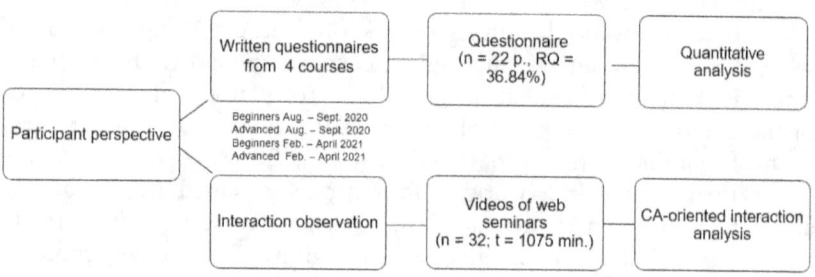

Figure 6.3 Data collection

participants actively took part in the survey, the majority is not covered. A qualitative limitation is the bias that it is mostly the active learners who participate in surveys. Thus, only data from a very selected group is available.

In order to describe typical practices, we conducted conversation analysis–oriented studies on a sample of 32 videotaped online courses from which we collected sequences focusing on participant interactions. From this, statements can be made about how learners themselves make the classroom their learning space and how online courses offer opportunities for interactive learning. From the collection of videos containing interactive practices, we transcribed and carried out sequence-oriented microanalysis. Typicality is based on the following three criteria: first, the sequences should capture examples of typical, i.e. frequently recurring, interactive practices in the online courses; second, they should capture the relevant participants, e.g. not only beginners; and third, in their contextualised form, they should provide insights into authentic lessons, e.g. the progression of the beginners course (T1_B3-T7_B8). Based on these criteria, the examples can be considered typical in terms of practices and the constellation of participants and contexts. The identifiers for the transcripts are composed of the sequence number (T1-T10), the course level (B: Beginners, A: Advanced learners), the lesson (1-8) and the excerpt per lesson (cf. Table 6.1 in Appendix 6.A).

Findings

Agency: Who are the learners and why do they participate?

The target audience of the online courses was teachers with or without Low German language skills, as the courses were among the offers made by the CCTLG for teachers' continuous professional development. The courses were advertised on a central platform accessible to all teachers. Division of the federal state into four school district areas means that teachers often only look for courses in their local area. This is the first advantage of the online seminars: they are accessible for all teachers regardless of their school district. Figure 6.4 shows a map of Mecklenburg-Western Pomerania. The location points indicate where the participants in 2020 and 2021 came from. Participants from other countries or other federal states in Germany are not shown on the map. One of the participants lived in Norway while taking part in the course, another in Sweden. Three others lived in Kiel (Northern Germany), Munich and Frankfurt/Main (both Southwestern Germany). Thus, it appears that people from across the country were engaged in translocal communication via the online courses. Teachers from bigger cities (Schwerin, Rostock, Neustrelitz, Neubrandenburg, Stralsund, Greifswald) could network with colleagues from smaller

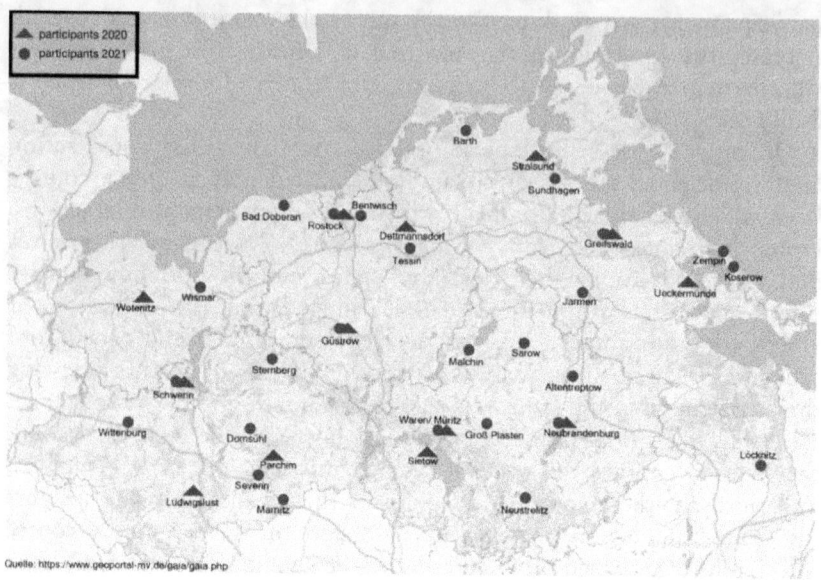

Figure 6.4 Location of learners in M-WP

towns and villages, which rarely ever happens in face-to-face events. The courses can thus facilitate collegial and cooperative exchange, which is particularly useful for mostly disadvantaged schools in rural areas.

The majority of participants were female (64%). The probable reason for this distribution lies in the gender structure of the German educational landscape, and especially that of Mecklenburg-Western Pomerania, where the majority of teachers are women (cf. Statistisches Amt, 2021: 6). Overall, the wide age range of the learners makes it clear that the new speakers are not necessarily young people: 56% were between 30 and 60 years old, 39% under 30, and 5% over 60. This means that the 'doubly excluded generation' of adult learners can indeed be addressed with online courses and that not only young people use these opportunities. The fact that the courses are part of the CCTLG's continuous professional development for teachers is likely to have played a role in this distribution. For teachers over 60 there is no need to develop new language competences because they will retire within the next five to seven years. One reason for them to participate might be that they still have some Low German skills learned from their parents or grandparents. Teachers under 30 are at the beginning of their career, and it is likely to be viewed positively by a new employer if teachers are actively striving to expand their skills and knowledge. Due to the target group, the main professions of the learners in the online courses are students (36%) or teachers (45%). The online format means that the courses can be opened to other interested learners without additional costs, which explains why 18% of participants have other professions (hotelier, pensioner, data protection officer, school social worker). These participants found out about the courses by chance; that is, they were not actively invited to take part. The group structure could look different if there were any official advertising beyond the aforementioned platform for teachers. The majority had good receptive skills before starting the courses (68%). About one third said they could speak well but with inhibitions (36%). This means the participants have partially heterogeneous primary receptive knowledge. The language is therefore not unknown to them.

In order to determine the participants' individual motivation for learning Low German, we asked them: What are the reasons for participating in one of the courses?

Overall, three aspects were dominant in the responses:

(1) Social aspects of belonging (family and region) and tradition.
(2) Individual interests (improving competences, interest in languages).
(3) Professional reasons (acquisition of additional qualifications).

As JP (beginner) writes, *Low German was my family's mother tongue, but now, almost two generations later, it is almost forgotten.* (JP-B); or, to quote JK (advanced): *[The language] is still spoken a lot in my surroundings. Lots of fishermen and the older generation... I want this too.* (JK-A). Interestingly, asked for their regional affiliation, both state that they feel European and Mecklenburgian or Western Pomeranian, respectively. Thus, regional identity does not exclude European identity. Even if regional awareness and the desire for social belonging play a role in interest in the language, identification does not seem to be automatically reduced to the region.

CR (advanced) details her reasons for participation as follows: *Overcoming language obstacles, developing knowledge, improving pronunciation.* (CR-A). She was one of the attendees who took the advanced learners' course as a follow-up to the beginners' course. Similarly, FL (advanced) explains *I grew up with Low German (grandfather, mother, region) and I always wanted to learn it.* (FL-A). Overcoming the inhibitions that prevent many participants from speaking the language is one of the individual motivations for taking part. In addition, the attendees recognise a need for grammar awareness and background information to underpin their existing knowledge in order to speak the language more confidently.

The third dominant aspect is the acquisition of additional qualifications (professional reasons). As CR (beginner) writes: *Try to acquire additional qualifications to make myself more attractive to schools.* (CR-B). Even though there is a general shortage of teachers in Mecklenburg-Western Pomerania (cf. State Government, 2021), certain subject combinations are less in demand than others, so a teaching qualification for Low German means a recruitment advantage.

The typical participant is thus an adult teacher learning Low German for social, individual and/or professional reasons. Online courses could nevertheless potentially form cross-generational and cross-professional learning groups in which different language skills and life experiences can support interactive learning.

Practices: Practices and norms in online courses

In the following, we present microanalytically oriented interaction analyses of authentic online courses. The following three examples illustrate norm negotiation, peer support and humour as typical interactive teaching/learning practices.

Interactive corrections: Contradictory norm orientation between prescription and autonomy of choice

Example 1 is taken from Transcript T4_B4_3 from the fourth session of a beginners' course in 2020 with 13 participants and the teacher; in the session, they are practising the grammatical phenomenon of the *daun*-periphrase. The example illustrates both a norm oriented towards linguistic correctness and a request for self-selected variation.

Example 1: Interactive corrections

Beginners/lesson 4; Transcript T4_B4_3; TE: teacher; A: Astrid (female student)

```
146   A:    moin ja (.)
            moin yes (.)
147         also ik dau gern läsen
            so I like to read
148         ähm mien mann daut nich gern malern
            renovieren
            um my husband doesn't like to decorate
149   TE:   hei deit nich giern malern
            he doesn't like to decorate
150   A:    hei deit nich giern malern
            he doesn't like to decorate
151         un miene kinner inner schuls schul
            and my children at school
152   TE:   in de schaul
            at school
153   A:    in de schaul äh: daun nich gern nä
            zuhören
            at school er: don't like *to listen*
154   TE:   tauhürn mhm
            listen mhm
```

155	A:	tauhürn
		listen
156	TE:	genau ich hab das hier nochmal mit
		hingeschrieben
		exactly, I have written this down here again.
157		de schaul oder de school je nachdem ne
		the school or the school depending on
158		wo man ist und wie man möchte so as man
		möchte
		where you are and how you want to, as you want to do.
159		un tauhürn willn se nich giern ja dat
		verståh ik
		and they don't like to listen, I understand that.
160		dat schriew ik ok nochmal dortau (.)
		I'll write that also (.)
161		tauhürn (.) äh na ich machs mal moment
		listen (.) uh well I'll do it just a moment
162		hüren ik schriew dat mal so (.)
		listen, I write it like this (.)
163		dat is ähm mit ein ü (.) as herrmann-
		winter dat schrifft
		that's with an ü (.) like hermann winter writes it
164		wunnerbor ik dank di
		wonderful, thanks

In line 148, the learner Astrid utters the grammatically incorrect sentence *he daut gern malern*, in which the wrong form of the verb *daun* (to do) is realised. This is implicitly criticised and explicitly corrected by the teacher with a repetition of the correct form in line 149 *hei deit nich giern malern*. The teacher thus produces the second part of the sequence, the other-initiated other-corrections, and with this 'instructional move' provides the guidance necessary for online learning (cf. Meskill & Anthony, 2015: 16f.). This correction sequence is concluded – in the classical way – in the third step by ratification in the form of a repetition of the correct form by Astrid in line 150. The following utterance sequences in lines 151–153 are devoted to the phonetically correct form of *schul – schaul* in the same three-part sequence structure and to the lexical translation of *zuhören – tauhüren* in lines 153–155. From line 160 onwards, the teacher reinforces the normative claim with reference to orthographic norms and, in line 164, concludes the communicative framework of language production for grammar acquisition for Astrid by thanking her. All in all, the above-mentioned lines convey norms based on clearly determinable correctness. The orientation towards a standard as a target norm is typical for language teaching. Nevertheless, this standard does not really exist for Low German, which can cause difficulties for the learning process. This can be seen in Example 1: in lines 157 and 158, namely, there is a metalinguistic reflection on pronunciation variants, depending on the place reference *the school or the school depending on/where you are and how you want to, as you want to do.* This discussion is correct from an object-language point of view, since the internal differentiation of Low German provides for heterogeneous pronunciation norms of the same lexemes. At the same time, however, it conveys a contradictory norm that opens up a field of tension between binary normality on the one hand and possible regional variance on the other. This makes it difficult for learners to systematically classify deviations. The target variety thus also becomes vague.

In Example 1, functionally differentiated code-switching is also noticeable. While the exercise is conducted in monolingual Low German, the teacher's metalinguistic explanations are partly High German and partly Low German. The High German phrases are in italics. In Example 1, a functional differentiation of variety use is realised in that Low German is the goal of the lessons and language exercises, but German is the dominant medium of the lessons. While the teacher does engage in internal code-switching, the learners' target norm is monolingual, 'pure' Low German language production (cf. the correction of lines 148, 151). This is noteworthy in that, on the one hand, it corresponds to typical practices of foreign language teaching, in which the target language is not the medium of instruction, and yet, on the other, the monolingual, purely Low German realisation of utterances does not really reflect the linguistic reality. Rather, in current language production among competent speakers, code-switching between German and Low German occurs as a matter of course, based not least on a linguistic equalisation process in the direction of German, which has been dominant for centuries, including in the language area being studied (Ehlers, 2018, 2021). In this respect, the monolingual norm ties in very well with traditional foreign language didactic concepts but only corresponds to a limited extent to recent linguistic reality. This norm of monolingualism can cause problems in contact with fluent speakers who use both languages in code-switching. However, this tension concerning standardisation processes does not only exist for digital forms of delivery but for face-to-face teaching and learning as well.

From the point of view of promoting interactive learning, the context can be characterised as action- and practice-oriented. The participants are expected to speak about their everyday life and personally significant content. The interactive learning opportunity is not due to a specific aspect of digital delivery, but to the analogy with f2f teaching. This is nevertheless made possible by digital technologies.

Peer support

The following example is from an advanced course with three participants and the teacher and focuses on peer support.

In order to train oral language production, the task in Example 2 is to read a dialogue out loud that was previously written in the chat. In the example, the two learners Lena (L) and Wilma (W), whose language competences are different, work together. The learners themselves constructively integrate these differently developed linguistic resources into their teaching/learning interaction by giving each other support.

Example 2: Peer support

Advanced learners/lesson 8; Transcript T8_A8_1; L: Lena (female student), W: Wilma (female student), TE: teacher

```
019    L:    äh:: ((räuspern))de katten kümmn alleen
              runner vun de boom un (.)
              uh:: ((clearing throat)) the cats get down from the tree by
              themselves and (.)
020           wenn dat ierst wind gäben moet (.) aber
              runder kam se: van (.) alleen:
              if there has to be wind first (.) but they get down by
              themselves
021    W:    aber: dat duert ok fö:=äh (.) fünfzig
              but that also takes uh (.) fifty
022           was heißt [fünfzig]?
              what is [fifty]?
023    L:              [föfftig]
                       [fifty]
024    TE:             [föfftig]
                       [fifty]
025    W:    ((kurzes Lachen)) föfftig jahr: (.) bi
              katten ut mäckelburg (2.0)
              ((short laugh)) fifty years with cats from Mecklenburg (2.0)
```

In line 21, Wilma marks uncertainty in the translation of the number 50 by the delay signal *äh* and the production of the number in German. The High German phrases are again in italics. In line 22, she makes her problems explicit by asking for the translation in Low German and initiates a self-initiated correction request. Lena reacts to this by delivering the desired correction in line 23, which is confirmed by the teacher in line 24. Then, in line 25, Wilma adopts the presented form, continues the dialogue and ends the linguistic correction sequence. The linguistic norm instantiated by the practised language use and specifically the correction of the German form *fifty – föfftig* can be described as monolingual Low German. Code-switching of German and Low German, as produced in line 21 by Wilma, is retrospectively marked as insufficient by the subsequent request for translation and confirmed by Lena and the teacher, who both provide the desired correction.

Peer support like that in Example 2 is found repeatedly in the data, especially in the advanced courses. This sequence is special in three ways.

Firstly, Lena feels it is her role as a knowledgeable speaker to provide support, and by successfully doing so she confirms to herself that she is a competent speaker. This can have a positive effect on her future learning from a motivational point of view. Secondly, Wilma experiences support from other learners, which simultaneously confirms the target norm from a peer perspective and frames it as possible. Thirdly, through the demonstrated peer support, a cooperative-collaborative learning situation is created by the participants themselves in situ. The fact that peers in particular can support each other in language learning and how they do so is shown not only by numerous studies on children's language acquisition in peer interactions (cf. Arendt, 2019; Cekaite *et al.*, 2014) but also by the cooperative learning approach (cf. Kunitz, 2018; Wocken, 2014).

For the above reasons, the sequence can be seen as supporting learning for both the recipient and the helper. The support aspects are on different levels, as the helper benefits on the motivational level, while the recipient benefits on the level of declarative-procedural language knowledge.

The interactive learning opportunity is basically analogous to Example 1. Here, too, the high degree of interactivity that is conducive to learning is made possible by digital technologies, but it is used by the teacher and the learners through their activities. In addition, the multimodality of the digital learning environment is used here to read aloud what was previously written in the chat and thus to train different competences.

Playful practices and challenging humour

The three participants of the advanced course (as in Example 2) act orally in Low German in a 'simulation globale' in the form of an imaginary village meeting in assigned roles. The aim is to discuss whether the fictional ducal castle should be rebuilt. We see Lena, Wilma and the teacher from Example 2 as well as Manuel.

Example 3: Challenging humour

Advanced learners/lesson 8; Transcript T8_A8_1; L: Lena (female student), W: Wilma (female student), M: Manuel (male student); TE: teacher

```
021   L:    und wat heff ick davun: (--)
             and what do I get out of it: (-)
022   TE:   [((lacht))]
             [((laughs))]
023   M:    [ja:] dat segg ick ok: (.) wat hettst
             du davon ne
             [yes:] that's what I say too (.) what do you get out of it?
```

```
024    L:     [((lacht))]
              [((laughs))]
025    TE:    [naja: (.)] du kannst villicht n schön
              hoffladen upmåken
              [well: (.)] maybe you can open a nice farm shop,
026           kiek mol dat is doch wunnerbor (.)
              see, that's wonderful,
027           wenn du denn de: de melk vun de kauhn
              richtig mal verbruken kannst
              if you can use the milk from the cow properly
028           för denn kääs und so wei=so wieder (-)
              for the cheese and so on.
029    L:     un denn hebben wi niks mehr tau fräden
              oder wat
              and then we won't have anything to eat or what?
030    TE:    [((lacht))]
              [((laughs))]
031    M:     [((lacht))]
              [((laughs))]
032    L:     [hm=hm] (-)
              [hm=hm] (-)
033    TE:    äh=wat ((…)) wat seggst du denn dortau
              (---)
              uh=what ((…)) what do you say (---)?
034    W:     wi bruken dat geld för de füerwehr
              we need the money for the fire brigade
035    TE:    [((lacht))]
              [((laughs))]
036    L:     [((lacht))]
              [((laughs))]
037    M:     [((lacht))]
              [((laughs))]
```

The target norm of the dialogue is Low German and is adhered to by all participants as much as possible. This becomes explicitly visible in the self-initiated self-correction in line 28 by the teacher, who replaces *wei=(ter)* with *wieder*.

In Example 3, however, the humour orientation adds another, rather ambivalent requirement. Humour is known from peer learning research to be a supportive characteristic and can be described with the maxim 'Be entertaining!' (Cekaite & Aronsson, 2014). The numerous laughs in lines 22, 24, 30, 31, 35, 36, 37 from Lena, Manuel and the teacher frame the entire interaction as humorous. The fact that humour has aspects which promote learning has been well established, not only in language didactic research (cf. Cekaite & Aronsson, 2014; Kiphard, 2004). Humour leads to a potential relaxation of the situation and thus to a reduction of speech anxiety and an increase in active speech production. This was ultimately also one of the reasons named for participation in the online courses. However, the humour orientation also increases demands on the participants in that their contributions must also be funny. Humour in a foreign language, even if it is only situational, represents one of the greatest demands on communicative competence of all. In this respect, laughter and humour are ambivalent requirements, but their positive effect is likely to outweigh their ambivalence.

The interactive learning opportunity is basically analogous to Example 1 and 2. Here, too, the high degree of interactivity that is conducive to learning is made possible by digital technologies. The entire dialogue makes high receptive and productive demands on the learners and can be seen as an extremely challenging interactive learning opportunity. The 'simulation globale' is a core method of communication- and action-oriented language teaching. Analogous to the gamification approach (cf. Biebighäuser, 2016; Jones, 2016), as an important component of CALL, this simulation also combines global practices of narrative sense-making with game aspects that promote learning. The result is a 'space of uncertainty from which new meaning can emerge' (Jones, 2016: 141).

Evaluation: How do participants evaluate the online courses?

In order to evaluate their digital language learning experience, the attendees were asked to assess the course structure and their personal progress as well as the fact that the courses are delivered digitally. All three areas were evaluated positively. The learning opportunities provided in the receptive competence areas reading and listening were rated 'just right' (reading 91% of responses, listening 80% of responses). For the productive competences speaking and writing, opportunities were also rated 'just right', but slightly lower (speaking 64%, writing 70% of responses). These findings show that online courses are by no means only passively received and can and do also address productive competences, which is appreciated and desired by the learners.

As the following quotations illustrate, the most frequently mentioned results of the online courses were that they encourage speaking, increase declarative and procedural knowledge, and provide further impulses: *At least I dared to speak in Low German.* (CR-B; BR-A; JK-A); *My vocabulary and grammar knowledge has improved.* (LL-A) and *I became more attentive. When I speak German, I notice more expressions that are Low German but also occur in my everyday German. Since I started listening to radio, audio books and videos in Low German, my listening comprehension has improved. I now try to build in those things in my everyday life regularly [...]. I also started to read Low German texts, for the moment children's books and poems, then later hopefully longer ones.* (JP-B). The latter aspect in particular is important, as a course length of eight sessions must be seen as the bare minimum. An ability to act in the target language cannot be achieved in eight 60-minute sessions. In addition to the course teaching the basics and reducing language inhibitions, one of its primary goals can and must be to strengthen existing interest and encourage further – preferably regular – engagement with the language.

The evaluation of the digital delivery of the course was positive, as JK (beginner) put it: *Super, little effort, great effect, no stress upon arrival.* (JK-B). For MW (beginner), the recordings of the session were 'a stroke of luck': *In my personal situation with two small children, the online course was a godsend for me. I rarely managed to attend the event live, so the recordings were great for me. I always dealt with it exactly when I had enough time for it.* (MW-B). Through the recordings, the learning process is not only individualised with regard to the point in time but also enhanced with regard to the possibility of repetition. A third aspect mentioned was the removal of spatial restrictions on participation, and not only by JP-B, participating from Norway. MK (beginner) writes: *An online course can save me a lot of driving time and enables access to offers from other locations. As a result, the range is much broader for me. If the course hadn't been online, I wouldn't have taken part, and I wouldn't have been able to.* (MK-B). Nevertheless, there are also disadvantages: *There is no direct exchange with the other participants,* writes ET (beginner).

Accordingly, the advantages of the digital delivery are savings in terms of time and travel costs, individualisation of learning processes (through recording), and translocal communication. The danger with online courses lies in the creation of one-to-many situations, which lead to purely receptive behaviour on the part of the participants. The survey results show that concepts which repeatedly demand interaction from both beginners and advanced learners and give them opportunities to speak can also be successfully implemented in online courses.

Summary and Discussion

Starting from a theoretical basis of (1) mediatisation, (2) interactive computer-assisted language learning and (3) new speakers and ambivalent norm concepts of AML, the chapter has examined online courses from a participant's perspective in terms of opportunities for interactive language learning which meet the special needs of the 'doubly excluded generation' of many adult AML speakers. The objects of investigation were agency, practice and evaluation.

On the basis of a questionnaire survey with a low response rate and microanalytical interaction analyses, the case-study produced the following findings. (1) *Agency:* the typical learner of the presented digital course can be characterised as an adult teacher. Reasons given for participation were social aspects, individual interests and professional reasons. Mediatisation – on the one hand – creates translocally organised spaces necessary for AML learning, which are particularly embraced by adults, the 'doubly excluded generation' of AML speakers. On the other hand, although mainly social and individual motives for participation are mentioned, most participants are teachers who use the online course for professional reasons. This offer is therefore only used by a small and specific group and the reach is comparatively low. (2) *Practices*: the typical teaching/learning practices established interactively by the learners and the teacher show a dominant monolingual norm orientation through numerous corrections, peer support and demanding humorous interaction patterns. Digital mediatisation thus enables practices very similar to interactive f2f-learning in school. The following three aspects are particularly relevant for the teaching of AML to new speakers. Online courses offer virtual spaces for necessary norm discussions of non-standardised varieties, for cooperative learning to integrate heterogeneous language competences and for playful and humorous use of language for everyday use outside of the institutional learning context. At the same time, however, the time frame is significantly shorter than in school lessons, which can reduce the long-term learning success. (3) *Evaluation*: in the evaluation, the participants confirmed that the digitally delivered course helped to encourage speaking and provided further language learning impulses. Savings in terms of time and travel costs, as well as the individualisation of learning processes, were named as advantages of the digital format. The opening of additional virtual spaces as an effect of mediatisation is rated particularly positively by learners. Through the use of highly developed audio and video technology, it is possible to interact in meditated learning spaces in a comfortable way, quasi from the sofa. Video recordings offer flexible learning opportunities. The practical possibilities that exist in online courses mean that the high level of motivation and desire to learn can be satisfied and the special needs of the adult 'doubly excluded generation' can also be met, which makes such courses particularly attractive for AML teaching to adult learners. To put it in other words, the online courses are not just a random offer, but they are particularly suitable for the important target group of adult semi-speakers, as they meet the special needs of the 'doubly excluded generation'. Our research thus debunks most of the negative prejudices. Digital technologies for communication enable language teaching that can be similar to good face-to-face classes.

At the same time, the following limitations of this optimistic view need to be discussed. Firstly, the analyses of the practices, which reconstructed both ambivalent norm concepts and monolingual and partially purist-oriented norms, reveal insights into a complex and potentially problematic field of conflict for the learners. The targeted monolingual Low German norm, which follows the concepts of traditional foreign language teaching, hardly corresponds to the current linguistic reality of Low German, which is characterised by numerous bilingual practices such as code-switching and translanguaging in various forms. Contradictory norm orientations are evident here, which can become a problem for the new speakers' language use outside the teaching/learning context when communicating with competent speakers (cf. Arendt, 2021; Hornsby & Vigers, 2018). This could be the case if the new speakers' purist use of language is perceived as artificial and interaction with them is therefore rejected. This potential response is not only due to the purist norms but also because the taught variety, at least the orthographically standardised teaching variety, sometimes meets with vehement resistance in linguistic as well as lay linguistic discussions as being 'artificial' (cf. Arendt & Langhanke, 2021). Basically, this problem area is more about the different concepts from a language didactic and (socio)linguistic perspective and less about the general processes of digital mediatisation. However, the latter cannot be viewed in isolation from the fundamental discussions of norms and concepts and occupies an ambivalent position in this respect. In the online courses studied, a standard-oriented regional language concept is taught, passing on a monolingual standard with functional differentiation. The latter initially excludes Low German as a medium of instruction and thus limits its functional scope. Although this is problematic, it can also be explained by Low German's traditional mode of existence as a regional language. This means that corpus planning with regard to scientific terms, didactic operators, etc., must first be carried out in order to ensure equal use of the variety Low German as a medium of instruction. Secondly, there are also limits to the positive evaluation, in the form of contact restrictions (only online and temporally restricted), limited group sizes, technical limitations and restricted sustainability. To increase sustainability, learners require further, preferably ongoing, language learning and language use opportunities. For this purpose, it seems necessary to familiarise learners with language learning strategies to enable them to use further open educational resources like apps or videos in a meaningful way after the end of the course (see Hodges & Prys, in this volume). This can be achieved, for example, by encouraging reflection on their individual learning process and by raising student awareness on the learning medium itself (Jones, 2016: 156). Fundamentally, however, all the potentially positive learning opportunities mentioned depend on the concrete practice of teachers and participants – that is, how they use the interactive digital possibilities.

What do the results mean for language maintenance and language vitality? There is no easy answer. If language maintenance means that non-speakers become new speakers by first becoming semi-speakers who increasingly use their language actively (Jaffe, 2015: 24), online courses can only support one stage of the development. As we have seen, digital resources can offer good teaching and learning opportunities to turn non-speakers into semi-speakers and possibly new speakers. However, whether and in what form learners use the language outside the online courses cannot be decided in the courses themselves. A crucial aspect of language maintenance is digital vitality. Language courses can strengthen this if they succeed in teaching digital literacy (Jones & Hafner, 2021; Knobel & Lankshear, 2015; Warschauer, 1999, 2004), which enables learners to use the language in a variety of online contexts. This can encourage them to act in translocal communities, and temporally limited communities of learners can become more stable communities of practice (Angouri, 2015; Eckert & McConell-Ginet, 1999; Gee, 2005). We are convinced that online language courses can make a decisive contribution in this area and that the model presented here could also be transferred to other small languages.

Note

(1) We would like to thank all reviewers for their helpful comments on previous versions of this paper.

Appendix 6.A

Table 6.1 Overview of transcript corpus

Transcript number	Participants (+ teacher)	Content	Length	
			pages	minutes
T1_B3	7 + 1	Obelix	2	6
T2_B4_1	13 + 1	Beginning	1	4
T3_B4_2	13 +1	Popeye	2	3
T4_B4_3	13 + 1	*Daun*-periphrase	6	14
T5_B5	11 +1	Greetings	8	17
T6_B8_1	12 + 1	Origin	6	13
T7_B8_2	12 + 1	Plural	4	7
T8_A8_1	3 +1	Reading aloud	1	2
T9_A8_2	3 + 1	Village meeting	6	17
T10_A8_3	3 +1	Evaluation	5	13
Total	16 + 1		41	1 h 36 min.

References

Adler, A., Ehlers, C., Goltz, R., Kleene, A. and Plewnia, A. (2016) *Status und Gebrauch des Niederdeutschen 2016*. Eigenverlag des Instituts für Deutsche Sprache.

Androutsopoulos, J. (2016) Theorizing media, mediation and mediatization. In N. Coupland (ed.) *Sociolinguistics. Theoretical Debates* (pp. 282–302). Cambridge University Press. https://doi.org/10.1017/CBO9781107449787.014.

Angouri, J. (2015) Online communities and communities of practice. In A. Georgakopoulou and T. Spilioti (eds) *The Routledge Handbook of Language and Digital Communication* (pp. 323–338). Routledge.

Arendt, B. (2019) Discourse acquisition in peer talk – The case of argumentation among kindergartners. *Learning, Culture and Social Interaction* 23, (100342). https://doi.org/10.1016/j.lcsi.2019.100342.

Arendt, B. (2021) A long-lasting CofP of new and native speakers—Practices, identities of belonging and motives for participation. *Languages* 6 (1), 30. https://doi.org/10.3390/languages6010030.

Arendt, B. and Langhanke, R. (eds) (2021) *Niederdeutschdidaktik. Grundlagen und Perspektiven zwischen Varianz und Standardisierung*. Peter Lang.

Auer, P. (ed) (1998) *Code-Switching in Conversation: Language, Interaction, and Identity*. Routledge.

Biebighäuser, K. (2016) Immersion und Interaktivität – Fremdsprachenlernen mit Avataren und Agenten. In T. Zeyer, S. Stuhlmann and R.D. Jones (eds) *Interaktivität beim Fremdsprachenlehren und-lernen mit digitalen Medien* (pp. 111–138). Narr.

Caruso, C. and Hofmann, J. (2018) A task-based approach to tablets and apps in the foreign language classroom. *Currents in Teaching and Learning* 10 (2), 68–77.

Council of Europe (2001) *Common European Framework of Reference for Languages: Learning, Teaching, Assessment* (pp. 101–130). Cambridge University Press.

Cekaite, A. and Aronsson, K. (2014) Language play, peer group improvisations, and L2 learning. In A. Cekaite *et al.* (eds) *Children's Peer Talk. Learning from Each Other* (pp. 194–213). Cambridge University Press.

Cekaite, A., Blum-Kulka, S., Gröver, V. and Teubal, E. (2014) Children's peer talk and learning: Uniting discursive, social and cultural facets of peers' interaction. In A. Cekaite *et al.* (eds) *Children's Peer Talk. Learning from Each Other* (pp. 3–19). Cambridge University Press.

Cenoz, J. (2009) *Towards Multilingual Education: Basque Educational Research from an International Perspective*. Multilingual Matters.

Crystal, D. (2006) *Language and the Internet*. Cambridge University Press.

Debyser, F. (1984) *Simulations Globales: L'Immeuble*. Hachette.

Eckert, P. and McConell-Ginet, S. (1999) New generalizations and explanations in language and gender research. *Language in Society* 28 (2), 185–201.

Ehlers, K.-H. (2018) *Geschichte der mecklenburgischen Regionalsprache seit dem Zweiten Weltkrieg. Teil 1: Sprachsystemgeschichte*. Peter Lang.

Ehlers, K.-H. (2021) Welches Niederdeutsch unterrichten? Ein kritischer Problemaufriss vor dem Hintergrund der jüngeren Entwicklung des Niederdeutschen in Mecklenburg-Vorpommern. In B. Arendt and R. Langhanke (eds) *Niederdeutschdidaktik. Grundlagen und Perspektiven zwischen Varianz und Standardisierung* (pp. 29–60). Peter Lang.

European Charter for Regional or Minority Languages (1992) See https://www.coe.int/en/web/european-charter-regional-or-minority-languages (accessed June 2022).

Nic Fhlannchadha, S. and Hickey, T.M. (2018) Minority language ownership and authority: Perspectives of native speakers and new speakers. *International Journal of Bilingual Education and Bilingualism* 21 (1), 38–53.

García, O. and Li, W. (2014) *Translanguaging: Language, Bilingualism and Education*. Palgrave Macmillan.

Gee, J. (2005) Semiotic social spaces and affinity spaces. In D. Barton and K. Tusting (eds) *Beyond Communities of Practice. Language Power and Social Context* (pp. 214–232). Cambridge University Press.

Gee, J. (2007) *Good Video Games + Good Learning. Collected Essays on Video Games, Learning and Literacy*. Peter Lang.

Gumperz, J. (1982) *Discourse Strategies*. Cambridge University Press.

Hornsby, M. and Vigers, D. (2018) "New" speakers in the heartland: Struggles for speaker legitimacy in Wales. *Journal of Multilingual and Multicultural Development* 39 (5), 419–430.

Jaffe, A. (2015) Defining the new speaker: Theoretical perspectives and learner trajectories. *International Journal of the Sociology of Language* 231, 21–44.

Jones, C. and Hafner, R. (2021) *Understanding Digital Literacies. A Practical Introduction* (2nd edn). Routledge.

Jones, R.D. (2016) A playful approach to interactive media in the foreign language classroom. In T. Zeyer, S. Stuhlmann and R.D. Jones (eds) *Interaktivität beim Fremdsprachenlehren und -lernen mit digitalen Medien* (pp. 139–162). Narr.

Kelly-Holmes, H. and Atkinson, D. (2017) Perspectives on language sustainability in a performance era: Discourses, policies, and practices in a digital and social media campaign to revitalise Irish. *Open Linguistics* 3, 236–250.

Kiphard, E. (2004) Lachen, Humor und Clownerie in Pädagogik und Therapie. In St. Kuntz and J. Voglsinger (eds) *Humor, Phantasie und Raum in Pädagogik und Therapie* (pp. 59–66). Modernes Leben.

Knobel, M. and Lankshear, C. (2015) Digital media and literacy development. In A. Georgakopoulou and T. Spilioti (eds) *The Routledge Handbook of Language and Digital Communication* (pp. 151–165). Routledge.

Kunitz, S. (2018) Collaborative attention work on gender agreement in Italian as a foreign language. *The Modern Language Journal* 102, 64–81.

Kytölä, S. (2015) Translocality. In A. Georgakopoulou and T. Spilioti (eds) *The Routledge Handbook of Language and Digital Communication* (pp. 371–388). Routledge.

Maak, D. (2011) „Geschützt im Mantel eines Anderen" – Die „globale Simulation" als Methode im DaF-Unterricht. *Informationen Deutsch als Fremdsprache* 38 (5), 551–565.

Meskill, C. and Anthony, N. (2015) *Teaching Languages Online* (2nd edn). Multilingual Matters.

Möller, F. (2008) *Plattdeutsch im 21. Jahrhundert. Bestandaufnahmen und Perspektiven.* Schuster.

O'Rourke, B. (2018) Just use it! Linguistic conversion and identities of resistance amongst Galician new speakers. *Journal of Multilingual and Multicultural Development* 39 (5), 407–418.

Peters, R. (2015) Zur Sprachgeschichte des norddeutschen Raumes. In M. Hundt and A. Lasch (eds) *Deutsch im Norden* (pp. 18–35). De Gruyter.

Pietikäinen, S., Kelly-Holmes, H., Jaffe, A. and Coupland, N. (2016) *Sociolinguistics from the Periphery. Small Languages in New Circumstances.* Cambridge University Press.

Puigdevall, M., Walsh, J., Amorrortu, E. and Ortega, A. (2018) 'I'll be one of them': Linguistic mudes and new speakers in three minority language contexts. *Journal of Multilingual and Multicultural Development* 39 (5), 445–457.

Reershemius, G. (2017) Autochthonous heritage languages and social media: Writing and bilingual practices in Low German on Facebook. *Journal of Multilingual and Multicultural Development* 38 (1), 35–49.

Reuter, H. (2021) Unterrichten ohne Norm: Niederdeutschunterricht an der Volkshochschule als Sprachpolitik von unten. In B. Arendt and R. Langhanke (eds) *Niederdeutschdidaktik. Grundlagen und Perspektiven zwischen Varianz und Standardisierung* (pp. 389–409). Peter Lang.

Schmidt, I. and Blume, C. (2016) Wir müssen reden. Interaktive Anwendungen zum fremdsprachlichen Sprechtraining. In T. Zeyer, S. Stuhlmann and R.D. Jones (eds) *Interaktivität beim Fremdsprachenlehren und -lernen mit digitalen Medien* (pp. 211–236). Narr.

Schroeder, R. (2017) *Social Theory after the Internet? Media, Technology and Globalization.* UCL Press.

Seljan, S., Berger, N. and Dovedan, Z. (2004) Computer-Assisted Language Learning (CALL). In *Proceedings of the 27th International Convention MIPRO 2004* (pp. 262–266). Liniavera.

Statistisches Amt Mecklenburg-Vorpommern (2021) *Statistische Berichte. Lehrkräfte an allgemeinbildenden und beruflichen Schulen in Mecklenburg-Vorpommern.* Schuljahr 2020/21. Schwerin.

Stellmacher, D. (2000) *Niederdeutsche Sprache.* Weidler.

State Government. (2021) See https://www.regierung-mv.de/Landesregierung/bm/Aktuell/?id=169121&processor=processor.sa.pressemitteilung (accessed November 2021).

Stieler-Hunt, C. and Jones, C. (2019) A professional development model to facilitate teacher adoption of interactive, immersive digital games for classroom learning. *British Journal of Educational Technology* 50 (1), 264–279.

Thurlow, C., Lengel, L. and Tomic, A. (2012) *Computer Mediated Communication: Social Interaction and the Internet.* Sage.

UNESCO *Atlas of the World's Languages in Danger.* See http://www.unesco.org/languages-atlas/index.php?hl=en&page=atlasmap (accessed June 2022).

Warschauer, M. (1999) *Electronic Literacies. Language, Culture, and Power in Online Education.* Lawrence Erlbaum Associates.

Warschauer, M. (2004) Technological change and the future of CALL. In S. Fotos and Ch.M. Brown (eds) *New Perspectives on CALL for Second Language Classrooms* (pp. 15–26). Lawrence Erlbaum Associates.

Wocken, H. (2014) *Zum Haus der inklusiven Schule. Ansichten – Zugänge – Wege* (2nd edn). Feldhaus.

Woolard, K. (2004) Codeswitching. In A. Duranti (ed.) *A Companion to Linguistic Anthropology* (pp. 73–94). Blackwell.

Zichermann, G. and Cunningham, C. (2011) *Gamification by Design. Implementing Game Mechanics in Web and Mobile Apps.* O'Reilly.

Part 3
Multilingual Practices on Social Media

7 North Frisian in Social Media: Looking for Computer-Mediated Communication in a Very Small Language

Hauke Heyen

Introduction

The use of minority languages, regional languages or small languages in computer-mediated communication (CMC), is often discussed in regard to terms like 'language vitality', where 'language death' (Crystal, 2000) is its opposite. Kornai (2013) for example coined the term 'digital language death' and developed a conceptual framework to describe the status of language use in the digital sphere, based on the premise that the representation of a language in CMC is an important indicator that the language community continues to work creatively and innovatively with the language and is capable of using it in new technological areas (see also Crystal, 2006: 234–235). In the framework outlined by Kornai, only user-generated content is considered as reference to a language on the web, in contrast to automatically generated content like machine translations. This approach emphasises the relevance of speaker practices rather than simply counting appearances of language produced on the web. It aligns with what Pietikäinen and Kelly-Holmes (2011; also Kelly-Holmes & Atkinson, 2017) framed the 'performance era' in media consumption and media production, seeing individual participants more and more as 'prosumers', a role that combines the consumer and producer in one person. Media content is no longer just received, but also created. Applied to social media communication, it has become commonplace for users to create and receive media every day, using the language they prefer and adapting their style to the language their audience requires. But what role do languages like North Frisian play that are actively used as a family language but only by some 5000 to 10,000 speakers? How do they engage in the performance era and show practices of their everyday language use online? At first glance, publicly available North Frisian content in CMC such as websites, Wikipedia entries or social media posts appears to be scarce, yet speakers claim to include their language in their digital communication habits (Heyen, 2020).

This chapter addresses the first of this volume's main questions, whether social media is able to provide new communicative domains for speakers of autochthonous heritage languages like North Frisian. After an overview on the sociolinguistic background of North Frisian and its speakers' social media use, this question will be addressed in a discussion of two case studies: one exemplifies how the approach of virtual breathing spaces can be applied to virtual Frisian communities (Belmar & Heyen, 2021) and the other examines how Frisian identities can be expressed in a multilingual setting through playful use of hashtags (Heyen, 2022). The overarching objective of this study is to discuss the mediatisation (Androutsopoulos, 2016) of North Frisian, focusing on practices that are not limited to the exclusive use of the heritage language, but acknowledge the multilingual reality the speakers are living in.

Setting the Scene

Traditionally, the North Frisian-speaking community is located in the uppermost North of Germany in a district called *Nordfriesland* ('North Frisia'), a rural area next to the Danish border on the North Sea coastline and a couple of islands. The actual areal distribution of the community of speakers over the last 200 years is, however, remarkably smaller than the district itself. Consequently, of North Frisia's roughly 165,500 inhabitants, only a few are believed to speak North Frisian. Since there is no census data on language use, these figures can only be estimated and would commonly be assumed to be some 5000 to 10,000 speakers, also counting speakers living outside the historical area (cf. Århammar, 2008; Walker, 2001). Due to new patterns of mobility in the post-war era and economic change from mainly agricultural sources of employment towards tourism, as well as a lack of institutions for higher education, speakers do not necessarily remain in their traditional region. In areas that are more popular among tourists, like the islands, the pressure of deciding to leave or remain in their home is especially high, as Walker (2001) points out, due to increasing house prices and a limited labour market. Speakers of North Frisian usually grow up at least bilingual Frisian–German, acquiring German at school at the latest, although they have a high probability of being in touch with German earlier, for example in mixed-language families, kindergarten, etc., because of the dominance of German in almost all domains of language. In fact, in administration, education, (inter-)regional trade and, to a certain degree, also cultural work and written language, North Frisian has not been present throughout history. North Frisian has always been the language of family or the local community, while Low German (historically) has been the language of trade, and Standard German the language of church and administration. Århammar (2008) describes this situation, which lasted into the 19th century, as a 'stable diglossia', followed by an ongoing shift to German in all domains. The restriction of North Frisian language use to intimate and local domains prevented the development of a standard variety, leading to the division of North Frisian into numerous varieties that can be grouped together into Island North Frisian and Mainland North Frisian. Walker notes that some of the varieties 'are to a certain degree mutually incomprehensible' (Walker, 2001: 266), but that inter-North Frisian communication is possible if speakers are trained to have a passive knowledge of other varieties (Walker, 2020: 112). This reflects also in literature and textuality: there is an orthographic convention for each variety. It is, however, hard to claim a North Frisian tradition of writing since there was, with a few exceptions, no North Frisian literature before the 19th century. Since school education is in German only, except for foreign language teaching, this is a context in which the role of North Frisian has often been discussed. There are schools offering Frisian classes, but, with one exception, where Frisian is an elective for the high school diploma, Frisian classes are usually offered on a voluntary basis, if at all, and include both L1 speakers as well as students learning it as a foreign language, placing the didactic focus on the latter, as Walker (2001: 272) concludes. As a consequence of Frisian education only being available on this basis, literacy skills and academic language skills are primarily acquired in German and not for Frisian. Thus, North Frisian never was perceived as a language of writing and was historically tied to the domains of family, home or the immediate local environment (Århammar, 2008).

The lack of literacy skills is significant, especially when it comes to computer-mediated communication, since a lot of interpersonal exchange takes place in written form, despite the growth of platforms with a focus on visual formats, like Instagram, Snapchat and TikTok (which might also contain embedded written language). Even if we acknowledge that the vast majority of speakers are supposed to be speaking one of the two varieties Århammar (2008) describes as the strongest varieties, with at least 2000 speakers each, the above-mentioned issues of inter-comprehensibility and different orthographic conventions still apply. This emphasises the need to be aware of different subgroups using their own variety rather than assuming some sort of standard variety all speakers would communicate in, especially since 'each Frisian speaker regards his dialect as the epitome of the Frisian language and generally speaking little notice is taken of the other dialects' (Walker, 2001: 270), which also reflects in identity constructions that are closely connected to the immediate surroundings (Kleih, 2019). It will be discussed later how using Frisian might affect the language community's interaction, since it reduces the potential number of peers and audiences in everyday communication if the communicative range of the language is as limited as described here.

Data on the use of North Frisian in computer-mediated communication was first gathered in 2017 and is presented in Heyen (2020). In the following, the most important outcomes on platform choice and language choice will be described. The data is based on a survey taken by 90 participants and modelled after a survey that was conducted for speakers of West Frisian and their language use in social media (Jongbloed-Faber, 2014; Jongbloed-Faber *et al.*, 2016). In contrast to its West Frisian counterpart, the survey in Heyen (2020) not only focuses on teenagers, but also considers older age groups. However, the results must be interpreted with caution. The 90 participants in the study only represent a small portion of the language community, and it can be assumed that a survey of this kind may well lead to a biased result, since it was only offered as an online questionnaire and thus possibly captures a group of respondents who are more willing to try out and use online formats anyway, although the sample of respondents shows a fair share of different age and gender groups. Also, a comparison of habits in social media platform use among the North Frisian-speaking respondents from Heyen (2020) with the average habits of users based in Germany over the same period from Schlobinski and Siever (2018) shows a tendency to similar social media use: almost 90% (87% in Heyen, 89% in Schlobinski & Siever) of all people use WhatsApp as opposed to Twitter, which might be present in public debates but is hardly used (6% among speakers of North Frisian versus 4% in general). While these are general trends over all age groups, Facebook and Instagram use differs depending on age. Instagram is clearly more popular among younger users and Facebook among older users, although the use of both platforms over all age groups appears to be higher in the North Frisian study than in national comparison (Heyen, 2020; Schlobinski & Siever, 2018). This suggests that the surveyed speakers of North Frisian follow the same trends observable nationwide and thus among speakers of German.

The most important point for further discussion in this chapter, however, is the way North Frisian is used on social media. With regard to types of posts with different outreach, as in direct messaging (private posts), group chats (group posts) and Facebook status updates, tweets or Instagram posts (public posts), the chance that a speaker would use North Frisian decreases the wider the potential audience grows. Even in group posts, the use of Frisian would be considered to be rather unlikely by the vast majority of the participants, reflecting on their own patterns of language use (Heyen, 2020: 64–67). This comes as no surprise and has been observed for other communities of small languages (for example Jongbloed-Faber *et al.*, 2016; see also Chapter 8 of this volume). These observations show that the patterns of use cannot be attributed solely to a connection with CMC and an unknown or only vaguely known group of recipients of posts. Speakers of North Frisian also adapt their offline communication strategies to online practices when it comes to audience planning: if the audience is not clearly defined as Frisian speaking, posters choose a common shared language instead (Heyen, 2020: 81; see examples for other languages on this matter in Chapters 4 and 8 of this volume). Considering the small size of the Frisian language community, it appears quite reasonable that a speaker would not reach many of their followers by posting in Frisian, given the very likely case that their followers do not form a Frisian-only community. In addition to the potential communicative range, normative pressure seems to prevail, which manifests itself in the form of self-restriction, for example, in order to avoid violating orthographic norms. Among the 31% of speakers that are not using North Frisian in CMC, fear of violating norms is significantly stronger than among users that use Frisian online (Heyen, 2020: 81). Nevertheless, there are 62 participants – roughly 69% – who claim to use Frisian in some computer-mediated communication. The question remains, where and when they do so.

Online Communities as Breathing Spaces for Small Languages

The first case study to be discussed here applies the concept of breathing spaces to online communities. This approach goes back to Fishman (1991) as a proposed measure to support everyday language use in communities where the respective language is declining. Fishman suggests physical 'breathing spaces', like a community centre for example, as an environment in which speaking the language is not contested in any way. Establishing breathing spaces can be read as part of a 'physical "normalization"' (Fishman, 1991: 59):

> an effort at minimal balance, at boundary maintenance and demographic preponderance in at least a few areas of basic, normal daily interaction, so that Xish [i.e. the small language] can have some space to call its own, some space in which it is the normal and self-evident channel, expression and accompaniment of at least some crucial cultural transmission and maintenance processes. (Fishman, 1991: 59)

A transfer of this concept from actual physical spaces to virtual communities in CMC settings and social media networks has also been suggested by Cunliffe, who sees parallels in virtual communities that are considered as 'language-empathetic social media enclaves' which 'try to create an audience in which speakers of the minority language dominate' (Cunliffe, 2019: 467). A concept for working with online communities as breathing spaces is outlined by Belmar and Glass (2019), referring to ubiquitous social media communication as part of media use practices typical of the performance era (Pietikäinen & Kelly-Holmes, 2011): 'the concept of a virtual community has become normalized to the point that it is notable when someone does not have a social media presence' (Belmar & Glass, 2019: 12). They see computer-based communication practices as being commonly established and argue that dynamics have developed in the formation of identities and interests that create group affiliations based on language skills and common interest in language. In their view, this is also facilitated by the potentially worldwide networking and spatial independence social media networks offer. In particular, in the context of migration or diaspora communities, location-independent online exchange also allows for networking between language of origin communities and can create a unique opportunity for them to use their respective language (Belmar & Glass, 2019: 13). Belmar and Glass distinguish between four categories of breathing spaces:

(a) the minority language is the only language used in the community;
(b) the minority language is the preferred language of the community, although the use of other languages is accepted; this is often the case in communities of learners where the dominant language and/or English are sometimes used;
(c) the minority language (its sociolinguistic context, grammar, lexicon, etc.) is the subject of discussion, especially if these discussions take place *in* the minority language;
(d) the status of the minority language as *language* (rather than dialect) is not contested. (Belmar & Glass, 2019: 14; emphasis in original)

While category (d) at first glance might appear trivial or self-explanatory, it functions as a basic criterion for establishing a breathing space that does not need to be monolingual but acknowledges the multilingual practices and repertoires speakers are making use of (which, again, can also be linked to principles of media use in the performance era, as outlined by Pietikäinen & Kelly-Holmes, 2011).

Applying the idea of online communities as breathing spaces, Belmar and Heyen (2021) present a case study in which Facebook groups and Facebook pages are analysed as communities. For both West Frisian and North Frisian, five communities each were analysed that showed some affiliation to the respective Frisian area or variety. This had to be either a strong local connection as in a local online forum, a strong thematic connection to the language as well as arts and literature in the language or representing an organisation dedicated to working with the language community or to preserving the language. Activities in the communities were monitored from 1 January to 30 March 2019, and posts collected. According to the most frequent topical categories in the collection, the posts were categorised as either Frisian language, the Frisian area, arts/literature, news or other and analysed for language use.

Of 1127 posts, 343 were from groups or pages connected to North Frisian. Although there is a strong link to both the region of North Frisia and work on the Frisian language community in the groups and pages considered for this study, only a few of the posts (25 exactly) contained any Frisian content; sometimes Frisian was visible only in an attached image or video (see Belmar & Heyen, 2021: 293–299). In most cases, Frisian would appear along with predominantly German content or only in images designed as vocabulary quizzes. Generic posts in Frisian only occur in content created by institutions; actual content in Frisian generated by users other than the page owners can be limited to four reactions to posts and are created by only three individual user profiles. In contrast, the case study shows different results for West Frisian. Although in both cases groups were chosen that suggested strong topical links to the language or its community, such as Frisia as an area, Frisian language, Frisian arts and literature or very locally bound connections assuming that these were engaging topics regarding the users' language choice, there was no example in the North Frisian collection that contained a posting by an individual user.

Nevertheless, except for a single group from which no Frisian posts could be recorded in the collection, the examined North Frisian virtual communities can be classified as breathing spaces according to Belmar and Glass's (2019) conceptual layout. While this might not necessarily be understood as a space in which 'normal daily interaction' is observable, as suggested by Fishman (Fishman, 1991: 59), it still offers the language a space of its own that might even be somewhat protected, as it is managed by an institution and its community. Belmar and Heyen conclude that speakers in the North Frisian communities observed might follow a more top-down approach in their language choices (Belmar & Heyen, 2021: 311), using the language only or most likely when they are part of an environment that strongly encourages the use of the small language. This appears to be confirmed by projects like 'Floosetääl our WhatsApp', a WhatsApp-based writing project by Friisk Foriining, a Frisian association involved in activities to conserve and empower the Frisian language. In this creative writing project in late 2020, more than twenty users were engaged in writing a continuation story through WhatsApp text messages, initiated and led by the association.

Drawing conclusions from such virtual breathing spaces for North Frisian, we find an observable effect on language use. In this case, the community-building factor plays the most important role in setting the scene in which a Frisian-speaking audience is both encouraged to participate and engaged with the topic as well. The benefit of breathing spaces described by Belmar and Glass (2019) does not seem to be the absence of threats or depreciation of language use but rather the presence of a common interest that can be related to some degree to the language. However, the much lower participation among North Frisian-speaking users in communities as compared to West Frisian-speaking users might be an outcome of the language community's size and its fragmentation into different varieties with different orthographic standards some speakers might feel uncomfortable with, as mentioned above.

Hashtags as Indicators for Language Use

In order to analyse minority language content in social media, Johnson (2013) uses a keyword-based search to find user profiles on Twitter posting Welsh content. This seems to be a practical approach to collecting user-generated content and seems to be made even easier by using hashtags as search items. Following the basic functionality of hashtags as building a cross-referential keyword catalogue with searchable topic markers (Zappavigna, 2015; cf. also Heyd & Puschmann, 2017), posts using a minority language hashtag might easily identify user profiles using the language, opening the door to checks for further posts that have not been tagged. McMonagle et al. (2019), for example, build on this by looking explicitly for the use of language tags for Gaelic ('#gaeilge'), Welsh ('#cymraeg') and West Frisian ('#frysk') in order to analyse both the respective hashtag in use and a user profile's language use. This proves to be a useful way to access content and analyse linguistic practices, including tagging, in smaller languages. However, as they point out, one should not 'expect that everyday users of a given language tag their online content as such' (McMonagle et al., 2019: 40), and hence this method would only show a sample of the content available.

Originally aimed at compiling a corpus of North Frisian posts for text analysis, a case study presented in Heyen (2022) follows the approach as Johnson (2013; see above). Starting with a search for hashtags denominating the names of major (in terms of community size) Frisian varieties and single words strongly connotated with emotions relating to friends, family and the home, the initial search aimed to identify user profile pages and look for further posts containing North Frisian content. Unfortunately, adapting this approach to access North Frisian online content did not prove successful. Due to the multiple varieties of North Frisian, the self-designations for the Frisian language vary in each variety. Also, the proportion of speakers using Twitter is low, not only among speakers of Frisian but throughout internet users in Germany, as shown above. The approach was then adapted for Instagram, where hashtags are also widely established. Although this platform is aimed at posts containing pictures or videos, hashtags are commonly used in comments or descriptions added to the picture/video. Posting on Instagram can hence be understood as a combination of pictorial content and optional textual content.

Despite Instagram's greater popularity, a hashtag search for posts in North Frisian using language tags (e.g. '#fering' for the variety of Föhr) did not prove successful either. However, in contrast to Twitter there was a distinct use of single hashtags in North Frisian. Therefore, the study was redesigned to analyse the use of hashtags that can be interpreted as North Frisian lexical items and to find out how the use of Frisian hashtags reflects mediatised practices of constructing Frisian identities. Besides the platform's popularity, Instagram is less restrictive on character length for posts than Twitter (except for a maximum of 20 hashtags), which would allow users to also post multilingual content without creating long threads. In addition, hashtags are quite commonly used on Instagram in different functions. These include the 'traditional' way of using hashtags as topic markers or topic tags, but, as Wikström (2014) and Zappavigna (2015) show, hashtags can appear in different functions, such as to provide *additional information* not relating to the post's content itself but rather complementing it or to add another semantic context and emotional information; quite common on Instagram is also a *playful use* of hashtags, which might contain self-referential sarcasm or irony, for example referring to one's own excessive use of hashtags with a concluding *#hashtaghell*; and sometimes hashtags are used to make a *typographical distinction* from the main text because they are usually rendered in a different font style (cf. Wikström, 2014; Zappavigna, 2015).

When a posting using a Frisian hashtag was found, the user's account was checked for additional posts containing Frisian hashtags. In all, 68 posts were considered, with a total of 131 hashtags categorised as lexical Frisian items or phrases. Some of the outcomes will be summarised in the following; for more details see Heyen (2022).

A canonical use of hashtags as topic tags describing a post's pictorial content is the most common type, as in *#sanapgung* ('sunrise') tagging a picture of a sunrise. A special type of topic tags are language tags, as already mentioned in connection with McMonagle *et al.* (2019, see above). These tags refer to a main topic with strong ties to a language which might be in the pictorial part, the textual part or both parts. In the collected data, the example of an easter egg painted in the colours of the North Frisian flag accompanied by the comment *Fröiliken poosche* ('Happy Easter') is tagged with *#frasch* ('Frisian'). The same hashtag is used in another post in which it appears rather as a marker for additional information or meta information: an image showing a burning candle with '2020' written on it is accompanied by a commentary wishing the very best for the year 2020 in German and tagged with *#twuntitwunti* ('twenty-twenty') and *#frasch*. Here, *#twuntitwunti* serves as a topic marker relating to the turn of the year referred to in the image and text. The *#frasch*, however, provides additional information on the language used in the first tag. This meta information is even stronger in another example, in which the post solely contains an image showing a flower in bloom and a hashtag *#hoow* ('hope') in its textual part. In the context of the emerging COVID-19 pandemic and the first public restrictions coming into effect in early 2020, this hashtag frames the post as encouragement to get through the uncertainty of the pandemic.

The most creative use of hashtags in the collection referred to here is represented by a playful use function as in *#hokerbeest*, which reflects the phrase *hoker beest* ('who are you'). In the varieties of the islands Föhr (Fering) and Amrum (Öömrang), this phrase is used not only to ask for someone's name when meeting for the first time but also to probe each other's social network and family to check for possible mutual relatives or acquaintances. In the collected posts, this hashtag appears without any semantic connections to either the pictural or the textual part of the post or any other hashtags. Rather, this can be interpreted as a playful, almost self-ironic, presentation of a local identity that is expressed in this hashtag. The loss of the social function of the phrase in this example, reducing it to merely a marker of being part of the local community, could also reflect the practice of 'indexical/intertextual bleaching' in mediatised posts (Androutsopoulos, 2016). Crucially, there are only a few posts that actually contain more Frisian content than just the hashtags. These tags are mostly used without any other Frisian content in the posts (see comparable findings for Low German in Chapter 9 of this volume).

Nevertheless, the majority of the hashtags analysed are used to tag locations, from distinct landmarks like a church and graveyard to bigger places like a town or an island to North Frisia as a whole. Also, not all Frisian hashtags are used by speakers of Frisian (as far as this can be derived from their Instagram posts). Especially hashtags referring to Frisian locations are often used by visitors and those users who want to express some kind of emotional relation to Frisia or the Frisian language. In other posts by these latter users, often no further tagging in Frisian is observable, let alone content posted in Frisian.

A conclusion drawn from these observations is that hashtags on Instagram give users a low-key opportunity to include at least a few elements of North Frisian in a posting, along with content in the audience's main language, such as German (or English). Thus, they might also help users to construct an identity of some sort – either through feeling connected to Frisia or the language (i.e. in the case of tourists using Frisian toponyms, for example) or being Frisian and wanting to show it to their Instagram followers. Expressing and constructing an online identity in social media profiles has been discussed both for the use of functional hashtags (Zappavigna, 2014) and for the choice of minority or smaller languages (Jongbloed-Faber *et al.*, 2017). The construction of affiliations to North Frisia on Instagram may be linked to landscape, not only among tourists, but also among people who are from North Frisia (contrary to findings in Kleih, 2019, where landscape is not among the features that can be seen as identity constructing).

Conclusion

Given the low number of speakers and limited communicative range of languages with a very small speaker community like North Frisian, it seems rather unlikely that speakers would use Frisian in public posting formats, except in the case of a few individuals who are especially engaged in promoting the Frisian language. This is what speakers claim themselves in the survey published in Heyen (2020) and is also evident from the few posts openly available and searchable that contain North Frisian. However, as the examples of breathing spaces show, speakers are engaging in environments that share a common interest while ideally actively fostering the use of the Frisian language. For forms of low-key integration of language, it does not seem necessary to establish a virtual community, as speakers are capable of making use of their multilingual repertoires in order to both keep up with the linguistic demands and expectations of their audiences and express their linguistic identities. This is what Androutsopoulos (2013, 2015) describes for members of heritage language communities and what Jongbloed-Faber *et al.* (2017)show for regional languages.

The studies presented here show that, although North Frisian content is not available in large numbers in public posts, this absence of visible online content does not necessarily mean that the language is losing 'vitality'. Speakers of the language have developed practices to use their language as part of their linguistic repertoire. This is strongly driven by identities, as both the virtual communities and hashtag use show. While in virtual communities an overarching shared interest, topical focus or institutional engagement serves as a driving factor for communication and eliciting user reactions, in hashtags it is the emotional connection and the possibility of self-expression and presentation. The outcomes, however, differ. In virtual communities as observed in Belmar and Heyen (2021), the production of longer texts plays a more important role for creating both posts and reactions. In contrast, expressions using hashtags allow for fewer conflicts and insecurities, also among the less confident writers of a small language, because they might focus on single fossilised expressions they feel comfortable with and can use their language in a setting in which normative expectations are lowered as it per se is associated with a playful use of language. Thus, there appears to be at least a chance that social media provides new communicative domains for speakers of North Frisian. The speakers' 'Frisianess' is no longer bound to the domain of family and hidden in diglossia, but part of a mediatised multilingual identity that is being staged in online posts.

References

Androutsopoulos, J. (2013) Code-switching in computer-mediated communication. In S.C. Herring, D. Stein and T. Virtanen (eds) *Pragmatics of Computer-Mediated Communication* (pp. 667–694). De Gruyter Mouton. https://doi.org/10.1515/9783110214468.667.

Androutsopoulos, J. (2015) Networked multilingualism: Some language practices on Facebook and their implications. *International Journal of Bilingualism* 19 (2), 185–205. https://doi.org/10.1177/1367006913489198.

Androutsopoulos, J. (2016) Theorizing media, mediation and mediatization. In N. Coupland (ed.) *Sociolinguistics. Theoretical Debates* (pp. 282–302). Cambridge University Press. https://doi.org/10.1017/CBO9781107449787.014.

Århammar, N. (2008) Das Nordfriesische, eine bedrohte Minderheitensprache in zehn Dialekten: Eine Bestandsaufnahme. In H.H. Munske (ed.) *Sterben die Dialekte aus? Vorträge am Interdisziplinären Zentrum für Dialektforschung an der Friedrich-Alexander-Universität Erlangen-Nürnberg, 22.10.-10.12.2007*. https://opus4.kobv.de/opus4-fau/frontdoor/index/index/docId/664.

Belmar, G. and Glass, M. (2019) Virtual communities as breathing spaces for minority languages: Re-framing minority language use in social media. *Adeptus* 14. https://doi.org/10.11649/a.1968.

Belmar, G. and Heyen, H. (2021) Virtual Frisian: A comparison of language use in North and West Frisian virtual communities. *Language Documentation & Conservation* 15 (June), 285–315.

Crystal, D. (2000) *Language Death*. Reprinted. Cambridge University Press.

Crystal, D. (2006) *Language and the Internet* (2nd edn). Cambridge University Press.

Cunliffe, D. (2019) Minority languages and social media. In G. Hogan-Brun and B. O'Rourke (eds) *The Palgrave Handbook of Minority Languages and Communities* (pp. 451–480). https://doi.org/10.1057/978-1-137-54066-9_18.

Fishman, J.A. (1991) *Reversing Language Shift. Theoretical and Empirical Foundations of Assistance to Threatened Languages*. Multilingual Matters.

Heyd, T. and Puschmann, C. (2017) Hashtagging and functional shift: Adaptation and appropriation of the #. *Journal of Pragmatics* 116, 51–63. https://doi.org/10.1016/j.pragma.2016.12.004.

Heyen, H. (2020) *#friesisch: Beweggründe und Hindernisse für nordfriesische Kommunikation in digitalen Medien*. Estrikken. Kiel: Friesische Philologie/Nordfriesische Wörterbuchstelle, Christian-Albrechts-Universität zu Kiel.

Heyen, H. 2022. #hokerbeest: Auf der Suche nach Spuren digitaler nordfriesischer Kommunikation. In A. Walker, E. Hoekstra, G. Jensma, W. Vanselow, W. Visser and C. Winter (eds) *From West to North Frisia: A Journey along the North Sea Coast. Frisian Studies in Honour of Jarich Hoekstra* (pp. 134–147). NOWELE Supplement Series 33. John Benjamins Publishing Company. https://doi.org/10.1075/nss.33.09hey.

Johnson, I. (2013) Audience design and communication accommodation theory: Use of Twitter by Welsh–English biliterates. In E.H. Gruffydd Jones and E. Uribe-Jongbloed *Social Media and Minority Languages: Convergence and the Creative Industries* (pp. 99–118). Multilingual Matters.

Jongbloed-Faber, L. (2014) *Taalgebrûk Fan Fryske Jongerein Op Sosjale Media. Rapportaazje Ûndersyk Taalfitaliteit I*. Fryske Akademy–Mercator European Research Centre on Multilingualism and Language Learning.

Jongbloed-Faber, L., Van Loo, J. and Cornips, L. (2017) Regional languages on Twitter: A comparative study between Frisian and Limburgish. *Dutch Journal of Applied Linguistics* 6 (2), 174–196. https://doi.org/10.1075/dujal.16017.jon.

Jongbloed-Faber, L., Van De Velde, H., Van Der Meer, C. and Klinkenberg, E. (2016) Language use of Frisian bilingual teenagers on social media. *Treballs de Sociolingüística Catalana* 26, 27–54.

Kelly-Holmes, H. and Atkinson, D. (2017) Perspectives on language sustainability in a performance era: Discourses, policies, and practices in a digital and social media campaign to revitalise Irish. *Open Linguistics* 3 (1), 236–250. https://doi.org/10.1515/opli-2017-0012.

Kleih, R. (2019) *Föhrer, Friese, Friesländer? Eine empirische Untersuchung zur Beziehung von Sprache und Identität in Nordfriesland*. Estrikken. Friesische Philologie/ Nordfriesische Wörterbuchstelle, Christian-Albrechts-Universität zu Kiel.

Kornai, A. (2013) Digital language death. *PLOS ONE* 8 (10), 1–11.

McMonagle, S., Cunliffe, D., Jongbloed-Faber, L. and Jarvis, P. (2019) What can hashtags tell us about minority languages on Twitter? A comparison of #cymraeg, #frysk, and #gaeilge. *Journal of Multilingual and Multicultural Development* 40 (1), 32–49. https://doi.org/10.1080/01434632.2018.1465429.

Pietikäinen, S. and Kelly-Holmes, H. (2011) Gifting, service, and performance: Three eras in minority-language media policy and practice. *International Journal of Applied Linguistics* 21 (1), 51–70. https://doi.org/10.1111/j.1473-4192.2010.00257.x.

Schlobinski, P. and Siever, T. (2018) *Sprachliche Kommunikation in der digitalen Welt: Eine repräsentative Umfrage, durchgeführt von forsa*. Gottfried Wilhelm Leibniz Universität, Seminar für deutsche Literatur und Sprache. Networx Supplement 80. https://doi.org/10.15488/3088.

Walker, A. (2001) Extent and position of North Frisian. In H.H. Munske, N. Århammar, V.F. Faltings, J.F. Hoekstra, O. Vries, A.G.H. Walker and O.Wilts (eds) *Handbuch Des Friesischen/Handbook of Frisian Studies* (pp. 263–284). Tübingen: Max Niemeyer Verlag. https://doi.org/10.1515/9783110946925.263.

Walker, A. (2020) Die Friesen und das Friesische in Nordfriesland. In R. Beyer and A. Plewnia (eds) *Handbuch der Sprachminderheiten in Deutschland* (pp. 65–138). Tübingen: Narr Francke Attempto.

Wikström, P. (2014) Srynotfunny: Communicative functions of hashtags on Twitter. *SKY Journal of Linguistics* 27 (127–152).

Zappavigna, M. (2014) Enacting identity in microblogging through ambient affiliation. *Discourse and Communication* 8 (2), 209–228. https://doi.org/10.1177/1750481313510816.

Zappavigna, M. (2015) Searchable talk: The linguistic functions of hashtags. *Social Semiotics* 25 (3), 274–291. https://doi.org/10.1080/10350330.2014.996948.

8 Unravelling Language Choice Online: Frisian Bilingual Teenagers on WhatsApp, Snapchat and Instagram

Lysbeth Jongbloed-Faber

Introduction

In many parts of the world where people have internet and a smartphone at their disposal, social media have taken a major place in daily communication. Some social media make it possible to communicate with the world, while other social media are mainly used for communication with an intimate circle of family and friends. What are the implications of these new forms of communication for the use of minority languages? Although the opportunities seem unlimited on the internet to preserve, spread and consume content in any language (Cunliffe & Herring, 2005: 131), the unequal power relations that exist in offline society between speakers of different language varieties are usually reproduced in online situations: it is often perceived to be impolite or a political statement to use a minority language that cannot be understood by one's entire audience (Cunliffe, 2007; Massaguer Comes et al., 2020). Moreover, a factor that may decrease the use of a minority language on social media is limited literacy, as in many cases, the minority language is not used or taught in education at all, or only to a limited extent.

This chapter investigates the language use of bilingual[1] Frisian–Dutch teenagers on WhatsApp, Instagram and Snapchat and attempts to explain the differences in language choice. It addresses the question

---

A previous form of this chapter has been published as a chapter in my dissertation: Jongbloed-Faber, L. (2021) *Frisian on social media. The vitality of minority languages in a multilingual online world.* Amsterdam: LOT publications. https://doi.org/10.26481/dis.20210903lj

posed in the introduction to this volume regarding whether social media can provide new communicative domains for speakers of autochthonous minority languages and is a case study of multilingual practices on social media (Reershemius & Arendt, this volume). It is a follow-up of a study among 2000 Frisian bilingual teenagers in 2013/2014 (Jongbloed-Faber *et al.*, 2016) that investigated the use of Frisian on Facebook, Twitter and WhatsApp. As the use of social media is volatile and many teenagers have given up using Facebook and Twitter (Newcom.nl, 2020), this follow-up study seemed necessary. The current study takes a novel approach as the influence of the audience on language choice on social media (cf. audience design by Bell, 1984, 2001) is investigated. In addition, extra attention is paid to regional orientation, as this has been shown to influence the (offline) use of dialect (Monka, 2014, 2020).

Over the last decade, several studies have investigated the use of regional, minority and/or heritage languages on social media (cf. Gruffydd Jones & Uribe-Jongbloed, 2013; Lillehaugen, 2019; McMonagle *et al.*, 2019). Most studies have analysed language use and choice on Facebook and Twitter. Studies on autochthonous minority language use on WhatsApp, Instagram and Snapchat are rare. Social media entail better opportunities for speakers to use autochthonous minority languages than for example on websites, as social media are more interactive and more similar to face-to-face communication (Cunliffe, 2019: 451). However, users of majority languages or national languages often have more resources and more technology available than speakers of minority languages (Lackaff & Moner, 2016), which causes a preference for communicating in those national languages on social media. So, although the internet may entail new opportunities to engage in digital culture, 'these opportunities are not equally distributed' (Ní Bhroin, 2019: 117). Interfaces in minority languages or keyboards for lesser-used scripts are not available or are being introduced on the market much later as commercial interests from the providers are small (European Parliament, 2018).

In contrast to the pre-2.0 web, where people were often writing *about* but not *in* smaller varieties such as minority languages or regional varieties, social media have become a space where communication in minority languages and regional varieties are no longer obstructed by purity norms and differences between varieties (Reershemius, 2017). Facebook has become such a space for many bilinguals to use their minority language (Cru, 2015; Cunliffe *et al.*, 2013). The use of a minority language in this new domain associated with modernity is far from the widespread stigma of lack of upward social mobility often attached to its regular use (Cru, 2015). Although online language use is often a reflection of offline communication patterns and power differences in public life (Cunliffe *et al.*, 2013: 85; McMonagle, 2019), social media provide opportunities to communicate more, spontaneously, and engage in literacy practices 24/7. Thus social media provide much more opportunities for speakers of minority languages to use their languages than in the past (McMonagle, 2019). Using a minority language on social media can construct closeness with the audience and feel more authentic (Jongbloed-Faber, 2018; Massaguer Comes *et al.*, 2020), however, it can also be considered a marked, political choice. In combination with the smaller size of the potential market, the use of minority languages by famous persons on for instance Instagram or YouTube is still limited (Massaguer Comes *et al.*, 2020).

Minority language speakers often make unconscious language choices on social media, making it hard to determine which factors influence their choices (Cunliffe, 2019: 460). Language choice is influenced by, among other things, language attitudes (Baker, 2006: 6). Attitudes may fluctuate, depending on the circumstances (O'Rourke, 2011: 6–7). Language attitudes are often a reflection of the status of different languages in society. Generally, two evaluative dimensions are distinguished in language attitudes: status (or power) and solidarity. The status dimension refers to the extent to which the use of a specific language variety might lead to upward social mobility, economic opportunity and power (Gardner & Lambert, 1972). The solidarity dimension refers to the extent to which a language variety evokes feelings of belonging. Generally, attitudes on the status dimension are more positive towards standard or high varieties than towards non-standard or low varieties, and speakers evaluate their own language variety more positively on the solidarity dimension (Kircher & Fox, 2019). Some scholars distinguish a third dimension, namely dynamism (Grondelaers & Speelman, 2013; Rosseel, 2017: 6). This dimension refers to the liveliness, coolness and trendiness of a language variety or its speakers. The presence of a minority language on social media shows the relevance of the language to modern life and accordingly how modern people consider the language. Its absence on social media may lead to decreasing relevance in society, especially for young people (Cunliffe, 2019: 452; Eisenlohr, 2004; UNESCO, 2003). Attitudes on the dynamism dimension might therefore have greater influence on the use of an autochthonous minority language on social media than other dimensions.

Another factor that may influence language choice on social media is the multi-layeredness of the audience. The Audience Design Model (Bell, 1984, 2001) is a framework that explains language variation in news media and personal communication through the multi-layeredness of the audience and can also be applied to bilingual language choice. Bell (1984, 2001) argues that intraspeaker variation is mainly influenced by the intended audience. Within an audience, several layers can be distinguished: direct addressees or second persons who are known, ratified and addressed by the speaker, and a peripheral audience that is not directly addressed. The peripheral audience, so-called third persons, consists of auditors who are known and ratified, overhearers who are known, but non-ratified and unaddressed, and finally, eavesdropper of which the speaker is totally unaware. Not only can an addressee influence the speaker's language variety, other (non-target) audience members can do so as well.

When a bilingual speaker is confronted with a language choice, Bell even expects a larger influence of peripheral audience members than in monolingual style shift (Bell, 1984: 176). On social media platforms where a message can reach a wider audience, language choice may thus not be the sole result of the language that is normally spoken between the interlocutors, but may also be influenced by peripheral audience members. A lesser spoken variety may then easily be replaced by one spoken/understood by a large(r) part of the audience. A study on language choice on Twitter showed that Welsh–English bilinguals often tweeted in English when monolingual English speakers were present in addition to Welsh-speaking bilinguals, while Welsh was mainly used in tweets when directly addressing other bilinguals (Johnson, 2013: 114–116). The same patterns were found in a study comparing the use of Limburgish, Frisian and Dutch in tweets. To address a wider audience, often the national language Dutch was used while in reactions and tweets directed at particular audience members, Limburgish or Frisian were often used (Jongbloed-Faber *et al.*, 2017).

In addition, Bell (1984, 2001) makes a distinction between audience design, where speakers are responsive to their audience, and referee design, where speakers do not adapt their language to their audience, but use a language (style) of another absent social group they want to belong to. Bell defines this as initiative style shift (Bell, 1984: 187–189, 2001: 162–163). The latter is comparable to theories concerning social identity construction: individuals are considered to have control over their linguistic repertoire and use linguistic resources to construct their social identity (cf. Coupland, 2009; Johnstone, 2010;). An example of initiative style shift /identity construction on social media would be the use of (the high status variety) English on Instagram although one's audience exists of speakers of Frisian and Dutch only, or the use of Frisian in front of a Frisian–Dutch multilingual audience.

Frisian in the Netherlands

Frisian[2] is the second official language in the province of Fryslân in the Netherlands, next to the national language Dutch. The province of Fryslân has almost 650,000 inhabitants, two thirds of which live in the countryside and one third in one of the four biggest cities (Provinsje Fryslân, 2020). Frisian is the first language for 48% of the inhabitants, while another 13% were raised bilingually speaking Frisian and mainly Dutch (Klinkenberg *et al.*, 2018). In general, Frisian is spoken more in the countryside than in cities (Gorter & Jonkman, 1995; Klinkenberg *et al.*, 2018).

The majority of the inhabitants are able to understand Frisian (very) well (84%), 64% can speak it (very) well, but only 16% indicate that they can write it (very) well (Provinsje Fryslân, 2020: 7–8). At home, 43% speak Frisian with their partner and 45% speak Frisian with their children (Provinsje Fryslân, 2020: 7–8). People's attitudes in Fryslân towards Frisian are mixed: while most Frisian speakers take a positive stance towards Frisian and its use, a minority of the province's population does not favour its use (usually those not speaking Frisian) (Gorter *et al.*, 2001; Klinkenberg *et al.*, 2018).

Over the past centuries, Dutch has managed to acquire a dominant position in education and many other domains in Fryslân. Most individuals learn Frisian as a first language at home, but develop their literacy skills through Dutch in educational contexts (Günther-Van der Meij, 2018: 15). As a result, Frisian is mostly a spoken language which results in the writing proficiency among Frisian-speakers to be low (Stefan *et al.*, 2015). The 2013–2014 study (Jongbloed-Faber *et al.*, 2016) revealed that predominantly teenagers with solely Frisian as home language use Frisian on WhatsApp, Twitter and Facebook: they use Frisian more frequently on WhatsApp and in private or addressed messages than in (semi-)public status updates or tweets. Teenagers' offline language use with their peer group, language attitudes and writing proficiency were found to be the most reliable explanatory factors for the use or non-use of Frisian on social media (Jongbloed-Faber *et al.*, 2016).

According to the UNESCO Interactive Atlas of the World's Languages in Danger (Moseley, 2010), Frisian is vulnerable. In 1998, Frisian was recognised as a regional or minority language under parts II and III of the European Charter for Regional or Minority languages (ECRML), which obliges the Dutch government to protect and promote Frisian in all fields of public life, such as education, public administration and services, and the media. Particularly the position of Frisian in primary education, however, is still vulnerable and in need of further improvement (Council of Europe, 2020).

In this chapter, I will use the term 'minority language' to refer to languages such as Frisian because this concept reflects the unequal power relations between speakers of a majority and minority language well, which often includes a difference in status between (speakers of) the two languages (Gardner & Lambert, 1972; Kircher & Fox, 2019). For speakers of minority languages, there are often fewer opportunities to use their language in all domains, in particular in 'official' domains, such as in communication with public authorities, in education and in court. Although in theory the ECRML ensures equal rights for the use of minority languages in official domains, in practice this may not be the case in many situations. As a consequence, many speakers of minority languages do not have access to (the same quality of) education in their minority language, and they may even face inferior literacy in their minority language in comparison to the majority language. This in turn can have a negative impact on the use of the minority language in writing, also on social media.

Materials and Methods

An online questionnaire containing 63 questions was developed in Frisian and Dutch to answer the research questions. The questionnaire is a partial replication of the questionnaire used in Jongbloed-Faber et al. (2016), and was supplemented with questions about audience design, attitudes and regional orientation. Schools providing secondary and vocational education throughout the province of Fryslân were contacted to participate in the survey. Eventually, 25 schools[3] gave permission to conduct the survey. Ten of the participating schools were located in one of the four major towns in Fryslân (Leeuwarden, Drachten, Sneek and Heerenveen), and 15 schools in the countryside. The survey was rolled out between October 2019 and January 2020. The data were collected during classes, to avoid a bias as a result of self-selection. Some schools gave the participants the possibility to choose between the Dutch and Frisian questionnaire. Other schools provided the link to the questionnaire in just one of the two languages. Participation was anonymous. The full questionnaire can be found in my dissertation (Jongbloed-Faber, 2021) at https://doi.org/10.26481/dis.20210903lj.

In total, 2507 teenagers filled in the questionnaire. Not all of them, however, met the criteria for participation in this study. To enable a comparison with the 2013/2014 study, only data from participants between the ages of 14 and 18 were used. Other criteria were that participants gave permission to use their answers for scientific research, they resided in the province of Fryslân and it took them at least 7 minutes to complete the questionnaire. The criteria resulted in the selection of 1982 participants for this study.

The following factors are incorporated in this study.

Home language

The teenagers reported which language(s) they speak at home with various family members and which language(s) these family members speak to them. Home language was defined as the language(s) the parents speak to the teenagers. For the purpose of this study, the teenagers were consequently split up into three different groups:

- L1 teenagers: teenagers who were exclusively raised in Frisian.
- L1-2 teenagers: teenagers to whom parents speak both Frisian and Dutch.
- L2 teenagers: teenagers to whom the parents speak Dutch.

Proficiency in Frisian

The teenagers were asked to report on their proficiency of Frisian for understanding, speaking, reading and writing on a five-point Likert scale with the following scales: not at all, with difficulty, reasonably, well and very well.

The use of Frisian and Dutch in offline situations with peers

The teenagers were asked to report on their offline language use with peers by reporting how often (never, sometimes, often or all the time) they speak Frisian, Dutch, English and other languages with their friends.

Attitudes

The teenagers were asked to rate ten word pairs on an eleven-point (0–10) semantic differential sliding scale to evaluate their attitude towards Frisian. The different word pairs all tap into one of the three dimensions of attitudes. The 10 word pairs together have a Cronbach's alpha of 0.97, suggesting they tapped into the same underlying construct. See Table 8.1 for an overview of the word pairs in English, Dutch and Frisian.

Table 8.1 Attitude word pairs

English	Dutch	Frisian
does not - does belong to me	hoort niet - wel bij mij	heart net - wol by my
not useful - useful for later	Niet - wel nuttig voor later	net - wol nuttich foar letter
rigid - relaxed	stijf - relaxed	stiif - relaxed
whiny - happy	zeurderig - vrolijk	seurderich - bliid
dull - cool	saai - cool	saai - cool
strange - familiar	vreemd - vertrouwd	frjemd - fertroud
not useful - useful with friends	niet - wel handig met vrienden / vriendinnen	net - wol handich mei freonen / freondinnen
ugly - beautiful	lelijk - mooi	net moai - moai
old-fashioned - modern	ouderwets - modern	alderwetsk - modern
unimportant - important	niet belangrijk - belangrijk	net belangryk - belangryk

Regional orientation

The regional orientation of teenagers was operationalised as follows. First of all, the teenagers were asked where they would like to live when they are an adult. The teenagers could choose between:

- where I currently live;
- in a village close to where I currently live;

- in a big(ger) town close to where I currently live;
- in a village or big(ger) town elsewhere in Fryslân;
- in a big(ger) town elsewhere in Fryslân;
- outside Fryslân;
- outside the Netherlands.

Following this, the teenagers were asked to indicate to what extent they (dis)agreed with the following statements measuring their orientation towards Frisian popular culture on a five-point Likert scale:

- I like contemporary Frisian music such as De Hûnekop, The Bounty Hunters or De Doelleazen.
- I follow Frisian accounts on Instagram that share funny Frisian memes/movies (for those having an Instagram account).

Audience

To measure the influence of the audience on the teenagers' language choice they were asked to fill in two audience matrixes as displayed in Table 8.2: one matrix for speaking and one for understanding Frisian.

Table 8.2 Audience matrix: what proportion of your contacts can speak/understand Frisian (estimate)?

	(Hardly) anybody	Less than half	About half	Over half	(Almost) all
Classmates					
Friends whom you meet outside school					
WhatsApp contacts					
Instagram contacts					
Snapchat contacts					

In addition, to measure the teenagers' awareness of their language choices and audience on social media, they were asked to indicate to what extent they (dis)agreed with the following statements on a five-point Likert scale:

- When I post a message on social media, I sometimes doubt which language I will/should use.
- The language choice of my posts depends on who I want to reach/from whom I would like to receive a reaction.
- The language I use on social media is the same as the language I speak with the receiver.
- When I post a message on social media, I do not think about who will see the message.

Finally, those who indicated to use Frisian sometimes or often on social media, were asked to indicate to what extent they (dis)agreed with the following statement on a five-point Likert scale: I write social media messages in Frisian less often than I would like to, because I would like everyone to understand my messages.

Results

The assumption that teenagers no longer intensively use Facebook and Twitter and that a follow-up study including other social media platforms was necessary turned out to be correct. In comparison to 2013/2014 (Jongbloed-Faber *et al.*, 2016), the use of Facebook and Twitter has decreased drastically as evident in Figure 8.1.

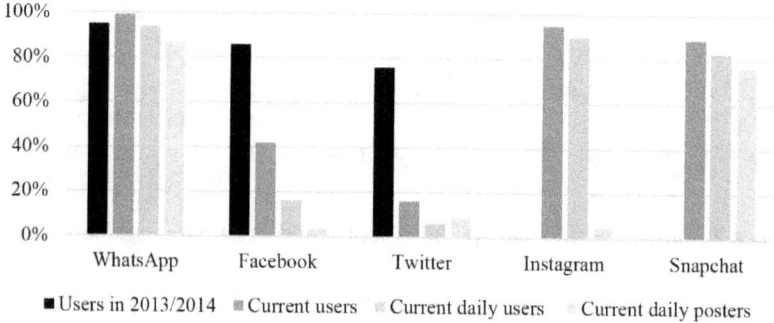

Figure 8.1 Social media use

WhatsApp is still the most used social media platform by teenagers: 99% use WhatsApp. Instagram proves to be platform where it is more important to see than to be seen. While 95% of the teenagers use Instagram, only 55% of them report that they hardly ever post an update and primarily watch others' posts. Snapchat is slightly less popular among teenagers than WhatsApp and Instagram: 89% of the teenagers use this platform. Nevertheless, the share of Snapchat users that post at least once a day is much higher than on Instagram: 77% compared to 5%.

The most popular social medium to chat with friends is Snapchat (51%), followed by WhatsApp (38%). To communicate about practical matters such as homework and dinner plans, teenagers prefer using WhatsApp (82%).

Language use on WhatsApp, Instagram and Snapchat by all teenagers

Figure 8.2 illustrates how often on average Dutch, Frisian, English, other languages and solely emojis are used on WhatsApp, Instagram and

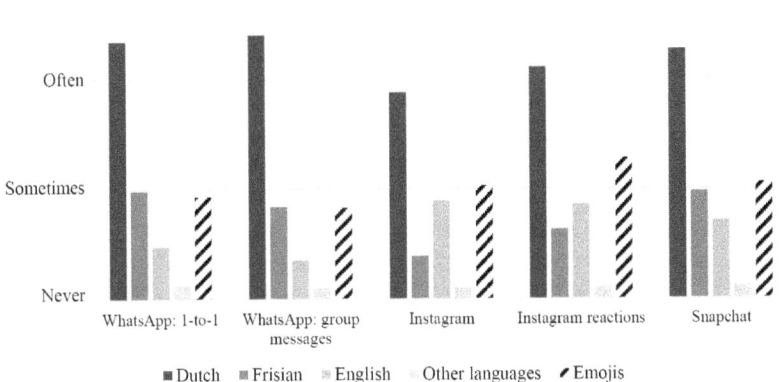

Figure 8.2 Language use on social media (all teenagers)

Snapchat. Dutch is the language that is used most on all media, followed by Frisian on WhatsApp and Snapchat, and by English on Instagram. On Instagram and Snapchat, on average, participants post messages consisting of just emojis more frequently than Frisian and English (sometimes in addition to a picture or video). Fifty-seven percent of all teenagers use Frisian to some extent on at least one of the three social media platforms.

Figure 8.3 shows the use of Frisian split by the teenagers' home language. On WhatsApp and Snapchat, the average frequency in use lies between sometimes and often. On Instagram, Frisian is used the least, also by L1 teenagers. While in Instagram reactions, on average, the L1 teenagers sometimes use Frisian, in Instagram posts the average lies even lower, in between never and sometimes. The L2 teenagers hardly use

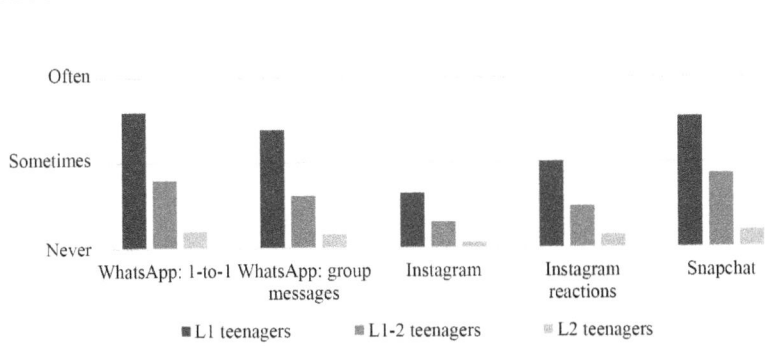

Figure 8.3 Use of Frisian on social media (all teenagers)

Frisian on social media, while L1-2 teenagers show an average between the L1 and L2 teenagers. The effect of home language is significant in all cases (WhatsApp-1-on-1 messages: $F(2, 1952) = 711.58$, $p < 0.001$; WhatsApp-group messages: $F(2, 1946) = 536.21$, $p < 0.001$; Instagram posts: $F(2, 1855) = 143.25$, $p < 0.001$; Instagram reactions: $F(2, 1855) = 260.96$, $p < 0.001$; Snapchat posts: $F(2, 1697) = 453.59$. Post hoc tests revealed significant differences between all groups ($p < 0.001$). L1 teenagers use Frisian on social media most frequently.

The next sections focus on the use of Frisian by L1 teenagers on the different social media platforms as these teenagers communicate in Frisian most in daily offline life. The other teenagers do not often use Frisian in daily life and their use of Frisian on social media is minimal on average. This focus on L1 teenagers will result in more insight into how audience on social media, literacy, regional orientation, and attitudes influence their online use of Frisian.

Language use on WhatsApp by L1 teenagers

Figure 8.4 shows the distribution in use of Frisian on WhatsApp by L1 teenagers in 1-on-1 messages and groups in general. Fifty-nine percent of the L1 teenagers use Frisian often or all the time in 1-on-1 messages, whereas this share is 48% in group messages.

A comparison in the use of Dutch and Frisian on WhatsApp reveals that 26% of the teenagers report using more Frisian than Dutch in 1-on-1 messages and 23% in group messages. Dutch is used more frequently by 42% of the teenagers in 1-on-1 messages and by 52% in group messages on WhatsApp. Thirty-two percent of the participants use Frisian as often as Dutch in 1-on-1 messages and

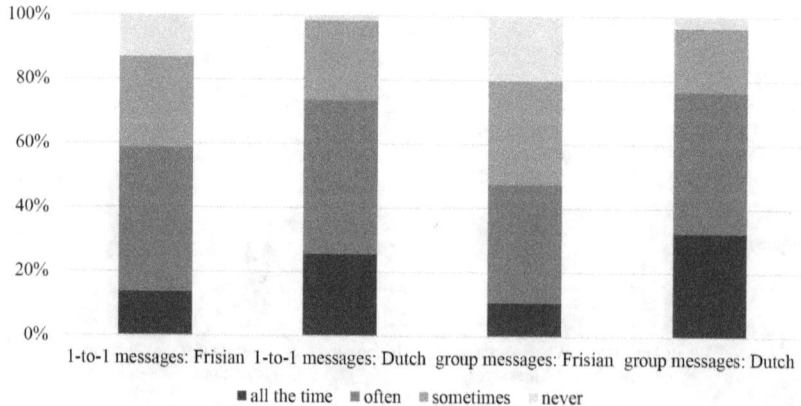

Figure 8.4 Use of Frisian and Dutch on WhatsApp by L1 teenagers (n = 1005 & n = 1002)

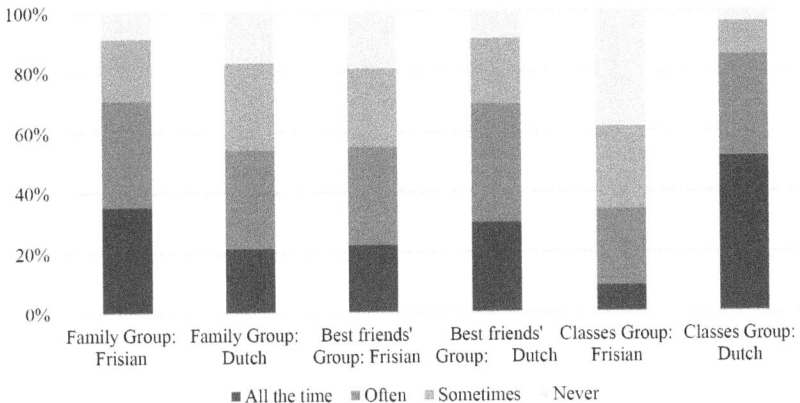

Figure 8.5 Use of Frisian and Dutch in WhatsApp Groups by L1 teenagers (n = 910, n = 975 and n = 873)

25% do in group messages. Besides reporting on the language use of the teenagers themselves, the teenagers also reported on the language use in three different WhatsApp groups: family, best friends and school class.

Figure 8.5 shows how often Frisian and Dutch is used in those WhatsApp Groups. In 70% of the family WhatsApp groups, Frisian is used often or all the time, and in 9% of these WhatsApp Groups Frisian is never used. Interestingly, in a large part of these groups of 'monolingual' Frisian families, both Frisian and Dutch are used. While the results of the questionnaire show that in oral communication at home Frisian is used most by far, Frisian is often combined or alternated with Dutch in social media messages: in just 17% of these family groups Dutch is never used. Social media is thus a space where both Frisian and Dutch are used, also among predominantly Frisian-speaking people. Generally, social media messages are thus for a large part a bilingual practice. In the WhatsApp groups with best friends of the L1 teenagers, in over half of the groups Frisian is used often or all the time. However, in these best friends' groups, Dutch is even used more often. In the WhatsApp group with classmates, Frisian is used the least: in 38% of those groups no Frisian is used at all. In contrast Dutch, is used all the time in 52% of the cases.

Table 8.3 compares the use of Frisian on WhatsApp by L1 teenagers in the current survey and Jongbloed-Faber *et al.* (2016). The mean use of Frisian on WhatsApp by L1 teenagers has not changed: 87% of the L1 teenagers still use Frisian on WhatsApp and 13% do not. Fifty-nine percent of the L1 teenagers use Frisian often or all the time in 1-on-1 messages and 48% still do so in WhatsApp group messages.

Table 8.3 The use of Frisian by L1 teenagers on WhatsApp: current survey compared to Jongbloed-Faber et al. (2016)

	WhatsApp: 1-to-1 messages		WhatsApp: Group Messages	
	2013–2014	2019–2020	2013–2014	2019–2020
Mean use of Frisian (scale 1-4)	2.6*	2.6*	2.4*	2.4*
Share using Frisian on WhatsApp				
Never (1)	13%	13%	20%	20%
Sometimes (2)	33%	28%	33%	32%
Often (3)	40%	45%	35%	37%
All the time (4)	15%	14%	12%	11%

*No significant differences observed ($p < 0.001$)

Language use on Instagram by L1 teenagers

Instagram is a different type of medium than WhatsApp and Snapchat. Although all three media have roughly the same functionalities, Instagram differs in two important aspects. First of all, Instagram has the possibility to connect and interact with people one does not personally know. Many people use the medium to follow (famous) others in addition to broadening one's own audience. The nature of this medium is also different. Interviews with teenagers revealed that they tend to present their unfiltered self on WhatsApp and Snapchat, while on Instagram it is more about keeping up appearances. This may also affect language choice and increase the use of higher status language(s).

Many teenagers report using Instagram to watch funny memes and movies: 74% of the L1 teenagers who are active on Instagram often watch funny memes/movies on Instagram and 40% specifically follow Frisian accounts that post funny Frisian memes/movies on Instagram.

The teenagers themselves do not use Frisian very often on Instagram. Most communication on Instagram happens through Dutch and emojis only, also by L1 teenagers. Fifty-seven percent of the L1 teenagers active on Instagram never use Frisian in their updates and 34% never use Frisian in reactions to posts of others. Seventeen percent use Frisian often or all the time when posting an update on Instagram, in reactions this share increases to 30%. These outcomes confirm that the nature of Instagram affects the use of Dutch and English at the cost of Frisian. This mirrors the conclusions drawn in an earlier study about language use patterns on Twitter which showed that a Tweet in the national language might very well get a continuation in a shared regional language (Jongbloed-Faber et al., 2017). Although many teenagers never post in Frisian, they respond in Frisian to Instagram posts of others more often. See Figure 8.6 and Figure 8.7 for the use of the different languages and emojis by L1 teenagers in Instagram posts and in Instagram reactions respectively.

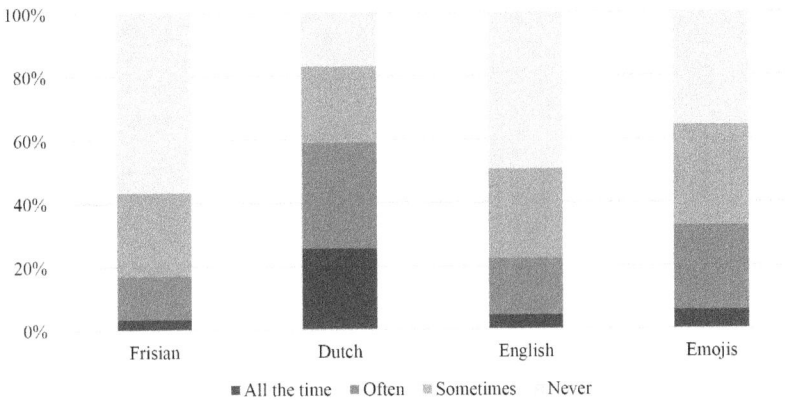

Figure 8.6 Language use in Instagram posts by L1 teenagers (n = 966)

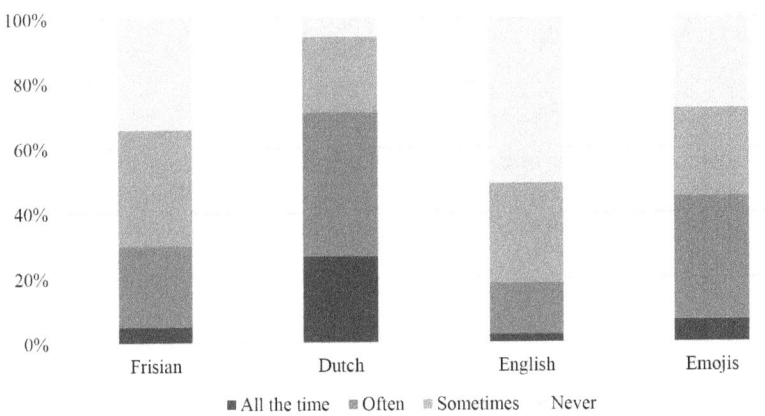

Figure 8.7 Language use in Instagram reactions by L1 teenagers (n = 966)

Language use on Snapchat by L1 teenagers

Snapchat has become a very important social media platform for teenagers: 89% of the teenagers use Snapchat, 83% use it daily and of the users, and 77% post something on Snapchat once or several times a day. The language use of L1 teenagers on Snapchat is shown in Figure 8.8. On average, Dutch is used most by L1 teenagers: 74% use it often or all the time. For Frisian, the average use lies a little lower: 57% use Frisian often or all the time in Snapchat messages. 24% of the L1 teenagers sometimes use Frisian on Snapchat, and 19% never. A quarter of the L1 teenagers report to use more Frisian than Dutch, one third of

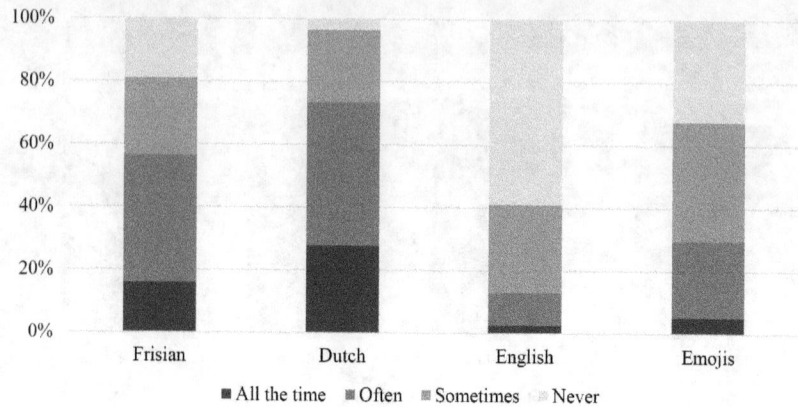

Figure 8.8 Language use on Snapchat by L1 teenagers (n = 885)

the L1 teenagers use Frisian as often as Dutch, and 42% use more Dutch than Frisian. English is not used very often in Snapchat messages by L1 teenagers. Messages with emojis only are more common.

Factors in the use of Frisian on social media

As discussed in the introduction, the following factors are expected to influence the use of Frisian on social media (the first three factors were found to be a significant explanatory factor in Jongbloed *et al.* (2016)):

- Offline language use with peers.
- Writing skills.
- Attitude towards Frisian.
- Audience.
- Regional orientation.

A regression analysis showed that six factors explain 61% of the variance in the use of Frisian on Snapchat, 64% of the variance on WhatsApp in 1-on-1 messages, and 58% of the variance in group messages. These factors are: offline language use with peers, the share of their contacts on Snapchat/WhatsApp that speak Frisian, self-reported writing skills, attitude towards Frisian and two variables indicating the teenagers' orientation towards Frisian popular culture. Important to note is that home language and share of one's audience that understands Frisian are not significant in this model. The extent to which teenagers thus use Frisian on social media can be largely predicted by *productive* habits and skills of the teenager and their peers, and not by the *receptive* skills of their peers. See Table 8.4 for an overview of the optimal models to explain the variance in use of Frisian on Snapchat and WhatsApp.

Table 8.4 Regression model explaining the variance in the use of Frisian on Snapchat and WhatsApp by all teenagers

Independent factors	Snapchat ($R^2 = 61\%$)		WhatsApp 1-to-1 messages ($R^2 = 64\%$)		WhatsApp group messages ($R^2 = 58\%$)	
	β	Sign.	β	Sign.	β	Sign.
Speaking Frisian with friends	0.324	0.000	0.377	0.000	0.333	0.000
Share of audience on Snapchat / WhatsApp that speaks Frisian	0.241	0.000	0.153	0.000	0.208	0.000
Own writing skills	0.167	0.000	0.218	0.000	0.198	0.000
Attitude towards Frisian	0.102	0.000	0.109	0.000	0.085	0.001
Liking contemporary Frisian music	0.081	0.000	0.077	0.000	0.096	0.000
Following funny Frisian Instagram accounts	0.058	0.002	0.039	0.029		n.s.

So the more frequently the teenagers speak Frisian with their friends, the larger the share of one's audience that speaks Frisian, the better one's literacy in Frisian, the more positive one's attitude towards Frisian, and the more one likes Frisian popular culture the more often the teenagers will use Frisian on Snapchat and WhatsApp. These factors thus have a positive effect on the use of Frisian on social media

The main difference is the relative importance of the different independent factors. While offline language use with peers has the strongest predictive power in all three models, the predictive power of the audience's ability to speak Frisian is stronger than writing skills for Snapchat and group messages on WhatsApp. Writing skills, however, are stronger in the model for 1-on-1 WhatsApp messages. Writing skills in this last model are less important for the use of Frisian on Snapchat, which might explain why the L1-2 and L2 teenagers use Frisian slightly more on Snapchat than on WhatsApp. The initial function of WhatsApp, sending text messages via the internet, and Snapchat, sharing (audio) visual material, might explain this difference.

Interestingly, the teenagers are not very concerned about and aware of their language choice on social media. Moreover, there is little difference in agreement with statements about language choice and audience awareness between L1, L1-2 and L2 teenagers while language choice is more straightforward for speakers of a majority language than of a minority language.

Regarding the attitudes towards Frisian, a Kaiser-Meyer-Olkin index (0.967) and Bartlett's Test of Sphericity (sign. <0.001) show that the 10 word pairs designed to measure the attitude towards Frisian are suitable for factor analysis. A factor analysis (Maximum Likelihood) shows that the 10 word pairs that all load onto one factor (eigenvalue of 7.9, explaining 79% of the variance, factor loadings between 0.779 and

Table 8.5 Regression model explaining the variance in the use of Frisian in Instagram reactions and posts by all teenagers

Independent factors	Instagram reactions ($R^2 = 43\%$)		Instagram posts ($R^2 = 29\%$)	
	β	Sign.	β	Sign.
Speaking Frisian with friends	0.274	0.000	0.192	0.000
Share of audience on Instagram that speaks Frisian	0.183	0.000	0.164	0.000
Own writing skills	0.179	0.000	0.123	0.000
Liking contemporary Frisian music	0.114	0.000	0.127	0.000
Following funny Frisian Instagram accounts	0.086	0.000	0.080	0.001
Language depends on audience	0.050	0.007	0.090	0.000

0.923) and no distinction can be made between the different dimensions of attitudes.

Of the independent variables that represent regional orientation, the (dis)liking of contemporary Frisian music and following funny Frisian Instagram accounts have a significant predictive value. In contrast to outcomes of other research (Monka, 2014, 2020), where teenagers would like to live in later life does not have a significant predictive value. What thus remains of regional orientation is the orientation towards Frisian popular culture.

It is more difficult to explain the variance in the use of Frisian on Instagram. The optimal model explains 29% of the variance in Instagram posts and 43% of the variance in Instagram reactions with six factors. Five factors in this model are the same as for Snapchat and WhatsApp, namely offline language use with peers, the share of the audience that speaks Frisian, writing skills and orientation towards Frisian popular culture. The last factor that has a small predicting value is the extent to which teenagers agree with the statement that their language on social media depends on the audience they want to reach. In contrast to the predictive models for WhatsApp and Snapchat, the teenagers' attitude towards Frisian does not have a significant predictive value for Instagram. The most probable explanation is that the orientation towards Frisian popular culture suppresses the effect of their attitudes. See Table 8.5 for an overview.

Predicting the use of Frisian on social media by L1 teenagers

Models predicting the use of Frisian on social media by L1 teenagers are able to explain less of the variance in use than for all Frisian teenagers together. See Table 8.6 for the optimal models predicting the use of Frisian on Snapchat and WhatsApp by L1 teenagers. Also in the model for L1 teenagers only, offline language use with peers, writing skills, attitude towards Frisian and teenagers' orientation towards Frisian

Table 8.6 Regression model explaining the variance in the use of Frisian on Snapchat and WhatsApp by L1 teenagers

Independent factors	Snapchat (R^2 = 38%)		WhatsApp 1-to-1 messages (R^2 = 43%)		WhatsApp group messages (R^2 = 38%)	
	β	Sign.	β	Sign.	β	Sign.
Share of audience on Snapchat / WhatsApp that speaks Frisian	0.302	0.000	0.218	0.000	0.253	0.000
Speaking Frisian with friends	0.190	0.000	0.234	0.000	0.181	0.000
Own writing skills	0.135	0.000	0.230	0.000	0.178	0.000
Liking contemporary Frisian music	0.124	0.000	0.120	0.000	0.135	0.000
Attitude towards Frisian	0.079	0.023	0.140	0.000	0.133	0.000
Following funny Frisian Instagram accounts	0.071	0.020	n.s.		n.s.	

popular culture influence the use of Frisian on WhatsApp and Snapchat. The factor explaining the largest share of the variance in the use of Frisian on group messages on WhatsApp, Snapchat and Instagram is the percentage of the audience speaking Frisian. The audience's speaking skills are thus of very high importance for L1 teenagers in the choice of whether or not to use Frisian on social media. These results show that the language practices with their audience in offline situations steers their language choice more than to what extent their wider audience will understand their messages.

Also for L1 teenagers, the audience has relatively more influence on the use of Frisian on Snapchat than it has on WhatsApp. The relative importance of offline language use and writing skills is higher on WhatsApp.

Two conclusions can be drawn from this model. First of all, language use on WhatsApp reflects language use in offline life more. Secondly, one's productive writing skills are of more importance when one making a language choice on WhatsApp than on Snapchat. A possible explanation for this is that in WhatsApp messages people actually write more and make less use of other semiotic resources than on Snapchat. Snapchat once started as a picture messaging app, and added an instant messaging feature later while for WhatsApp, the message feature was the main feature from the beginning. Furthermore, 82% of the teenagers prefer using WhatsApp to communicate about practical matters such as homework and dinner plans. For such purposes, teenagers with inferior writing skills in Frisian may turn to Dutch.

The variance in the use of Frisian on Instagram by L1 teenagers only is again less straight forward to predict: six independent factors can predict 24% of the variance in Instagram posts and 29% in Instagram reactions. The independent factors are the same as for all teenagers together. The relative importance of the factors is different, however.

Table 8.7 Regression model explaining the variance in the use of Frisian on Instagram reactions and posts by L1 teenagers

Independent factors	Instagram reactions (R^2 = 29%)		Instagram posts (R^2 = 24%)	
	β	Sign.	β	Sign.
Share of audience that speaks Frisian	0.189	0.000	0.151	0.000
Liking contemporary Frisian music	0.166	0.000	0.147	0.000
Speaking Frisian with friends	0.166	0.000	0.132	0.000
Own writing skills	0.115	0.000	0.098	0.016
Attitude towards Frisian	0.104	0.004	0.090	0.003
Following funny Frisian accounts on Instagram	0.080	0.012	0.128	0.000

The orientation towards Frisian popular culture is relatively more important in this model than in other models. See Table 8.7 for the optimal model predicting the use of Frisian on Instagram.

Obstructions to use Frisian on social media

Generally, participating teenagers chose three main reasons why they do not use Frisian on social media. The main obstruction is the teenagers' writing skills: writing in Frisian is difficult, and may cost too much time. The second reason is that not all friends understand Frisian. Finally, for L2 teenagers the main reason is that Frisian is not their home language.

For teenagers who do use Frisian on social media their audience is the most important reason why they do not use Frisian more often. Their writing skills are not their biggest concern, they are more annoyed by the autocorrect function on their smartphones. However, two third of the teenagers still find writing in Dutch easier than in Frisian. Half of the teenagers using Frisian on social media often write Frisian phonetically and do not use diacritics either. This because it is too much work or they do not know where to put them. The more frequently teenagers use Frisian on social media, the more they feel they can better express themselves in Frisian, the more they write Frisian phonetically and the more they disagree with the statement that Dutch is easier to write than Frisian. It is unclear what the cause and effect is in this relationship: whether the perceived ease of writing in Frisian increases the use of Frisian or the increased use leads to an increased perception of competence.

Conclusions and Discussion

This paper investigated the use of the autochthonous minority language Frisian on social media by Frisian–Dutch bilingual teenagers.

The results show that Frisian is predominantly used in the more private contexts on social media, such as WhatsApp and Snapchat. It was used less on Instagram. Especially teenagers who were raised exclusively in Frisian by their parents (L1 teenagers) communicate in Frisian on these platforms.

Frisian was found to have acquired a stable position on WhatsApp. Compared to six years ago (Jongbloed-Faber *et al.*, 2016), there are no significant changes in the use of Frisian by L1 teenagers on WhatsApp. Eighty-seven percent of the L1 teenagers use Frisian to some extent on WhatsApp. Almost 60% of the L1 teenagers use Frisian often or all the time on WhatsApp and Snapchat and a quarter of the L1 teenagers use Frisian more often than Dutch. Most teenagers however use more often Dutch than Frisian, also those teenagers who were raised exclusively in Frisian. L1 teenagers thus show very bilingual behaviour, even on the more intimate social media platforms such as WhatsApp and Snapchat. Although in everyday face-to-face communication most families solely speak Frisian to one another, in family WhatsApp groups of these L1 teenagers Dutch is used besides Frisian in many families' group messages, although Frisian is used more often than Dutch.

On Instagram, Frisian is used least of all: 26% of the L1 teenagers active on Instagram post in Frisian sometimes and 17% use Frisian often or all the time. In reactions on Instagram, 30% of the L1 teenagers use Frisian often or all the time and 36% sometimes use Frisian. In posts, Dutch, English and emojis only are used more frequently than Frisian.

The factors that influence the use of Frisian by Frisian teenagers on social media most are offline language use with peers, the share of contacts that speak Frisian on the particular social media platform, writing skills, attitude towards Frisian and orientation towards Frisian popular culture. Six factors explain almost two third of the variation in the use of Frisian on WhatsApp and Snapchat, and roughly one third on Instagram. To explain the variation in use by L1 teenagers alone the same factors can be used. For L1 teenagers the factor audience is of relatively higher importance than for all teenagers together.

The fact that offline language use with peers influences the use of Frisian on social media is not surprising. This study also shows that language attitudes influence language choice on social media like they do in offline contexts. In addition, although the future regional orientation does not have an impact on the extent to which Frisian is used on social media, their current orientation towards Frisian popular culture does.

Another important factor in the use of Frisian on social media is writing skills. Writing skills are a factor that can only influence one's language choice if the skills are inadequate or are imbalanced in different languages which often are a majority and minority language. The Frisian writing skills of the teenagers, even of those with Frisian as home language, lag far behind their understanding, speaking and reading skills of the language. Although Frisian has been an obligatory subject in primary school in the province of Fryslân since 1980 and in secondary education since 1993, 73% of the primary schools and 61% of secondary schools are not able to offer Frisian writing lessons of sufficient quality to their pupils (Varkevisser & Walsweer, 2018: 36, 166). This insufficient education in Frisian explains the outcomes: two third of the teenagers who use Frisian on social media find writing in Dutch easier than in Frisian. The less they use Frisian the more they agree with the statement. Moreover, over half of the teenagers using Frisian on social media often write Frisian phonetically.

When taking a closer look at the role of the audience on the use of Frisian on WhatsApp and Snapchat, it is not the share of audience that understands Frisian but the share of audience who speaks Frisian that significantly explains the variation in use. It is thus not a matter of choosing a language on social media that everyone can understand as Androutsopoulos (2014) finds but choosing the language that is used in offline communication and the habit of speaking Frisian with one's audience. Communication and language choice on WhatsApp and Snapchat thus resemble face-to-face interaction more than in mass media, and the peripheral audience is therefore less influential on language choice than a model like the audience design model from Bell (1984, 2001) would expect. The Frisian–Dutch bilingual teenagers are thus generally responsive to their addressees, and converge their language towards their second-person audience, and not so much towards peripheral audience members. In contrast, on Instagram, the variation in language choice can less clearly be explained from the factors identified for WhatsApp and Snapchat. On Instagram, one's orientation towards Frisian popular culture is relatively important. Moreover, referee design – diverging one's linguistic practices away from their audience towards an absent outgroup – plays a larger role. The use of a more prestigious language variety such as Dutch or English is more prevalent, even though for L1 teenagers on average still half of their audience on Instagram speak Frisian. The different objective of the medium, instead of communicating with peers it is more about exposing a polished self to the world, consciously constructing oneself on Instagram, will probably be a better explanation for the less clear language choice patterns.

Furthermore, the results confirm Cunliffe's statement (2019: 460) that language choice is often an unconscious process for minority language speakers. Frisian bilingual teenagers do not seem very concerned about and aware of their language choices on social media. There is little difference in (dis)agreement with statements about language choice and audience awareness between those teenagers speaking Frisian, Dutch or both at home while one would expect speakers of a majority language to be less concerned with their language choices than minority language speakers.

While Bell (1984, 2001) expected that 'the peripheral audience members influence bilingual language choice far more than they do monolingual style shift' (Bell, 1984: 176), this research shows that the actual speaking practice in daily life is actually very important for language choice on social media for bilingual speakers. The share of one's audience on social media understanding the minority language has little explanatory power. Therefore, communication on WhatsApp and Snapchat can be considered as a new way of communication that resembles face-to-face communication more than it does traditional mass media, although one can reach a much larger audience than in face-to-face communication. The wider audience is ignored more on those social media platforms than traditional audience design models would predict and language choice is less affected by the peripheral audience members. Moreover, few minority language speakers seem really concerned with their language choice. They do not consider it too much and 'just' do what they would do in offline life, provided that their poor writing skills do not inhibit them to use the minority language.

Acknowledgements

I am grateful for the constructive feedback on the set-up of the study and during the writing process of this chapter from my PhD supervisors Hans Van de Velde, Leonie Cornips and Edwin Klinkenberg.

Notes

(1) Like many teenagers in the world, a considerable part of the Frisian–Dutch teenagers are very proficient in English as well. Although that part could be considered to be tri- or multilingual, not all of them are.
(2) Frisian is the name commonly used to refer to West Frisian, the variety of Frisian spoken in the Netherlands (Tiersma, 1999).
(3) There are approximately 110 secondary and vocational school locations in Fryslân.

References

Androutsopoulos. J. (2014) Languaging when contexts collapse: Audience design in social networking. *Discourse, Context and Media* 4–5, 62–73.
Baker, C. (2006) *Foundations of Bilingual Education and Bilingualism* (4th edn). Multilingual Matters.
Bell, A. (1984) Language style as audience design. *Language in Society* 13 (2), 145–204.
Bell, A. (2001) Back in style: reworking audience design. In P. Eckert and R. Rickford (eds) *Style and Sociolinguistic Variation* (pp. 139–169). Cambridge University Press.
Council of Europe (2020) *European Charter for Regional or Minority Languages: Sixth report of the Committee of Experts in respect of the Netherlands*. Committee of Ministers.
Coupland, N. (2009) The mediated performance of vernaculars. *Journal of English Linguistics* 37 (3), 284–300. https://doi.org/10.1177/ 0075424209341188.

Cru, J. (2015) Language revitalisation from the ground up: promoting Yucatec Maya on Facebook. *Journal of Multilingual and Multicultural Development* 36 (3), 284–296. https://doi.org/10.1080/01434632.2014.921184.

Cunliffe, D. (2007) Minority languages and the internet: New threats, new opportunities. In M. Cormack and N. Hourigan (eds) *Minority Language Media: Concepts, Critiques and Case Studies* (pp. 133–150). Multilingual Matters.

Cunliffe, D. (2019) Minority languages and social media. In G. Hogan-Brun and B. O'Rourke (eds) *The Palgrave Handbook of Minority Languages and Communities* (pp. 451–480). Palgrave Macmillan.

Cunliffe, D. and Herring, S. (2005) Introduction to minority languages, multimedia and the web. *New Review of Hypermedia and Multimedia* 11 (2), 131–137. https://doi.org/10.1080/13614560512331392186.

Cunliffe, D., Morris, D. and Prys, C. (2013) Investigating the differential use of Welsh in young speakers' social networks: A comparison of communication in face-to-face settings in electronic texts and on social networking sites. In E.H. Gruffydd Jones and E. Uribe-Jongbloed (eds) *Social Media and Minority Languages: Convergence and the Creative Industries* (pp. 75–86). Multilingual Matters.

Eisenlohr, P. (2004) Language revitalization and new technologies: Cultures of electronic mediation and the refiguring of communities. *Annual Review of Anthropology* 33 (1), 21–45.

European Parliament (2018) *European Parliament Resolution of 11 September 2018 on Language Equality in the Digital Age.* European Parliament.

Gardner, R.C. and Lambert, W.E. (1972) *Attitudes and Motivation in Second-Language Learning.* Newbury House.

Gorter, D. and Jonkman, R.J. (1995) *Taal yn Fryslân: op 'e nij besjoen.* Fryske Akademy.

Gorter, D., Riemersma, A. and Ytsma, J. (2001) Frisian in the Netherlands. In G. Extra and D. Gorter (eds) *The Other Languages of Europe* (pp. 103–118). Multilingual Matters.

Grondelaers, S. and Speelman, D. (2013) Can speaker evaluation return private attitudes towards stigmatised varieties? Evidence from emergent standardisation in Belgian Dutch. In T. Kristiansen and S. Grondelaers (eds) *Language (De)standardisations in Late Modern Europe: Experimental Studies* (pp. 171–191). Novus Press.

Gruffydd Jones, E.H. and Uribe-Jongbloed, E. (eds) (2013) *Social Media and Minority Languages: Convergence and the Creative Industries.* Multilingual Matters.

Günther-van der Meij, M.T. (2018) *The Impact of the Degree of Bilingualism on L3 Development.* Leeuwarden/Groningen: Fryske Akademy/University of Groningen.

Johnson, I. (2013) Audience design and communication accommodation theory: Use of Twitter by Welsh-English biliterates. In E.H. Gruffydd Jones and E. Uribe-Jongbloed (eds) *Social Media and Minority Languages: Convergence and the Creative Industries* (pp. 99–118). Multilingual Matters.

Johnstone, B. (2010) Indexing the local. In N. Coupland (ed.) *Handbook of Language and Globalization* (pp. 386–405). Wiley-Blackwell.

Jongbloed-Faber, L. (2018) Local identity construction in dialect pop music: Songs, narratives, and social media posts. *Us Wurk, Tydskrift foar frisistyk*, 67 (3-4), 104–136.

Jongbloed-Faber, L. (2021) *Frisian on Social Media. The Vitality of Minority Languages in a Multilingual Online World.* LOT publications. https://doi.org/10.26481/dis.20210903lj.

Jongbloed-Faber, L., Van de Velde, H., Van der Meer, C. and Klinkenberg, E.L. (2016) Language use of Frisian bilingual teenagers on social media. *Treballs de Sociolingüística Catalana* 26, 27–54. https://doi.org/10.2436/20. 2504.01.107.

Jongbloed-Faber, L., van Loo, J. and Cornips, L. (2017) Regional languages on Twitter: A comparative study between Frisian and Limburgish. *Dutch Journal of Applied Linguistics* 6 (2), 174–196. https://doi.org/10.1075/dujal.16017.jon.

Kircher, R. and Fox, S. (2019) Attitudes towards multicultural London English: Implications for attitude theory and language planning. *Journal of Multilingual and Multicultural Development* 40 (10), 847–864. https://doi.org/10.1080/01434632.2019.1577869.

Klinkenberg, E., Stefan, N. and Jonkman, R. (2018) *Taal yn Fryslân. De folgjende generaasje.* Fryske Akademy.

Lackaff, D. and Moner, W.J. (2016) Local Languages, Global Networks: Mobile Design for Minority Language Users. *Proceedings of the 34th ACM International Conference on the Design of Communication.*

Lillehaugen, B.D. (2019) Tweeting in Zapotec: Social media as a tool for language activists. In J.C.G. Menjívar and G.E. Chacón (eds) *Indigenous Interfaces: Spaces, Technology, and Social Networks in Mexico and Central America* (pp. 202–226). University of Arizona Press.

Massaguer Comes, M., Flors-Mas, A. and Vila, F.X. (2020) *Català, youtubers i instagramers: Un punt de partida per promoure l'ús de la llengua.* Biblioteca Tècnica de Política Lingüística.

Newcom.nl (2020) *Nationale Social Media Onderzoek 2020.*

McMonagle, S. (2019) Aspects of language choice online among German-Upper Sorbian bilingual adolescents. *International Journal of Bilingual Education and Bilingualism* 25 (1), 59–79. https://doi.org/10.1080/13670050.2019.1624686.

McMonagle, S., Cunliffe, D., Jongbloed-Faber, L. and Jarvis, P. (2019) What can hashtags tell us about minority languages on Twitter? A comparison of #cymraeg, #frysk and #gaeilge. *Journal of Multilingual and Multicultural Development* 40 (1), 32–49. https://doi.org/10.1080/01434632.2018.1465429.

Monka, M. (2014) Sproget afhænger af stedet: - om sprogforandring i virkelig tid i Jylland. *Maal og Minne* (2), 92–130.

Monka, M. (2020) Southern Jutland: Language ideology as a means to slow down dialect leveling. In M. Maegaard, M. Monka, K.K. Mortensen and A.C. Stæhr (eds) *Standardization as Sociolinguistic Change: A Transversal Study of Three Traditional Dialect Areas* (pp. 70–118). Routledge.

Moseley, C. (ed.) (2010) *Atlas of the World's Languages in Danger* (3rd edn). UNESCO Publishing. Online version: http://www.unesco.org/culture/en/endangeredlanguages/atlas.

Ní Bhroin, N. (2019) Indigenous, Nordic and Digital? How Sámi-language users negotiate access to digital media. In A. Sparrman (ed.) *Making Culture: Children and Young People's Leisure Cultures* (pp. 115–126). Kulturanalys Norden, IV.II.

O'Rourke, B. (2011) *Galician and Irish in the European Context: Attitudes Towards Weak and Strong Minority Languages.* Palgrave Macmillan.

Provinsje Fryslân (2020) *De Fryske taalatlas 2020. Fryske taal yn byld.* Provinsje Fryslân.

Reershemius, G. (2017) Autochthonous minority languages and social media: Writing and bilingual practices in Low German on Facebook. *Journal of Multilingual and Multicultural Development* 38 (1), 35–49. https://doi.org/10.1080/01434632.2016.1151434.

Rosseel, L. (2017) *New Approaches to Measuring the Social Meaning of Language Variation: Exploring the Personalized Implicit Association Test and the Relational Responding Task.* KU Leuven.

Stefan, M.H., Klinkenberg, E.L. and Versloot, A.P. (2015) Frisian sociological language survey goes linguistic: Introduction to a new research component. In A.J. Brand, E. Hoekstra, J. Spoelstra and H. Van de Velde (eds) *Philologia Frisica Anno 2014. Lêzings fan it tweintichster Frysk Filologekongres fan de Fryske Akademy op 10. 11 en 12 desimber 2014*, vol. 1091 (pp. 240–257). Ljouwert: Fryske Akademy and Afûk.

Tiersma, P.M. (1999) *Frisian Reference Grammar.* Ljouwert: Fryske Akademy.

UNESCO (2003) *Convention for the Safeguarding of the Intangible Cultural Heritage.* See https://ich.unesco.org/en/convention Last accessed 2 May 2022.

Varkevisser, N.A. and Walsweer, A.P. (2018) *It is mei sizzen net te dwaan. Rapport Taalplan Frysk. Ynventarisaaske nei de stân fan saken oangeande it (fak) Frysk yn it primêr en fuortset ûnderwiis.* Provinsje Fryslân.

9 'Moin mitnanner': Digital Practices and Low German on Instagram

Gertrud Reershemius

Introduction

Low German is the English name for *Platt* or *Plattdütsch*, as the language is referred to by its speakers who currently number approximately 2.5 million, mainly in northern Germany (Adler *et al.*, 2016; Arendt & Stern, this volume). Speakers of Low German are bilingual and use Low German alongside German. For some time, Low German has been in the process of a shift towards German due to an increasing loss of communicative domains and decreasing transmission across generations in the family. In 1999, the Low German varieties were recognised as an endangered regional language as part of the European Charter for Regional or Minority Languages. Although Low German is in steady decline as a vernacular used for day-to-day communication, it has become increasingly popular and more visible in the public space in recent years (Reershemius, 2011, 2020). Low German is often used to establish proximity and closeness in communication and to connect people to a concept of place, even if they no longer live in the Low German-speaking regions. It is drawn on as a resource for identity construction and, in addition to its communicative functions, also increasingly serves symbolic or postvernacular purposes such as emblematic use or communicating about the language rather than in it (Reershemius, 2009). Low German tends to be associated with discourses of tradition and authenticity, making it subject to commodification processes in the context of advertising and tourism (for example Freese & Launert, 2004; Jürgens, 2016; Reershemius, 2011).

Digital communication and the use of social media have increasingly become part of day-to-day life for individuals and groups. A substantial number of users are also speakers of smaller or lesser used languages such as Low German and tend to find that domains for these varieties in daily communication are decreasing rapidly offline (Cormack, 2013;

Cunliffe, 2019). Thus, it is of considerable importance to speakers, language planners and researchers to find out what happens when speakers of smaller languages use computer-mediated communication, particularly social media: Will social media provide communicative digital spaces for them, connect them across geographical divides and raise the image of the languages in question; or could the effects be detrimental? How do users apply their bi- or multilingual repertoires on social media? How are emerging digital writing practices likely to shape these languages?

For the majority of its speakers, Low German is a predominantly oral language, with German serving as the dominant standard language for written and professional purposes. Studies and surveys predating the advent of social media have shown that most Low German speakers at the time were uncomfortable writing in Low German (Möller, 2008; Reershemius, 2002), despite the existence of a considerable corpus of literature in Low German since medieval times, to which a literary scene has added ever since (Möhn & Goltz, 2016). Computer-mediated communication in Low German initially served mainly as a new medium to showcase events organised by the Low German cultural scene offline (Reershemius, 2010). At this earlier stage, interactive content such as chatrooms did not play a significant role at all. On the few occasions where chat in Low German could be observed, communication tended to be dominated by (self-proclaimed) language activists, who attempted to impose their notions of correct spelling and considered the use of German elements sacrilegious, thus smothering most meaningful exchanges in Low German. This has changed considerably with the popularisation of user-generated content systems, in particular social media: in a study conducted only six years later, Reershemius (2017) showed that Low German speakers had by then created digital spaces, for example on Facebook, where an increase in the use of spontaneously written Low German mainly for entertainment purposes could be observed without any attempts by individuals or institutions to influence how users applied orthography or to criticise them if they engaged in bilingual practices such as code-switching. While the study of Low German on social media is still very much in its infancy, several recent studies have explored various aspects of this form of communication. Schürmann (2016), for example, examines humour in the Low German exchanges of a WhatsApp group chat. The exchanges presented are entirely in Low German, although it remains unclear whether the four members of the group conduct all their communications in Low German or just those intended to be humorous, or whether this particular chat group had been specifically set up for the purpose of using Low German. Fenske (2021) analyses two Instagram accounts which contain a comparatively large number of contributions relating to Low German. She concludes that even these two rather well-known content creators still only reach a small number of followers. Interestingly, she also observes that the overall numbers of users contributing to various hashtags related to Low German is increasing. It remains to be seen whether changing literacy practices and the increased interaction with written language triggered by social media could potentially lead to a changed attitude towards writing in Low German.

This article focuses on the question of how Low German-speaking social media users apply their multilingual repertoires on Instagram, in line with this volume's overall focus on digital practices: Do users develop new multimodal writing practices and forms of digital literacy for Low German? Recent studies have shown that the average social media user contributes to more than one platform on a daily basis. If these polymedial practices (Madianou & Miller, 2012) have become the norm for how users communicate digitally, why would it still be worthwhile to look at one specific platform – Instagram in this case – in relation to a particular language, Low German? The reasons are threefold: first, the size of Instagram – it is currently one of the most popular social media platforms, with 1386 million active users worldwide; second, its appeal to younger generations of users; and third, its particular set-up which combines images with writing. All content posted on Instagram in users' feeds or stories, which can be public or private, contains images or videos. These are generally accompanied by text in the form of captions often including hashtagged words or phrases (e.g. #Plattdeutsch), which are searchable by other users and thus serve to link content by different creators. Other users can comment on content posted by creators.

Currently, 23.8% of Germans use Instagram. While people over the age of 65 make up less than 2% of users, Instagram is most popular among the 25 to 34 age group (Statistica). This generational trend is relevant when analysing digital practices in Low German, since fewer younger speakers use heritage languages (Adler *et al.*, 2016: 12 ff.).[1] Finally, Instagram is based on a set-up that combines posted images with writing, which lends itself to an examination of the visualising practices of Low German-speaking Instagram users. Each social media platform provides a distinct social context for its users based on its behavioural privacy settings, following mechanisms and modality, as outlined by Waterloo *et al.* (2018: 1816). Instagram, for example, allows its users to either make their posts accessible only to their followers or to the public, for the whole of the worldwide Instagram community to see. Consequently, public Instagram posts are nonreciprocal, which means that their followers do not have to be followed in return. Instagram – like Twitter – is therefore 'a microblogging site where users can follow others without the need for approval or reciprocation' (Waterloo *et al.*, 2018: 1817). In terms of modality, Instagram is a platform that focuses on the sharing of images, which can lead to a focus on identity work and projects of the self (see, for example, Lup *et al.*, 2015; Sheldon & Bryant, 2016). It is relevant for the analysis of smaller languages such as Low German to establish which discourses and functions the language serves in its users' identity construction projects on social media. Although Instagram posts consist of at least one image or video clip, they also contain writing of varying lengths. Users normally post a text and some 'hashtags' to indicate the topical contexts they situate their posts in. Followers can then respond, and in some cases they are actively encouraged to do so by questions in the text. Thus, while its focus is on the sharing of images, Instagram as a social media platform also actively promotes communication in writing. This raises the question of how Low German-speaking users go about writing in a language most of them do not normally use as their written medium of communication.

The main research questions for this study are:

(1) Agency: Who is posting and what are the main communicative aims for using Low German on Instagram?
(2) Using the heritage language: How do users employ Low German on Instagram and how do they write it?
(3) Visual practices: How do users visualise posts in relation to Low German?

Theoretical Framework

There are four major concepts of analysis that underpin the theoretical framework for this study. Firstly, the study is based on the concept of *digital practices*, tools and texts as outlined by Jones *et al.* (2015). Secondly, it acknowledges the *polymedial realities of user practices* (Madianou & Miller, 2012). Thirdly, it analyses social media user activity as processes of *sharing* and creating *events* (Androutsopoulos, 2014b); and finally, it examines linguistic practices on social media as the application of *multilingual repertoires* (see, for example, Matras, 2020).

The concept of digital practices is based on the notion of practice articulated in literacy studies (see, for example, Barton, 2006) and mediated discourse analysis (Scollon, 2001), 'in which practice is seen less as a matter of dispositions or regimes of knowledge and more as a matter of the concrete, situated actions people perform with particular mediational means (such as written texts, computers, mobile phones) in order to enact membership in particular social groups' (Jones *et al.*, 2015: 2). This approach defines digital tools as the means to perform digital practices. These encompass websites, software, physical objects and semiotic tools such as talking, writing or using images in various ways. Digital practices result in digital texts which 'include conversations – both written and spoken – videos, photographs, drawings, paintings, street signs, websites, software interfaces, video games, and any other aggregate of semiotic elements that can function as a tool for people to take social action' (Jones et al., 2015: 5). The digital practices of Low German speakers have changed rather dramatically over the last decade. My first study of Low German online was conducted before social media became widespread and showed that Low German speakers online mainly mirrored and showcased the activities of the Low German cultural scene actually happening offline (Reershemius, 2010). Twelve years on, a distinction between digital and 'real' life no longer seems to apply:

> Social media has already become such an integral part of everyday life that it makes no sense to see it as separate. In the same way no one today would regard a telephone conversation as taking place in a separate world from 'real life'. It has also become apparent that research on social media is no longer the particular purview of either media or of communication. Our research provides considerable evidence that social media should be regarded rather as a place where many of us spend part of our lives. (Miller et al., 2016: 7)

Thus, events on social media normally do not necessarily simply mirror communicative realities in analogue mode anymore – social media has become an integral part of social life for an increasing number of people (see also Bolander & Locher, 2020), a process also theoretically conceptualised as mediatisation (see, for example, Androutsopoulos, 2014a; Krotz, 2014) in which (new) media fundamentally change the way people communicate and organise their lives. Accordingly, studies of social media ought to focus on what users post and how they communicate on various platforms, ideally also analysed in connection with their non-digital communicative contexts and practices (Miller et al., 2016: 1). Based on an extensive study of digital practices, in particular of younger people, Madianou and Miller (2012) introduced the term *polymedia* to describe their observation that most users regularly frequent more than one social media platform, in addition to other digital practices. Anecdotally, a short survey among 47 undergraduate students in one of my classes at a British university in 2019 confirmed this observation: my students used an average of six social media platforms, with WhatsApp, YouTube and Instagram being the most popular at the time. Thus, it is important to keep in mind when analysing Low German speakers posting on Instagram that this very likely represents just a fraction of their overall online activity, and not all of it necessarily contains Low German (see also Jongbloed-Faber, 2021, and in this volume on Frisian in the Netherlands).

This chapter takes a user-centric approach, focusing on how people *share* posts in or about Low German on Instagram. Androutsopoulos

(2014b: 5–6) defines 'sharing' as a complex practice consisting of three stages: selecting, styling and negotiating. Selecting involves the process of choosing significant moments in a person's life to be retextualised when turned into posts on social media. These moments are then processed by semiotic practices such as writing or producing and reworking images (styling). Finally, they are posted on Instagram and potentially encourage other users to engage in forms of dialogue, for example by 'liking' the posts or by responding (negotiating). The sequences resulting from selecting, styling and negotiating will be analysed as 'events' in the following.

Finally, for this study, all events consisting of more than one language will be analysed as posts by users with a multilingual repertoire, encompassing the linguistic structures multilingual speakers have at their disposal:

> This repertoire is not organised in the form of 'languages' or 'language systems'; ... elements of the repertoire (word-forms, phonological rules, constructions, and so on) gradually become associated, through a process of linguistic socialisation, with a range of social activities, including factors such as sets of interlocutors, topics, and institutional settings. ... Context-appropriate selection does not necessarily conform to a separation of 'languages': In some contexts, certain types of cross-linguistic 'mixing' and 'inserting' may be socially acceptable and may constitute effective goal-oriented communication. (Matras, 2020: 4)

Multilingual repertoires are not necessarily balanced. Some multilingual speakers can fully function in more than one language, while others may have access only to a limited set of communicative resources involving elements from languages other than their most dominant one. Between these two extreme points on the multilingual continuum, an indefinite number of levels of multilingual practices are potentially possible, depending on personal life trajectories and linguistic biographies (Busch, 2012).

Data and Methodology

The methodological approach chosen for this study combines quantitative and qualitative methods of analysis. It is based on two stages of observation and data collection: for the first stage, an orientation period lasting two months (1 June until 31 July 2021), I searched for hashtags containing 'Plattdeutsch', 'Platt', 'Plattdütsch/ Dütsk', 'Niederdeutsch', 'Nedderdütsk' and 'Low German' in order to get an overview of communication in or around Low German on Instagram. Hashtags form a linguistic innovation in microblogging by allowing users to add metadata to individual posts. Hashtagging originated on Twitter and was spread as a practice by users to other social media platforms, such as Facebook or Instagram. On Instagram, tagging:

> is a writing space situated within an assemblage of other writing spaces, images and layout. Whether they are creating the page or looking at the page, people are making meaning in relation to the whole page, including the tags. Tags are not just separate 'metadata' but they can be a central part of the meaning making, contributing to the overall coherence of the page. ... Hashtags indicate what the post is about according to its producer and adds it to a new or existing collective, thus potentially forming discursive communities around certain topics. (Zappavigna, 2016: 277)

Some hashtags, for example #MeToo, have become powerful focal points in social movements by providing a forum for communicating about specific issues on social media, in this case the abuse of women by powerful men. Hashtags are also a semiotic resource allowing users to create specific contexts for their posts that may not be apparent from the content, writing or imagery of the post itself (see also Heyen in this volume). They also make social media such as Instagram searchable (McMonagle *et al.*, 2019), not only for researchers but also for users who are looking for specific communities online: if a user wants to find other users interested in, for example, Low German, they will search for hashtags around their topic of choice.

For the second phase of data collection, I systematically observed the most popular hashtag, #Plattdeutsch, for one month (1–31 August 2021) by recording all publicly viewable posts on a daily basis and labelling them according to their agency, language use and dialogicality. #Plattdeutsch consisted of 28,600 events in September 2021, having grown since the end of August 2020 by 9700 events (Fenske, 2021: 82). The overall number of posts analysed for this study is 608. For the qualitative analysis, representative events were chosen and examined in detail. Finally, I conducted six semi-structured interviews with contributors to #Plattdeutsch in order to capture user motivation, the users' communicative goals when posting on Instagram, and to cross-check my own interpretation of the data.

Results

Who posts on #Plattdeutsch and what are their communicative aims?

The following section shows the results of a quantitative analysis of agency in the events observed and then examines representative examples of the different categories of agency qualitatively. Ten categories of agency emerged during the orientation phase: (1) Low German theatre,

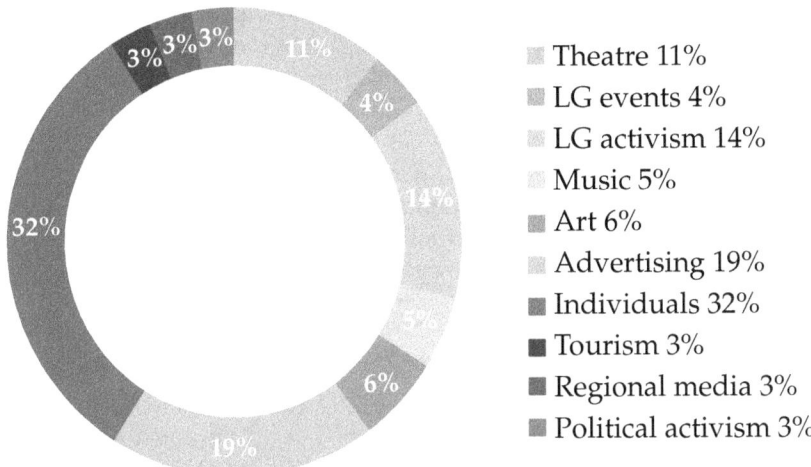

- Theatre 11%
- LG events 4%
- LG activism 14%
- Music 5%
- Art 6%
- Advertising 19%
- Individuals 32%
- Tourism 3%
- Regional media 3%
- Political activism 3%

Figure 9.1 Distribution of agency (#Plattdeutsch; n = 608)

(2) cultural events, such as public readings or language festivals, (3) Low German language activism, (4) music, (5) art, (6) advertising, (7) individuals posting, (8) tourism, (9) regional media and (10) political activism independent from Low German. The 608 events observed during the second phase of observation were tagged accordingly; Figure 9.1 shows the distribution of agency.

Strikingly, the same structures of agency as observed in Reershemius (2010) before the advent of social media in the digital world of Low German still seem to be in place, with theatre, music, language activism, art and cultural events motivating 40% of the posted events with #Plattdeutsch. This reflects the activities of the Low German culture scene, with professional and amateur theatre productions, concerts, exhibitions, public readings, a Low German festival and posts by institutions engaged in Low German language maintenance efforts. Very much in line with observations in Reershemius (2010), these posts mainly showcase offline events. However, different from a decade ago, they now invite responses or 'likes' and can be spread easily by users reposting them with different hashtags, or on other social media platforms. Social media has become a flexible and effective way of sharing news and information within and about the Low German culture scene. Using #Plattdeutsch allows people interested in Low German to form a loose community and keep informed about events and initiatives.

An interesting innovation compared with the digital world of Low German in 2010 is the relatively high number of advertisements posted during the observation period (19%), indicating an increased use of Low German for commodification purposes (see Heller, 2010, for the concept of linguistic commodification). These are posts by users aiming to sell products, not advertisements put up by Instagram itself. Adverts published in connection with #Plattdeutsch fall into two categories. The first are adverts for products where the language is part of the product itself, for example printed t-shirts with slogans in Low German, baseball caps brandishing greetings in Low German (*Moin*), postcards with Low German mottos, etc., very much following the design of Event 1.[2] Due to copyright regulations, Instagram images do not belong to the public domain and cannot be replicated for research purposes. The images will therefore be described in the following:

Event 1

Image: Two images, one showing the Low German motto *Sabbel nich, dat geiht*! 'Don't talk, it works', the second depicting a mug with a Low German print *Kannst keen Platt Fehlt di wat*! 'If you don't speak Low German, you are missing out'

Text: *Auf Hochdeutsch: Quatsch nicht, das geht! Shop für XXX T-Shirts, Tassen und Büdels in der Profil Beschreibung.* 'In High German: Don't talk, it works! Shop for XXX t-shirts, mugs and bags in bio'

Hashtags: #Plattdeutsch #platt #norddeutsch #niederdeutsch #heimat #dorfkind #land #landleben #plattdütsch #schnacken #valentinstag #niedersachsen #ostfriesland #norddeutschland #schleswigholstein #nordsee #moin # norden #meer #Sprache #liebe #plattschnacken #unsernorden #dasbesteamnorden #norddeutschland #Sprüche #sprichwörter #heimatliebe #heimat #dorf #plattdüütsch

Likes: 568

Responses: Four, three of which respond with more mottos in Low German

Event 1 shows a remarkably high number of hashtags referring to geographical entities (13 out of 32), thus placing the event in the context of northern Germany. Four out of 32 hashtags refer to living in the countryside as a specific lifestyle, ten out of 32 focus on language. By selecting these hashtags, the advert addresses potential consumers who feel an affiliation with northern Germany and in particular its rural environments and who 'do' Low German, which does not necessarily include speaking it. In Event 1, Low German is employed in the form of mottos as part of the images, with a single Low German word (*Büdel* 'bag') in the comment. *Büdel* belongs to a small repository of Low German words that are well known to speakers of German in northern Germany and frequently referred to by people who are 'doing' Low German, or, in other words, involved in postvernacular practices (Reershemius, 2009; Shandler, 2005).

For the second category, the products or services to be sold are not constructed with or around Low German; rather, the language is used as a contextualisation cue.[3] This works in two ways. For example, in an advertisement for a hotel in northern Germany, the image shows a photograph of the hotel building in its rural surroundings. In addition, a short text in Standard German and eight hashtags are provided, two of which put the hotel in the context of Low German-speaking northern Germany, probably in an attempt to add what can be perceived as authenticity,[4] working with the widespread notion that 'real' northerners speak Low German so that the hotel is shown embedded not only in the northern German rural countryside but also in its cultural heritage.

A different advertising strategy which still uses Low German as a contextualisation cue is followed, for example, by a medium-sized business selling mechanical tools. This event shows a photograph of a shopfront and a text in Low German which contemplates the changing of the seasons without any mention of the business or its products. It has five hashtags, including #Plattdeutsch. Text and image seem to be unrelated at first, but by posting in Low German, the owner presents themselves as part of the (Low German-speaking?) local community, which may make potential customers more inclined to consider their products. Both models of advertising under #Plattdeutsch are applied in order to attract customers by localising and authenticating the businesses or their products. The observed advertising events are normally posted by smaller businesses, usually with a company website as part of the posting user's bio, which is the 150-character description under the username on Instagram profile pages.

The third group of contributors to #Plattdeutsch are individuals. At 32%, this is the largest category, as can be expected in the context of a social media platform such as Instagram with a focus on the self-presentation of individuals. In all observed cases in this category, #Plattdeutsch is only one of a number of contextualising hashtags. Within this group, holidaymakers stand out: these are people who have spent their holidays in northern Germany, predominantly the coastal areas, and post pictures of landscapes or local landmarks, sometimes as a selfie or as a snapshot of friends and family members, as shown by Event 2:

Event 2

Image: Four photographs of Hamburg's *Elbphilharmonie* concert hall

Text: Travelers told me it's a tourist duty to photograph this architectural landmark – so welly, welly, brothers & sisters – here are my perspectives: ze Elb philly …

Hashtags: #hamburg #hanse #hansestadt #ginsul #plattdeutsch #fischbrötchen #hamburgerhafen #ichwillmeer #deichtorhallen

#art   #museum   #architecture   #hamburgerhafen   #reeperbahn
#harbour   #deichkind   #elbphilharmonie   #flaneur   #herzogdemeuron
#schmuddelwetter   #cigarjournal   #americanbars   #ontheroad
#wanderlust   #nomad   #traveller   #jester   #wienerbarbuch   #booze
#ratpacktoursvienra

Likes: 42

Responses: –

The user posting Event 2 adds a text in English to their snapshots of Hamburg's landmark concert hall, thus addressing an international audience. The added hashtags suggest that the user sees themselves as a flaneur/nomad/traveller/jester, who is 'on the road' and happens to be in Hamburg. Eleven out of 30 hashtags refer directly to Hamburg as a geographical or cultural entity. Low German is part of both, together with a local culinary treat, the fish sandwich (#fischbrötchen), and the notoriously murky weather conditions (#schmuddelwetter).

By following up on holidaymakers' individual user profiles, I found that #Plattdeutsch is not normally part of their Instagram posts. Many other individual users posting with #Plattdeutsch, however, integrate this particular hashtag into most of their posts, whether directly related to Low German or not. An example of the latter would be a user who regularly posts photographs of a garden with texts in German and a number of gardening hashtags, plus, a bit incongruously, #Plattdeutsch. Another regularly posts highly stylised photographs of a particular rural region in northern Germany, normally without written comment but with #Plattdeutsch among a number of other hashtags. One of the questions I put to my interviewees was whether they normally use the same hashtags for their posts. The majority of them do, usually adapting their standard lists of hashtags to the images they are posting by adding new ones or leaving out others. One of the interviewees – an ardent hobby crafter – was quite specific:

> Ich poste entweder für meine Freunde, also Leute, die ich kenne, oder für die XXX. Und da nehme ich schon unterschiedliche Hashtags. … Ich weiß natürlich, dass alle alles sehen können, und da pass ich das ein bisschen an. 'I post either for my friends, that's people I know, or for the XXX. And I do use different hashtags. … I know that everyone can see everything, so I adapt here and there.'

My interviewee posts publicly and has over 200 Instagram followers, navigating between a closed, local group of friends and an (international) crafting community. They see themselves as part of two Instagram communities – local friends and the crafter forums – and explicitly use #Plattdeutsch as an emblem of their identity in both.

The analysis of agency for #Plattdeutsch shows an increased level of commodification and commercialisation, rather casual encounters with Low German, as the example of the holidaymakers shows, but also the emergence of loosely structured digital communities for which Low German is not necessarily a focus or a means of communication but rather contributes to concepts of cultural identity. In many cases, Low German is used as a token of identity or a contextualisation cue by which individual users position themselves in specific geographic and cultural environments.

The use of Low German

All 608 events recorded during the observation period of this study were tagged according to the different ways in which users applied Low German both in images and texts, distinguishing between events that in Low German contained (1) no words or phrases, (2) just one word or phrase, (3) two to three words or phrases and (4) four or more words or phrases. This tagging system endeavours to capture the use of Low German either as a base language, a code, or a symbol (Androutsopoulos, 2010; Androutsopoulos & Ziegler, 2019). As a base language, Low German is used as the main language for a communicative event; as a code, elements of Low German such as words and phrases are integrated into predominantly German communicative events; as a symbol, highly indexicalised single words, greetings or proper names are used in an otherwise predominantly German communicative event. Figure 9.2 shows the overall distribution.

Probably the most striking result here is that 27% of all events observed as part of #Plattdeutsch did not contain a single Low German word or phrase. The content of these events is varied and includes, for example, Low German amateur theatre groups showcasing photographs

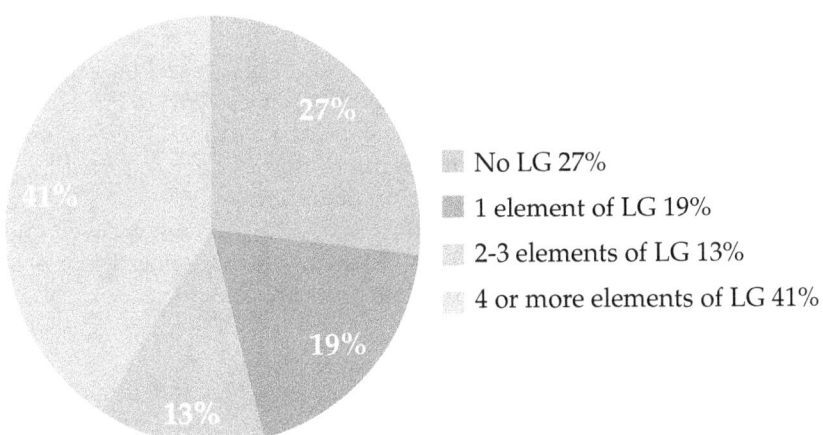

Figure 9.2 The use of Low German (#Plattdeutsch; n = 608)

of their latest production, gardeners posting pictures of trees and flowers, or amateur photographers uploading images of northern Germany. Some of the events in this category consist of images and hashtags only, while others include texts and responses of varying lengths, mostly in German, as for the example in Event 3[5]:

Event 3

Image: Photograph of sun setting behind trees

Text: *Urlaub – und eine Woche neigt sich langsam dem Ende – es ist doch ganz erholsam …*

'Holidays – and a week comes to its end – it is indeed rather relaxing …'

Hashtags: #platt #Donnerstag #forest #nordsee #mehrvomsommer #meinostfriesland #ostfriesland #ostfrieslandliebe #ostfrieslandmomente #landschaftsfotografie #sonydeutschland #samyang #fotografie #wundergut #naturephotography #yourshotphotographer #sonyalpha #meinedeutschlandliebe #sonyphotography #mittag #wald #moin #norden #plattdeutsch #nordennorddeich #landscape #shotonsony #germany #germany_travel #ostfriesland_travel

Likes: 39

Responses: Three, one in German, two in English

Event 3 uses #Plattdeutsch in order to place the event geographically. The post seems to be addressing a community of viewers interested in landscape photography. The user posting the event applies the hashtags to define the user's potential audience while at the same time constructing their own profile as a photographer from northern Germany engaged in landscape photography of the area.

While some of the content of posts without any Low German elements seems to have no connection with Low German, in other cases the event's main topic clearly does, such as in the Low German amateur theatre groups' posts. The events in this category indicate that engagement with Low German on Instagram can mean as little as adding a hashtag. Although many of the events in this category received likes and responses, none of the latter were in Low German.

Roughly one third of all events observed (32%) contain between one and three words or phrases in Low German. The following Event 4 is representative for the way many of these posts are constructed:

Event 4

Image: Photograph from theatre production

Text: *Herzlich willkommen im XXX.Theater! Ihr möchtet unsere aktuelle Komödie „Teemlich beste Frünnen" gern sehen, aber wagt euch nicht an die plattdeutsche Sprache heran? Kein Problem: Denn heute geht's wieder los mit unserem Platt-Vorspiel! Das ist eine stückbezogene Einführung ins Plattdeutsche, immer donnerstags um 19 Uhr. Das Platt-Vorspiel bei „Teemlich besten Frünnen" leitet unsere Kollegin XXX. Die Teilnahme ist kostenlos. Jetzt gibt es keine Ausrede mehr! ;-)*

'Welcome to the XXX Theatre! You would love to see our current show "Teemlich beste Frünnen" but don't dare to because of the Low German language? No problem: today we'll start again with our Low German introduction! It is an introduction to Low German in connection with the play, every Thursday at 7pm. The Low German introduction will be run by our colleague XXX. There is no charge. Now there are no excuses left! ;-)'

Hashtags: #xxxtheater #xxxtheater Hamburg #plattdeutsch #plattdüütsch #nordishbynature #theaterliveerleben #komödie #ziemlichbestefreunde #theaterhamburg

Likes: 131

Responses: Two, both in German

Event 4 is closely connected with Low German since it deals with a high-profile Low German theatre production and offers an introduction to Low German language. However, the only actual Low German used here is the title of the play, which is put in inverted commas. This is a strategy frequently observed: Low German is used sporadically in an otherwise German text but is written in capital letters or inverted commas, thus turning it into a marked form. Another widespread practice is to integrate Low German mottos or greetings to start off or end an otherwise German post – for example, *Moin mitnanner!* 'Beautiful (day) to all of you'. This application of Low German falls mainly into the category of symbolic use (Androutsopoulos & Ziegler, 2019).

Of the events observed, 41% contain at least four words or phrases in Low German, and some are entirely written in the language, thus using Low German as a base language or at least a code. These events include, for example, a regular blog by a Low German–speaking cat called Fritz, posts by two individuals who have been named as *Plattfluencers* – 'influencers for Low German' – by a regional newspaper, or individuals like the Instagram user who posted Event 5:

Event 5

Image: Three photographs of apple trees and crates full of freshly picked apples

Text: *…. vandaag: de Begünn van de Appelarnt (Emoji of an Apple)*

'…. today: the beginning of the apple harvest'

Hashtags: #plattdeutsch #apfel #herbst #ernte #eigenernte #landwirtschaft #garten #naturephotography

Likes: Nine

Responses: –

Event 5 is an example of posts which contain German only in the hashtags and are otherwise in Low German as a base language without any German elements or translation. For the majority of events observed for the category of more than four words or phrases in Low German, translations are provided, thus clearly indicating that viewers of #Plattdeutsch are not expected to be competent speakers/readers of Low German.

Event 5 did not receive any responses apart from nine likes, which is in line with the vast majority of events observed for the purpose of this study: longer exchanges are very much an exception. Responses tend to be few, often consisting of affirmative emojis such as hearts or thumbs up, and only rarely contain Low German. Longer exchanges in Low German occur only rarely. Another result is that the observation did not show a single example of an intervention by language activists criticising the way Low German was applied in terms of orthography or transcription of regional phonological features. This is a remarkable difference compared to computer-mediated activities in Low German 12 years ago, before the widespread use of social media (Reershemius, 2010). It adds further evidence to the hypothesis that social media can have an empowering effect for users, allowing them to apply their bilingual repertoire even if they are not familiar with writing conventions in their heritage language.

To summarise, only in 41% of events observed is Low German used as a base language. For almost 60% it is connected to a fixed number of bilingual practices: Low German elements are either translated into German and/or marked by inverted commas in an otherwise German text. For the majority of events, the use of Low German tends to be restricted to a limited set of indexicalised words, phrases, greetings or mottos, thus being used mainly as a symbol.

Visual practices

On Instagram, 'new content requires a visual element – whether it is a photo, an illustration, a quote or rendered text, a video, or a text-oriented story, the presentation of this content is still predicated on the visual; there is no option to post a caption without a visual element' (Leaver *et al.*, 2020: 75). Which visual semiotic resources[6] do users apply when they add #Plattdeutsch to their posts? Due to Instagram privacy, the rights to posted images belong to their creators; images published on an Instagram account do not belong to the public domain. The following section therefore again relies on description.

Among the 608 events observed for the purpose of this study, three patterns of applying visual semiotic resources stand out: Firstly, as discussed above, many posts were based on images of northern German landscapes and landmarks, whether taken as holiday snapshots or (semi) professional photographs. Secondly, many images were created around coastal icons, for example drawings, paintings, photos or computer-generated images of lighthouses, seagulls, sailing boats, cows, anchors, seals or sea captains. In both cases, the images imply a connection between Low German and geographical entities in northern Germany, in particular its coastal areas.

The third pattern involves images created by turning Low German words, mottos or proverbs into pictures (see, for example, the images in Figure 9.3, created for this study following the observed practices as a demonstration of this common form of image).

In these practices, the language itself has become an emblem and part of the visual discourse. The fascination with Low German words or phrases in computer-mediated communication has been noted for some time. Even before the advent of social media, Goltz (2009) observed the proliferation of Low German online dictionaries and word collections on the internet. Institutions and individuals provided opportunities for users to contribute Low German words and phrases, and these opportunities were taken up enthusiastically: Goltz (2009) found nine such word collections for Low German; only six months later, Reershemius (2010) counted 13. In 2016, the most popular open Facebook group in relation to Low German was called *Lustige plattdeutsche Wörter* 'Funny words in Low German', and it encouraged Facebook users to contribute Low German words, now with the additional opportunity to share and discuss them (Reershemius, 2017). These collections are normally set

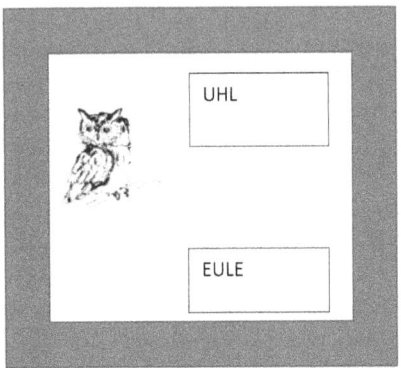 

Figure 9.3 'Owl'+ 'One person's owl is another person's nightingale'
Source: Klara Kamphues.

up by individuals and endeavour to preserve words perceived as old or quaint which users have heard from their parents and grandparents:

> Word-collecting activities suggest an active contribution to maintenance efforts. To participate, the individual user does not necessarily need to be a competent speaker; it is sufficient to remember the odd word here and there. ... the collections celebrate linguistic heritage while also providing a source of entertainment. (Reershemius, 2017: 40)

On Instagram, the popular focus on Low German words and phrases has turned into a visual practice by exhibiting elements of a heritage language in the process of language shift, using a variety of semiotic resources. The emblematic use of Low German words and phrases is also apparent in the many Instagram adverts for hats, t-shirts, bags, mugs and other products featuring well-known Low German elements such as the greetings *Moin* 'beautiful (day)' or *Munterholln* '(stay) lively'. Using and wearing these objects also stands for a form of exhibition.

Discussion and Conclusions

The analysis of all events posted under the steadily growing #Plattdeutsch during one month has revealed some remarkable continuities for computer-mediated communication in or around Low German since even before the advent of social media. A culture scene which had already used the internet early on to showcase offline events such as theatre productions, readings or concerts and which continued its efforts on social media, for example on Facebook, represents 40% of observed contributions to Instagram with #Plattdeutsch, fulfilling exactly the same role as 12 years ago. A significant difference is the higher level of interactivity now possible on social media platforms which allows viewers to acknowledge, like and respond to such posts. Overall, however, the levels of interactivity remain low and tend to consist mainly of affirmative responses and likes. Another difference to pre-social media digital practices is the disappearance of individuals or institutions policing the use of Low German online. As observed five years ago on Facebook (Reershemius, 2017), on Instagram users write in Low German as they see fit, a practice which serves the purpose of communicating in a written form of Low German without comprehension problems among speakers of different regional varieties.

Another tendency observed in earlier studies was the users' fascination with Low German words, phrases and mottos. While these were presented as online collections and amateur dictionaries before social media, they became the basis for entertainment and reminiscent exchanges on Facebook and have turned into forms of exhibition on Instagram. All three presentations are manifestations of the same intentions and their underlying problem: users want to preserve what they – often only just – remember, thus indicating the level of advanced language shift that is actually happening.

In addition to the overall high levels of commodification and commercialisation observed, another surprising result of this study is the fact that 27% of all events posted under #Plattdeutsch did not contain a single Low German word, although many of the posts' content displayed a clear connection to Low German. This emphasises the problem that engagement with heritage languages on social media does not necessarily lead to their use as base languages, but often rather to exchanges about them (see for example Alvarado Pavez, 2022; Sperlich, 2005). It also underlines a problem with certain solely quantitative approaches to the study of heritage languages on social media: the fact that #Plattdeutsch consisted of 28,600 events in September 2021 does not automatically indicate a lively use of Low German or the emergence of online domains for Low German as a base language. Engagement with a heritage language on Instagram can mean as little as adding a hashtag, a proper name, the title of a play in inverted commas or beginning a post with a greeting phrase. However, practices around Low German on social media such as Instagram will very likely contribute to the indexicalisation of a limited Low German repository of words and phrases to be referred to for purposes of identity construction and commodification strategies. Coming back to the overarching question this book raises about the potential development of digital practices in the heritage language in a time of increasing mediatisation, this means that patterns of digital multimodal writing practices can indeed be observed for Low German, although they focus on its use as a symbol or code rather than a base language.

Compared with the analysis of Low German on Facebook (Reershemius, 2017), where increased levels of interactivity and actual exchanges in Low German could be observed, the results of the present study of #Plattdeutsch on Instagram seem to show a different trend. Considering that Instagram tends to attract younger generations of users, this trend could be cause for concern for those engaged in language policy development or the learning and teaching of Low German.

Notes

(1) See also the contributions by Heyen and Jongbloed-Faber in this volume on the use of Instagram by younger speakers of autochthonous minority languages, in this case North Frisian and West Frisian.
(2) All events selected for detailed description and analysis were found to be representative of the category they were described in, for example, Event 1 stands for many similar commercially motivated posts.
(3) Contextualisation cue is a term introduced by Gumperz (1982) for communicative practices involving language alteration such as code switching.
(4) For the concept of 'authenticity' in linguistics, cf. e.g. Woolard (2016).

(5) Six posts contained comments in English, two in Spanish.
(6) Van Leeuwen defines the term semiotic resources as follows: '... the actions, materials and artifacts we use for communicative purposes, whether produced physiologically – for example, with our vocal apparatus, the muscles we use to make facial expressions and gestures – or technologically – for example, with pen and ink, or computer hardware and software – together with the ways in which these resources can be organised. Semiotic resources have a meaning potential, based on their past uses, and a set of affordances based on their possible uses, and these will be actualised in concrete social contexts where their use is subject to some form of semiotic regime' (Van Leeuwen, 2004: 285).

References

Alvarado Pavez, G. (2022) Language ideologies of emerging institutional frameworks of Mapudungun revitalization in contemporary Chile: nation, Facebook, and the moon of Pandora. *Multilingua* 41 (2), 153–179.
Adler, A., Ehlers, C., Goltz, R., Kleene, A. and Plewnia, A. (2016) *Status und Gebrauch des Niederdeutschen 2016. Erste Ergebnisse einer repräsentativen Erhebung.* IDS.
Androutsopoulos, J. (2010) The study of language and space in media discourse. In P. Auer and J.E. Schmidt (eds) *Language and Space. An International Handbook of Linguistic Variation* Vol. 1 (pp. 740–759). Boston: de Gruyter Mouton.
Androutsopoulos, J. (2014a) (ed.) *Mediatization and Linguistic Change.* de Gruyter.
Androutsopoulos, J. (2014b) Moments of sharing: Entextualization and linguistic repertoires in social networking. *Journal of Pragmatics* 73, 4–18.
Androutsopoulos, J. and Ziegler, E. (2019) Medien und areale Sprachvariation des Deutschen. In J. Herrgen and J.E. Schmidt (eds) *Sprache und Raum. Ein internationales Handbuch der Sprachvariation* Vol. 4 (pp. 828–844). de Gruyter Mouton.
Barton, D. (2006) *Literacy: An Introduction to the Ecology of Written Language* (2nd edn). Blackwell.
Bolander, B. and Locher, M.A. (2020) Beyond the online offline distinction: Entry points to digital discourse. *Discourse, Context & Media* 35, 1–8.
Busch, B. (2012) The linguistic repertoire revisited. *Applied Linguistics* 33 (5), 503–523.
Cormack, M. (2013) Concluding remarks: Towards an understanding of media impact on minority language use. In E.H. Gruffydd Jones and E. Uribe-Jongbloed (eds) *Social Media and Minority Languages: Convergence and the Creative Industries* (pp. 255–265). Multilingual Matters.
Cunliffe, D. (2019) Minority languages and social media. In G. Hogan-Brun and B. O'Rourke (eds) *Palgrave Handbook of Minority Languages and Communities* (pp. 451–480). Basingstoke: Palgrave MacMillan.
Fenske, J. (2021) Letzte Rettung Social Media? Die Verwendung des Niederdeutschen auf Instagram. *Korrespondenzblatt des Vereins für niederdeutsche Sprachforschung* 128, 80–89.
Freese, H. and Launert, U. (2004) "Nu bruuk ik Tee mit Kluntje!" Niederdeutsch und Werbung – Kurze Betrachtung eines Forschungsdesiderats. In M. Lehmberg (ed.) *Sprache, Sprechen, Sprichwörter. Festschrift für Dieter Stellmacher zum 65. Geburtstag* (pp. 107–120). Stuttgart: Steiner.
Goltz, R. (2009) Plattdeutsche Wortlisten im Internet. Eine Bestandsaufnahme. *Quickborn. Zeitschrift für plattdeutsche Sprache und Literatur* 99, 45–52.
Gumperz, J.J. (1982) *Discours Strategies.* Cambridge University Press.
Heller, M. (2010) The commodification of language. *Annual Review of Anthropology* 39, 101–114.
Jones, R.H., Chik, A. and Hafner, C.A. (2015) Introduction: Discourse analysis and digital practices. In R.H. Jones, A. Chik and C.A. Hafner (eds) *Discourse and Digital Practices: Doing Discourse Analysis in the Digital Age* (pp. 1–17). Routledge.

Jongbloed-Faber, L. (2021) *Frisian on Social Media. The Vitality of Minority Languages in a Multilingual Online World.* LOT.
Jürgens, C. (2016) Regionale Identität per Einkaufstüte. Eine Fallstudie zum Enregisterment des Niederdeutschen in Hamburg. In A. Bieberstedt, J. Ruge and I. Schröder (eds) *Hamburgisch. Struktur, Gebrauch, Wahrnehmung der Regionalsprache im urbanen Raum* (pp. 307–345). Lang.
Krotz, F. (2014) Mediatization as a mover in modernity: Social and cultural change in the context of media change. In K. Lundby (ed.) *Mediatization of Communication* (pp. 131–161). de Gruyter.
Leaver, T., Highfield, T. and Abidin, C. (2020) *Instagram.* Polity
Lup, K., Trub, L. and Rosenthal, L. (2015) Instagram #Instasad?: Exploring associations among Instagram use, depressive symptoms, negative social comparison, and strangers followed. *Cyberpsychology, Behavior, and Social Networking* 18 (5), 247–252.
Madianou, M. and Miller, D. (2012) *Migration and New Media.* Routledge.
Matras, Y. (2020) *Language Contact* (2nd edn). Cambridge University Press.
McMonagle, S., Cunliffe, D., Jongbloed-Faber, L. and Jarvis, P. (2019) What can hashtags tell us about minority languages on Twitter? A comparison of #cymraeg, #frysk and #gaeilge. *Journal of Multilingual and Multicultural Development* 40 (1), 32–49.
Miller, D., Costa, E., Haynes, N., McDonald, T., Nicolescu, R., Sinanan, J., Spyer, J., Shriram, V. and Wang, X. (2016) *How the World Changed Social Media.* UCL Press
Möhn, D. and Goltz, R. (2016) *Niederdeutsche Literatur seit 1945.* Olms.
Möller, F. (2008) *Plattdeutsch im 21. Jahrhundert. Bestandsaufnahmen und Perspektiven.* Schuster.
Reershemius, G. (2002) Bilingualismus oder Sprachverlust? Zur Lage und zur aktiven Verwendung des Niederdeutschen in Ostfriesland am Beispiel einer Dorfgemeinschaft. *Zeitschrift für Dialektologie und Linguistik* 69 (2), 163–181.
Reershemius, G. (2009) Post-vernacular language use in a Low German linguistic community. *Journal of Germanic Linguistics* 21, 131–147.
Reershemius, G. (2010) Niederdeutsch im Internet. Möglichkeiten und Grenzen computervermittelter Kommunikation für den Spracherhalt. *Zeitschrift für Dialektologie und Linguistik* 77 (2), 183–206.
Reershemius, G. (2011) Reconstructing the past? Low German and the creating of regional identity in public language display. *Journal of Multilingual and Multicultural Development* 32 (1), 33–54.
Reershemius, G. (2017) Autochthonous heritage languages and social media: Writing and bilingual practices in Low German on Facebook. *Journal of Multilingual and Multicultural Development* 38 (1), 35–49.
Reershemius, G. (2020) Semiotic rural landscapes and the performance of community in villages: A case study from Low German-Speaking Northern Germany. *Linguistic Landscape* 6 (2), 128–154.
Schürmann, T. (2016) Scherzkommunikation in niederdeutschen Whatsapp-Nachrichten einer Gruppe von L1-NiederdeutschsprecherInnen. In K. Arens and S. Torres Cajo (eds) *Sprache und soziale Ordnung. Studentische Beiträge zu sozialen Praktiken in der Interaktion. Wissenschaftliche Schriften der Westfälischen Wilhelms Universität Münster* (pp. 187–217). Westfälische Wilhelms Universität.
Scollon, R. (2001) *Mediated Discourse: the Nexus of Practice.* Routledge.
Shandler, J. (2005) *Adventures in Yiddishland: Postvernacular Language and Culture.* University of Californian Press.
Sheldon, P. and Bryant, K. (2016) Instagram: Motives for its use and relationship to narcissism and contextual age. *Computers in Human Behavior* 58, 89–97.
Sperlich, W. (2005) Will cyberforums save endangered languages? A Niuean case. *International Journal of the Sociology of Language* 172, 51–77.
Statistica (2022) See https://www.statista.com/statistics/1018019/instagram-users-germany/ (accessed June 2022).

Van Leeuwen, T. (2004) *Introducing Social Semiotics: An Introductory Textbook*. Routledge.
Waterloo, S.F., Baumgartner, S.E., Peter, J. and Valkenburg, P.M. (2018) Norms of online expressions of emotions: Comparing Facebook, Twitter, Instagram and WhatsApp. *New Media & Society* 20 (5), 1813–1831.
Woolard, K.A. (2016) *Singular and Plural: Ideologies of Linguistic Authority in 21st century Catalonia*. Oxford University Press.
Zappavigna, M. (2016) Social media photography: Construing subjectivity in Instagram images. *Visual Communication* 15 (3), 271–92.

Epilogue: Agency, Ideologies and the Continuum of Language Practices – Towards an Integrated Theory

Yaron Matras

The Hebrew Language Academy operates a Twitter account (@HebAcademy), which at the time of writing has a rather modest community of around 35,000 followers. New posts appear almost on a daily basis. They are usually accompanied by appealing and humorous original illustrations. Their content is educational and often corrective. For example, a pinned tweet from March 2021 calls on audiences not to omit the pronunciation of /h/ in casual speech. Another from January 2022 lists three phrases featuring common colloquialisms and asks readers to identify the 'mistakes'. In an accompanying post, the question 'What do we want?' is answered: 'For you to speak proper Hebrew' (*ivrít tiknít*). Some posts offer insight into the etymology of common expressions in a bid to raise awareness. The message also has its liberal moments. A post from March 2022 states that it is correct to alternate between two pronunciation formats of the verbal inflection template *nikíti* ~ *nikéti* 'I cleaned' (the latter considered a colloquialism) since such alternation is also found in Biblical Hebrew. Heritage is mobilised to license authenticity. The digital platform is used to broadcast regulatory positions including both prohibitions and concessions.

Some replies to the posts criticise 'progressive' decisions as giving in to the 'errors of the young generation'. Followers expect the Academy to serve as the guardian of proper language usage. They regard speakers as lacking not just competence but also authenticity as genuine co-owners of the language as well as agency to determine what is correct language. Hebrew is one of few, perhaps the only, language in the modern world that has been successfully revitalised. Its status as a spoken language of the home and the first language acquired by infants was gained gradually as part of a nation-building project beginning in the early 20th century (Kuzar, 2012; Nahir, 1998). This history is still present in the minds of many users who are surrounded by parents, teachers and community leaders who are not native speakers. Deference to the authority of the Academy is seen as part of a duty to protect the Israeli nation-building project. While the status of Hebrew speakers as an autochthonous population in historical Palestine remains contested, that project is regarded as still in progress. Several generations on, many descendants of Jewish immigrants consider themselves to be 'new speakers' of an ancient language.

Speakers of the languages of autochthonous populations in Western Europe are able to trace their continual presence in a territory or region to ancestry going back many generations. Yet some of the themes found in their online interactions around language bear similarities to the public discourse around revitalised (Modern) Hebrew: the question of agency and the authority to propose and modify usage norms; the authenticity of new speakers and co-ownership of language; the role of language in forging and reaffirming a feeling of belonging or sense of 'identity' and its relevance as part of a claim to historical precedence and ownership of the land.

The Hebrew Language Academy's social media engagement is an example of top-down standardisation shaping both literacy norms and speech. By contrast, many of the cases discussed in the preceding chapters represent bottom-up, open discussion processes that are hosted by digital platforms. As noted in the editors' Introduction, the internet serves as a meeting space that facilitates a virtual community of practice. Mediatisation refers in this context not just to ways of accessing information but also to changing patterns of social interaction that can shape ideologies and practices around lesser-used languages.

The effort to revitalise Hebrew was driven by the view that the language in its written form (including Biblical texts, prayers and rabbinical literature as well as poetry and a century-old practice of administrative correspondence) constitutes an important pillar of national heritage that is shared by all Jewish communities. As part of the nation-building project, that shared heritage was given institutional priority over the many different spoken and written languages of Jewish immigrant populations in Palestine and Israel. Interest in 'heritage language' in contemporary sociolinguistic research usually focuses on the diversity of background languages used by second-generation immigrants (Clyne, 1991; Edwards, 2001; Ricento, 2005). The terms 'regional minority' and 'indigenous' languages in turn capture the continuity over time in geographical space of languages spoken by numerical minority populations (and those who have become numerical minorities as a result of colonisation). A further emerging term is 'diaspora languages'. It is sometimes applied from the perspective of home or origin countries to denote the languages of communities that have emigrated but retain a linguistic affinity to their origin region and to one another. This can be considered in light of social-anthropological approaches to diaspora communities as networks of connections among people who partake in shared or common activities (cf. Brubaker, 2005; Cohen, 2008; Werbner, 2002): Promoting a heritage language can be understood as a 'diasporic stance'.

In their Introduction to this volume the editors report that speakers of Western European autochthonous regional languages do not see themselves as part of a minority but rather as people who share a common heritage including cultural and linguistic practices. In public discourses the emphasis on the (numerical) minority and regional status is there to justify the legal frameworks that aim to give such languages protection despite their secondary and sometimes even peripheral role in the institutional and public life of the nation states and societies in which they are spoken. Flagging them as 'autochthonous' serves to legitimise their claims for protection in a territory in which they have a claim to precedence. The added emphasis on heritage underscores ownership and authenticity. It can be seen as a step towards recognising similarities between the cultivation of the languages of second generation immigrants and that of regional autochthonous languages (i.e. those with a claim to territorial precedence). A further notion – 'indigenous languages' – is used mostly in the context of post-colonial societies. It is defined in relation to a localised historical timeline of colonialism: Indigenous languages are those that were there prior to colonisation. Their weaker status in society often as numerical minority languages is an outcome of colonial settlement and power structures.

Lending institutional recognition and authenticity to autochthonous or indigenous languages is not without contention. Critical studies of neoliberal ideologies have argued that the focus on creating a consumer-based community seeks to take a profit-oriented approach to multilingualism that turns language into a commodity. In that context the commitment to 'linguistic diversity' aims at increasing profitability by facilitating the mobility of professionals and experts and mobilising pride in regional identities in order to incentivise economic participation in peripheral regions. In this way pride in identity becomes an instrument of power and control of the state economy (cf. Allan & McElhinny, 2017; Heller, 2010; Heller & Duchêne, 2012).

The preoccupation with digital interaction platforms sheds light on the more spontaneous and personal dimension of identity discourses around regional languages, particularly the acceptance of partial forms of language competence, language use and learning. It also illuminates the symbolism that is associated with language when forging ideologies of regional belonging along with the fact that fractal competence replaces system-based perfection as participants assume agency in shaping what they regard as a part of their heritage. This is precisely where the notion of 'heritage language' helps shift the qualitative perspective. For Kalayil (2019: 128 ff.), 'heritage language' is a link between language and community culture while at the same time evoking a sense of distance. That distance enables one to avoid feelings of guilt for not showing complete proficiency in the language, which in turn legitimises and valorises different patterns of language usage.

Many researchers prefer the term 'heritage speaker'. It acknowledges the highly individualised nature of proficiency, patterns of usage and attitudes towards the language. In the context of immigrant community languages, heritage speakers are the children of immigrants born in the host country or immigrant children who arrived in the host country in childhood (Polinsky, 2018; Rothman & Bousquette, 2018; Wiley, 2001). They are the second generation of speakers who are either simultaneous or sequential bilinguals. Typical of heritage speakers is the fact that at some point during their early socialisation they experience a shift in competence: The language acquired in the home becomes the weaker language in terms of proficiency and frequency of use. The surrounding majority or national language becomes the primary language. Some researchers have referred to heritage speakers as 'interrupted native speakers' (cf. Hlavac & Stolac, 2021; Montrul, 2010, 2012; Tan, 2017).

Whereas the Hebrew Language Academy sees its role as regulating language wholesale, for Western European regional languages users' engagement patterns with online platforms might be seen as a series of individual acts each aimed at forging a narrative around particular choices. This reminds us of Deumert's (2018) definition of heritage as the act of 'choosing inheritance'. Through the lens of globalisation and transnationalism, users' repertoires of cultural practices and cultural skills – their cultural capital – are seen as broader and more fluid than fixed language systems with clear boundaries. In the social-anthropological study of globalisation concepts such as 'ethnoscapes' and 'super-diversity' (Appadurai, 1992; Vertovec, 2007) capture the multiplicity of social interaction options. These multiple connections transcend physical space and lead to a lower degree of predictability of links between language, place, identity and community. This has methodological implications for the analysis of relations between linguistic forms, participants, place and institutions (cf. Arnaut *et al.*, 2016; Blommaert, 2010; Blommaert & Rampton, 2011). Terms such as 'translanguaging', 'metrolingualism', 'heteroglossia' and 'crossing' have been used to capture the dynamic fluidity of moves among linguistic forms (Blackledge & Creese, 2010; García & Li, 2014; Li, 2018; Pennycook & Otsuji, 2015; Rampton, 1995). The notion of 'translanguaging' in particular has been celebrated almost with a sense of triumphalism: It stands for a paradigm shift that not only replaces the view of languages as fixed entities with clear demarcation boundaries but also calls for social engagement and intellectual resistance against ideologies that foster that view (cf. Creese & Blackledge, 2018; Moore et al., 2020).

The appreciation that increased mobility and new forms of mediality and institutional participation create ever more complex domains of interaction has strengthened the research focus on individual practice. New notions of linguistic repertoires problematise 'language' as a pre-defined set of structures and view it instead as a dynamic, emerging pattern of practices. They seek to describe such practices beyond fixed notions of groups or speech communities. Instead they view groups as emerging and evolving networks of practice with participants moving in between and among them (Blommaert & Backus, 2013; Busch, 2012). Multilingualism is being seen ever more often as a complex set of features blended together in an individual's overall repertoire. That repertoire includes acquired norms and conventions according to which in a given interaction context features and sets of features are selected and others inhibited (Jørgensen, 2008; Matras, 2009/2020). The view of language contact as one closed system interfering with another has been replaced by a view in which plurality of form is the default and closed systems or 'named languages' are derived social constructions. Some authors have even been critical of enumerations of languages, referring to it polemically as 'linguistic accounting', 'demolinguistics' or 'headcount of languages' (cf. King, 2016: 187–188; Pennycook & Otsuji, 2015: 19–49; Stevenson, 2017: 56–64). They juxtapose the listing of languages to first-hand investigations of linguistic practices, referred to as 'languaging'.

The preceding chapters show us however that there is a reality behind both: the dynamic fluctuation of features in an individual's repertoire attracts the active engagement of participants who set out to shape their own practice and sometimes that of others. In some cases, practices are mapped differently onto different media, with some forums attracting greater conversational engagement while others serve primarily emblematic functions, often linked to increased multimodal representations. At the same time we find an explicitly verbalised preoccupation with the metalinguistic perception of 'languages' as emblems of identity that can be enumerated, labelled, and evaluated and whose integrity can be either carefully maintained or intentionally disrupted and interrogated. The individualised deployment of single features and the meta-linguistic discourses around named languages thus constitute two poles on a continuum of practices. Both need to be accounted for in an integrated model of language practices. The ethnography of linguistic practices in online multilingual environments offers opportunities to draft a theoretical model that does justice to voluntary and cursory participation in practice communities around fragmented features of language as well as with ideas that are associated with language. The notion of heritage offers a shift of emphasis away from co-ownership of language as strictly rule based, essentialised notions of belonging that subscribe wholesale to the prescriptive ideologies and authority of recognised institutions. In that regard, the issues and practices around territorial languages, including those that are termed 'authochthonous' with reference to their claim to territorial precedence, come to resemble more and more those surrounding non-territorial, diasporic, trans-local and migrant languages. Common to these various types – regional-authothonous, heritage, community, diaspora and indigenous languages – is the realisation that there are multiple ways to try to compensate for the position of being the weaker language in a complex linguistic ecosystem. They include the fostering of individual agency in mediatisation around the shaping of structural features and of discursive narratives.

References

Allan, K. and McElhinny, B. (2017) Neoliberalism, language and migration. In S. Canagarajah (ed.) *The Routledge Handbook of Migration and Language* (pp. 79–101). Routledge.
Appadurai, A. (1992) Global ethnoscapes: Notes and queries for a transnational anthropology. In R.G. Fox (ed.) *Interventions: Anthropologies of the Present* (pp. 191–210). School of American Research.
Arnaut, K., Blommaert, J., Rampton, B. and Spotti, M. (eds) (2016) *Language and Superdiversity*. Routledge.
Blackledge, A. and Creese, A. (2010) *Multilingualism: A Critical Perspective*. Continuum International.
Blommaert, J. (2010) *Sociolinguistics of Globalization*. Cambridge University Press.
Blommaert J. and Backus, A. (2013) Superdiverse repertoires and the individual. In I. Saint-Georges and J.J. Weber (eds) *Multilingualism and Multimodality. The Future of Education Research* (pp. 11–32). SensePublishers.
Blommaert, J. and Rampton, B. (2011) Language and superdiversity. *Diversities* 132, 1–21.
Brubaker, R. (2005) The 'diaspora' diaspora. *Ethnic and Racial Studies* 28 (1), 1–19.
Busch, B. (2012) The linguistic repertoire revisited. *Applied Linguistics* 33 (5), 503–523.
Clyne, M. (1991) *Community Languages: The Australian Experience*. Cambridge University Press.
Cohen, R. (2008) *Global Diasporas. An Introduction* (2nd edn). Routledge.
Creese, A. and Blackledge, A. (eds) (2018) *The Routledge Handbook of Language and Superdiversity*. Routledge.
Deumert, A. (2018) The multivocality of heritage: Moments, encounters and mobilities. In A. Creese and A. Blackledge (eds) *The Routledge Handbook of Language and Superdiversity* (pp. 149–164). Routledge.
García, O. and Li, W. (2014) *Translanguaging: Language, Bilingualism and Education*. Palgrave Macmillan.
Edwards, V. (2001) Community languages in the United Kingdom. In G. Extra and D. Gorter (eds) *The Other Languages of Europe* (pp. 243–250). Multilingual Matters.
Heller, M. (2010) The commodification of language. *Annual Review of Anthropology* 39, 101–114.
Heller, M. and Duchêne, A. (2012) Pride and profit: Changing discourses of language, capital and nation-state. In A. Duchêne and M. Heller (eds) *Language in Late Capitalism: Pride and Profit* (pp. 1–21). Routledge.

Hlavac, J. and Stolac, D. (eds) (2021) *Diaspora Language Contact. The Speech of Croatian Speakers Abroad*. De Gruyter Mouton.

Jørgensen, J.N. (2008) Polylingual languaging around and among children and adolescents. *International Journal of Multilingualism* 5 (3), 161–176.

Kalayil, S. (2019) *Second-generation South Asian Britons Multilingualism, Heritage Languages and Diasporic Identity*. Lexington Books.

King, L. (2016) Multilingual cities and the future: Vitality or decline? In L. King and L. Carson (eds) *The Multilingual City: Vitality, Conflict and Change* (pp. 179–202). Multilingual Matters.

Kuzar, R. (2012) *Hebrew and Zionism: A Discourse Analytic Cultural Study*. De Gruyter Mouton.

Li Wei. (2018) Translanguaging as a practical theory of languages. *Applied Linguistics* 39 (1), 9–30.

Matras, Y. (2009) [2020] *Language Contact*. Cambridge University Press.

Montrul, S. (2010) Current issues in heritage language acquisition. *Annual Review of Applied Linguistics* 30, 3–23.

Montrul, S. (2012) Is the heritage language like a second language? *EUROSLA Yearbook* 12 (1), 1–29.

Moore, E., Bradley, J. and Simpson, J. (eds) (2020) *Translanguaging as Transformation: The Collaborative Construction of New Linguistic Realities*. Multilingual Matters.

Nahir, M. (1998) Micro language planning and the revival of Hebrew: A schematic framework. *Language in Society* 27 (3), 335–357.

Pennycook, A. and Otsuji, E. (2015) *Metrolingualism: Language in the City*. Routledge.

Polinsky, M. (2018) *Heritage Languages and their Speakers*. Cambridge University Press.

Rampton, B. (1995) *Crossing: Language and Identity Among Adolescents*. St. Jerome Publishing.

Ricento, T. (2005) Problems with the 'language-as-resource' discourse in the promotion of heritage languages in the USA. *Journal of Sociolinguistics* 9 (3), 348–368.

Rothman, J.R. and Bousquette, J. (2018) Heritage languages in North America: Sociolinguistic approaches. *Journal of Language Contact* 11, 201–207.

Stevenson, P. (2017) *Language and Migration in a Multilingual Metropolis. Berlin Lives*. Palgrave Macmillan.

Tan, E.K. (2017) A rhizomatic account of heritage language. In S. Canagarajah (ed.) *The Routledge Handbook of Migration and Language* (pp. 468–485). Routledge.

Vertovec, S. (2007) Super-diversity and its implications. *Ethnic and Racial Studies* 30 (6), 1024–1054.

Werbner, P. (2002) The place which is diaspora: Citizenship, religion and gender in the making of chaordic transnationalism. *Journal of Ethnic and Migration Studies* 28 (1), 119–133.

Wiley, T.G. (2001) On defining heritage languages and their speakers. In J. Peyton, D.A. Ranard and S. McGinnis (eds) *Heritage Languages in America: Preserving a National Resource* (pp. 29–36). Centre for Applied Linguistics.

Index

Note: References in *italics* are to figures, those in **bold** to tables; 'n' refers to chapter notes.

AAVE (African American Vernacular English) 36
Abalain, H. 77, 79
Adler, A. 37
affinity spaces 6
Alemannic 37
'algorithmic identity' 24
alignment 24–26
Amador-Moreno, C. 18
AML *see* autochthonous minority languages
Andalusian 42–43
  vs Spanish 43, 44
  unintelligibility myth 42, 43, 51n19
Androutsopoulos, J. 16, 58, 130, 165, 188, 196–197
anonymity 21–22, 23–24
Arabic
  'dialects' 36
  unintelligibility myth 47
Arendt, Birte 1–9
Århammar, N. 157
Atkinson, D. 155
Audience Design Model 170–171
Ausbau-centrism 35, 36–38, 42
authenticity 21, 22–24
autochthonous minority languages (AML) 1–2, 81, 90, 215, 218
  new speakers 3, 6, 78
  research 5, 9
  see also teaching Low German in online courses

Baldauf, R.B. 101, 104
Bangor University *see* Welsh Language Use in the Community: Research Study (2015)
Barton, D. 195
Bauman, R. 15

Bavarian 37
Beccaria, Gian Luigi 50n8
Bell, A. 170–171, 189
Belmar, G. 82, 160–161, 162, 165
Bermingham, N. 78
Bert, M. 78
Berthele, R. 37
Bliuc, A-M. *et al.* 27
Blommaert, J. *et al.* 16, 18, 90
Bonabeau, E. 17
breathing spaces 9
Breton 2, 77–79
Breton in the online context 1, 77–79
  Breizh-Izel 79
  discourse re standard Breton 85–87
  on the internet 79–80
  KerOfis 84
  language revitalisation 77–78
  néo-bretonnants (new speakers) 78, 79, 80–82, 90
  non-standard Breton online 87–90
  role of OPAB 84–85
  stereotypes 79
  terminology database 84–85
  TermOfis 84, 93, 94
  traditional speakers 78, 79
  translation service 84
  conclusion 95–98
Breton in the online context: research design
  contexts examined 81–83
  data sampling and analysis 83
  research questions 83–84
Breton on Facebook: *Facebook e brezhoneg!* 80, 81, 82, 90
  borrowings and neologisms 92–95, **94**
  orthographies and dialects 91–92
  theoretical considerations 90–91
Briggs, C.L. 15
Brocklebank, Ted 36

Brunstad, E. 55
Burnap, P. 26

Cameron, D. 18–19
Coluzzi, P. et al. 45
communities of practice 6
computer-mediated communication (CMC) 2
  see also North Frisian in Social Media
computer-mediated discourse analysis (CMDA) 15–16
conceptual orality 59
Cooper, R.L. 120
creole languages 36
Critical Discourse Analysis 32
critical literacy 3
crossing 216
Crystal, D. 2, 122, 155
cultural capital 216
Cunliffe, D. 3, 159–160, 188

Danish language: Faroe Islands 55, 56, 57
Darquennes, J. 110, 120
Davies-Deacon, Merryn 7–8
de factoism 21–22
Denmark 55, 58
Deumert, A. 216
dialectal variation 43, 44
diaspora languages 214–215
diatopic variation 43
digital language death 155
digital literacies, defined 2–3, 6
digital mediatisation 6
digital technology 1–9, 15–17
digital tools and practices 8, 195
discourse-centred online ethnography 16
Dołowy-Rybi ska, N. 37
Douglas, K.M. et al. 24
Dutch 171, 172, 174

endangered languages 2, 4–5
  see also Lombard
epilogue 9, 213–218
ethnoscapes 216
European Charter for Regional or Minority Languages (ECRML) 1, 54, 129, 172, 192
Expanded Graded Intergenerational Disruption Scale (EGIDS) 42

Facebook
  Ausbau-centrism 37
  Breton: *Facebook e brezhoneg!* 80, 81, 82, 90–95, **94**

Lombard 41, 45, 47, 50n4–8, 51n13–17
  Low German 193
  minority languages 169
  North Frisian 8–9, 158–159
  Welsh 108
  see also Frisian bilingual teenagers online
Far Lombard 45–46, 49
Faroe Islands 54, 55
  Danish language 55, 56, 57
  English 56, 57
  Føroyska Málnevndin (Faroese Language Committee) 57
  Málmørk (language policy) 57
  Málrádid (Language Council) 57
  medial diglossia 56, **56**
Faroese 2, 7, 54, 58
  'bottom-up Faroeisation' 72, **72**
  and Denmark 55
  Home Rule Act (1948) 56
  Insular Scandinavian 54–55
  linguistic, historical, sociocultural background 54–58
  literacy 55
  metalinguistic discourse 63–70
  non-native nouns in context of CMC 59–63, **60**
  orthography 55
  spelling 55–56
  conclusion and outlook 70–73, **71**
Fenske, J. 193–194
Fishman, J.A. 4, 9, 159, 161
Foriining, Friisk 161
Frisian 1, 9n2, 171
  in the Netherlands 171–173
  see also North Frisian; North Frisian in social media
Frisian bilingual teenagers online 168–171
Frisian bilingual teenagers online: materials and methods 173
  attitudes 174, **174**
  audience **175**, 175–176
  home language 173
  proficiency in Frisian 174
  regional orientation 174, 175
  use of Frisian and Dutch offline with peers 174
Frisian bilingual teenagers online: results 176, **176**
  all teenagers 176–177
  attitudes towards Frisian 183–184
  L1 teenagers on Instagram 180, **181**, **184**, 185–186, **186**

L1 teenagers on Snapchat 181–182, *182*
L1 teenagers on WhatsApp *178*, 178–179, *179*
language use 176–178, *177*
obstructions to use of Frisian 186
predicting use of Frisian on social media 184–185, **185**
social media use *176*
use of Frisian on social media *176*, *179*, **180**, *182*–184, **183**
writing skills 187–188
conclusions and discussion 186–189

Gaelic 1
German 156–157
Glass, M. 82, 160, 162
glosses 63
Gobber, Giovanni 40, 50n7
Goltz, R. 207
Grinevald, C. 78
Grondelaers, S. *et al.* 58

Hafner, C.A. 2–3
Hall, K.J. 116
Hammershaimb, V.U. 55
Hårstad, S. 58
hashtags as indicators for language use 108, 113
functions 163–164
North Frisian 162–165
Hebrew language 213–214
Hebrew Language Academy 213, 214, 216
Hemon, R. 79
heritage, defined 216
heritage languages 216, 218
heritage speakers 216
Herrieu, Loeiz 88
heteroglossia 216
Heyen, Hauke 8–9, 158, 160–161, 162, 163, 165
Hickey, R. 18
Hodges, R. 8, 105, 110–111, 112, 113
Hornsby, M. 78

Icelandic 58
Insular Scandinavian 54–55
written language 55
indigenous languages 215
Indigenous Tweets 80
Instagram 8–9, 158, 194–195
Frisian bilingual teenagers 180, *181*, **184**, 185–186, **186**
hashtags 163–164
Lombard 192–209

Low German 192–209
minority languages 170
North Frisian 158, 163
see also Frisian bilingual teenagers online
intelligibility 39, 44
Internet 19
Irish English 7, 18–20, 22
Irish Gaelic 7
Irish language 2, 17–18, 22
Irvine, J.T. 58
Italy *see* Lombard

Jakubowicz, A. *et al.* 19
Jamaican Creole 43
Jenkins, H. 4
Johnson, I. 162
Jones, M.C. 78
Jones, Rh. *et al.* 108
Jones, R.H. *et al.* 2–3, 195–196
Jongbloed-Faber, L. *et al.* 9, 158, 165, 179, 182, 196

Kalayil, S. 216
Kashubian Piedmontese 37
Kelly-Holmes, Helen 5, 7, 16, 155, 160
Kornai, A. 108, 155
Kristiansen, T. 16
Krotz, Friedrich 1
Kurdish 43, 44

La Repubblica 40
language, education and community in a digital age *see* Welsh digital resources case study
'language' as pattern of practices 217
language attitudes 43–44, **44**, 170
language choice 170–171
language contact 217
language death 155
language ideologies 3, 15–17
alignment 24–26
anonymity/de factoism 21–22
authenticity 21, 22–24
defined 15, 58
and digital technology 15–17
expertise 30–31
influence 26–27, **27**
Irish language and Irish English 17–22
language knowledge: preliminary model 20–21
the thread 18–20
validation 27–30
discussion 31–32

language policy and planning 104
language vitality 155
'languaging' 217
Lawson, R. 36
Leaver, T. *et al.* 206
Leonardi, M.M.V. 37
Liddicoat, A. 104
Limburgish 171
Lindqvist, Ch. 55
live and let live 25–26
Lombard 1, 2, 7, 37, 45, 46
    dialects 46
    on Facebook 41, 45, 47, 50–51n4–8, n13–17
    Far Lombard 45–46, 49
    on Instagram 192–209
    online 45–49
    speakers 47
    unintelligibility myth 38–49, 43, 50–51n4–17
    video interviews 46
    Zoom meetings 46
    conclusions 49–50
Low German 1, 2, 8, 9, 9n2, 37, 128–129, 157, 192
    on Facebook 193
    and social media 193
    WhatsApp 193–194
    see also teaching Low German in online courses
Low German on Instagram 192–195
    data and methodology 197–198
    results 198–203, *199*
    theoretical framework 195–197
    use of Low German *203*, 203–206
    visual practices 206–208, *207*
    discussion and conclusions 208–209
Lucal, B. 116

Madianou, M. 195
Mapudungun (Mapuzugun) 3–4, 5
Marshall, Huw 113
Matras, Yaron 9, 197
McAlister, F. *et al.* 108
McMonagle, S. *et al.* 162, 163
media convergence 4
media policies 5
media richness 27
mediatisation 1, 2, 129
medium, defined 1
Meillet, Antoine 50n2
metrolingualism 216
Miller, D. *et al.* 196
Milroy, J. 21
Milroy, L. 21

minority languages 1, 2, 3, 36, 122, 169, 170, 172–173, 215
    see also autochthonous minority languages (AML); regional/minority languages
'Minority Languages in the Digital Age' conference 10n3
Morvannou, Fañch 88–89
multilingual practices on social media 8–9
multilingualism 217
multi-modal discourse analysis 16
Musk, N. 104
myth busters 35

'names languages' 217
native authenticism 78
Netherlands
    Dutch 171, 172, 174
    Frisian 171–173
new speakers 6
Ní Bhroin, N. 169
Niue 3
North Frisian 2, 8–9, 157
North Frisian in social media 9, 155–156, 158–159
    hashtags as indicators for language use 162–165
    online communities as breathing spaces 159–162
    setting the scene 156–159
    conclusion 165–166
    see also Frisian bilingual teenagers online
North Germanic language communities 54, 57–58, *58*
Nuñez, M.R. 43

online platforms 35–38
    Lombard: recent maintenance activities 45–49
    unintelligibility myth 38–45
    conclusions 49–50

Pavez, Alvarado 4
Pearce, M. 15, 18
Petersen, N.M. 55
Pietikäinen, S. 5, 155, 160
Platt/Plattdüütsch see Low German
Pritchard, S. 108
Prys, C. *et al.* 104
Prys, Cynog 8

Reershemius, Gertrud 1–9, 81, 193, 199, 207, 208
referee design 171

regional/minority languages 1, 35, 36, 38, 39, 50n1, 54, 214, 215–216
   negative attitudes 35
   see also Faroese; teaching a regional language in online courses
Rumsey, A. 35

Sanchez-Alcolea, M.T. 43
Sandøy, H. 59, 70, 71
Sands, Bobby 25
Schacht, S. 116
Schiffman, H.F. 22
Schlobinski, P. 158
Schürmann, T. 193
Scollon, R. 195
Scots 36–37
shifting ideologies 7–8
Shklovsky, Viktor 50n2
Shohamy, E.G. 22
Siever, T. 158
sign languages 36
Sigurdsson, Jón 55
Simonsen, H. 59
Skaale, S. 70
Snapchat 9, 181–182, *182*
social identity construction 171
social media 4, 6, 16
   language choice 170–171
   see also North Frisian in social media
Soria, C. 37, 108
Spanish vs Andalusian 43, 44
Spanish–Portuguese bilinguals 37
spelling 4
   Faroese 55
Sperlich, W. 3
Stern, Ulrike 8
Stewart, B.J. 116
super-diversity 216
'super-localism' 21
Szabla, M. 90

Tamburelli, M. 7, 36, 37
teaching a regional language in online courses *see* teaching Low German in online courses
teaching Low German in online courses 128–130, 132–134
   beginners' course 133, *134*
   Competence Centre for the Teaching of Low German at Greifswald University (CCTLG) 132, 135, 136
   data and method *134*, 134–135
   interactive computer-assissted language learning (CALL) 131
   interactive corrections 138–140
   mediatisation 129, 130
   'new speakers' 131–132
   participants 132–133, *133*
   peer support 140–142
   playful practices, challenging humour 142–144
   practices 131
   spaces 130–131
   theoretical framework 130–132
teaching Low German in online courses: findings
   agency: learners and participation 135–138, *136*, 145–146
   evaluation by participants 144–145, 146
   potential problems 146–147
   practices and norms in online courses 138–144, 146
   results 147–148
   summary and discussion 145–148
   transcript corpus **148**
terminology 1, 9*n*2
translanguaging 216–217
tribes 25
Trudgill, P. 43
Turkish vs Kurdish 43, 44
Twitter 17, 18, 19–20, 24–25, 26, 27–28, 31–32, 158
   Breton 81–82
   German use 158
   Hebrew Language Academy 213
   Welsh 162, 171
   see also Frisian bilingual teenagers online

UNESCO 2, 105
   Atlas of the World's Languages in Danger 129, 172
unintelligibility myth
   Andalusian 42, 43, 51n19
   Arabic 47
   Kurdish 43, 44
   and language attitudes 43–44, **44**
   Lombard 38–49, *43*, 50–51n4–17
   conclusions 49–50
unravelling language choice online *see* Frisian bilingual teenagers online

Van Leeuwen, T. 210n6
Vikør, L.S. 57
virtual ethnography 16

Walker, A. 156, 157, 158
Waterloo, S.F. 193

Web 2.0 4–5, 7, 15
Weinreich, Ulrich 36, 50n2
Welsh 1, 2, 9n2, 19, 171
  on Facebook 108
  on Twitter 162
Welsh digital language revitalisation
  projects 103
    Ap Geiriaduron (Dictionary App) 113
    Coleg Cymraeg Cenedlaethol 113,
      114–116, 120
    Mentrau Iaith Cymru 111, 121
    Sociology Multimedia Resource Pack
      103, 110, 114–120, *116*, *117*, *119*,
      121–122
    Terminology Portal, Porth Termau
      Cenedlaethol Cymru 120
    A Toolkit for Promoting Use of Welsh
      in the Community (2017) 103,
      110–114, 121
    Yr Awr Gymraeg (The Welsh Hour)
      113
Welsh digital resources case study 8,
  103–104
    Bangor University 111, 113, 118,
      122–123
    Coleg Cymraeg Cenedlaethol 104,
      107, 114–115, 121–123
    Cymraeg 2050 108, 109–110, 112
    Education Reform Act (1988) 106

Mentrau Iaith Cymru 104, 122–123
Welsh in education 106–108
Welsh in the community 105–106
Welsh in the digital age 108
Welsh Language context 105–110
  discussion 120–123
  conclusions 123–124
Welsh Language Strategy, A Living
  language: a language for Living (2012)
  110–111
Welsh Language Use in the Community:
  Research Study (2015) 111
West Frisian 2, 158, 189n2
WhatsApp 9, 158
  Frisian bilingual teenagers *178*,
    178–179, *179*
  Low German 193–194
Wikipedia 37–38, 40–41, 43
Wikström, P. 163
Williams, M.L. 26
Woolard, Kathryn 20, 21, 22, 23

X *see* Twitter

Yiddish 36
YouTube 8, 22, 170

Zappavigna, M. 163, 198
Zieseler, Laura 7, 59

For Product Safety Concerns and Information please contact our EU Authorised Representative:

Easy Access System Europe

Mustamäe tee 50

10621 Tallinn

Estonia

gpsr.requests@easproject.com

www.ingramcontent.com/pod-product-compliance
Lightning Source LLC
Chambersburg PA
CBHW052036300426
44117CB00012B/1850